And the Tiger Leaps

Jeann Beattie

 McClelland and Stewart Limited Toronto/Montreal

The permission of *Maclean's Magazine* to use excerpts from two articles, 'I Became My Burglar's Best Friend' and 'Big Sister to the Saints,' is gratefully acknowledged.

The Canadian Publishers
McClelland and Stewart Limited
25 Hollinger Road, Toronto 374

To the Saints with affection
and especially to the one Saint, who understands
the real meaning of friendship.

Prologue

This story begins in 1957. It could have happened last night – or next week. It has never really ended.

The dialogue is the result of remembered conversations, as well as research interviews taped at the time for two magazine articles and for a CBC-TV documentary show.

The book is dedicated to the Saints, but it is dedicated as well to Father Orr, to the lawyers, probation officers, welfare workers, and the police – especially old Number Six – who were part of that time.

The names of some of the Saints have been changed, and time sequences have been altered to give continuity to the story. But all the people in the story are real . . . and all of it happened.

'One moment does not lead to another.
The door opens and the tiger leaps.'

'The Waves' Virginia Woolf

Book One

Chapter One

It began with a spectacular explosion of sound. While the noise echoed and re-echoed throughout my apartment, I jack-knifed off the pillow, trying, in that hour when all sense of being is faint, to identify the sounds. Of course. Someone was pounding wildly, hysterically, on my front door. Still wavering in that neutral dimension between sleep and consciousness, still immobilized by the sheer force of the sounds, I stared at the door, waiting for it to collapse.

Inexplicably the pounding stopped. The apartment was very still.

Apparently my heart had exploded with the noise. Pieces of it twitched and throbbed in every corner of my body. I looked at the luminous dial of the clock on the coffee table and I wondered, if my heart did not reassemble, if anyone would know that I had died at precisely four o'clock in the morning. Slowly the throbbing eased. Slowly I slipped back into sleep.

From a periphery of consciousness I knew with deadening certainty that somewhere in the darkness, possibly no further away than the edge of my skin, there was a menace. The silence was thick with it. I glanced again at the clock. Four-thirty. I had been asleep then, a deep, unknowing sleep. Now I was rigidly awake, alert to the menace, convinced that my slightest move would make it materialize like some terrifying ectoplasm.

Nothing moved in the apartment. There was no sound. The bar of yellow light under the front door, seepage from the corridor, was right where it should be. I could make out the edge of the coffee table, a chair, the chesterfield, the fireplace. This sensation had to be a backlash from the pounding. I turned over to face the wall. The light blanket didn't turn with me. I pulled. It resisted. Another tug, half irritation, half alarm. It must be caught on something. Yet there was nothing to hold it. I hesitated the length of a heartbeat and yanked again. It shifted easily under my hand.

Silence can be an unsettling companion for an active imagination. Mine clicked into high gear. I strained to penetrate the stillness. The

1

wall became a shadowed threat, barred with unlikely streaks of pale light from the window. For five minutes I waited for something to happen. Then, impatiently, I confessed I had a choice. I could lie, stiff and defenceless against the nameless horror until dawn, or I could get up, tour the apartment, prove to my imagination that nothing was wrong, and get back to sleep.

I threw back the covers, swung off the bed, picked up my robe from the end of the bed, and padded swiftly from the living room. I didn't look behind me. And I didn't turn on the living room lights. If I wanted light in that room I had to move through the darkness from lamp to lamp.

As I passed the bathroom on the way to the kitchen, I reached in automatically and flicked on the light. I didn't look inside. I didn't see the window.

The kitchen was empty of threat. Last evening's dinner dishes were piled on the counter. An ashtray, for no particular reason, sat on top of the refrigerator. Embarrassed and relieved, I poured a glass of milk and wondered about the pounding. This was a sedate dowager of a building in mid-town Toronto. Its tenants didn't fling themselves against strangers' doors at four in the morning. I knew no one in the building, beyond polite exchanges of weather observations with un-named tenants. Perhaps someone had been in trouble, pleading for help even from a stranger. Yet there had been no sounds from other doors. Or perhaps it was a passer-by, spurred by mischief. The building's front door was unlocked. My apartment, on the ground floor, was the first in the corridor to the right of the lobby. It would be a natural random target.

Then I saw the book, lying on the floor beneath the window's wide sill. That was odd. I wasn't the world's neatest woman, but I didn't usually leave books scattered on the floor. As I bent to pick it up, I glanced through the long window. Darkness piled against the sides of the two apartment buildings and blanketed the courtyard between. Trees were outlined against a paling sky and the light looked turned in upon itself. I felt like the only person alive in the city. That was a melancholy thought. Briskly I rinsed out the glass.

At the bathroom door, as I reached for the light switch, I glanced inside. The tub stretched across the back wall. Above it was a good-sized window. I paused, puzzled by the impression of something wrong.

Of course. The window. The frame had been recently repainted. I remembered pushing strenuously to open the window even an inch before I went to bed. Now it gaped open, slanting inward. That was wrong. The window pushed out. Not in.

Perhaps when danger is anticipated, the mind holds itself aloof from shock. There was no shock now, or even alarm. Only surprised relief. Here was the reason for my uneasiness. Someone had tried to get in. Probably the pounding had been someone warning of the attempted entry. Beaming with satisfaction I walked four steps into the bathroom, leaned over the tub and pushed the window. It wouldn't budge. I turned to step into the tub.

A hand, strong and firm, went around my mouth from behind. I knew an instant of total disbelief. I caught a glimpse of blue that had no business being in my bathroom, especially when it appeared to be part of a man's shirt and there appeared to be a man inside that shirt.

Something heavy crashed down on my skull.

There was no general return to consciousness, no clearing of vision, no murmured questions. A hand. The blue. Blackness. And, stingingly awake, I was sprawled in the tub, staring up at the blue. It was a shirt all right, and there was a man inside it. He was tall and young and he stood silent and motionless, staring back at me. Something covered the lower half of his face. His eyes were wide and brilliantly blue. Their expression changed, alarm dissolving into flat speculation. From one hand dangled something dark and heavy. And as we stared at each other, I could hear screaming, high, piercing, and uncontrolled, shriek after shriek bouncing off the walls out into the night. The man didn't look as if he were screaming. It had to be me.

My mind split into two halves, one a trapped animal, frantic in its helplessness, the other a calm recorder, aware of the inevitable. He was going to kill me. The calm self was washed with regret. I was no stripling, but even at thirty-three I had dreams of life. Regret gave way to a cold thrust of anger. My involvement with life was too passionate, my demand to live too intense to die needlessly and absurdly in my own bathtub. Still screaming, still staring at those sapphire blue eyes, I grabbed the edge of the tub to propel myself out of it.

The blue eyes listed, swung in reverse, blurred. Blackness dropped again.

Someone was shouting. The apartment was filled again with the sound of pounding. The bathroom was empty and I was huddled in the tub, like an animal lowered by a glimpse of life he doesn't like. I grabbed the tub's edge once more, annoyed this time by the noise. Surely people could be more quiet about a rescue, if indeed this were a rescue. I stepped out of the tub, deliberating the next move. And I screamed again, a final shrill blast of terror and frustration. Then, quietly, I opened the front door.

The apartment superintendent straightened the collar of his bathrobe with the chiding look of harassed superintendents. I smiled at him, wondering what I had to smile about, and apologized for the rumpus. A prowler had been in my apartment, I told the doubtful face. He had hit me over the head. 'You must have had a nightmare,' he said, 'a very bad, very loud nightmare.' I lifted his hand to my head. His eyes widened. There was a bump, the size of an egg, on the right side. 'Have you called the police?' he asked.

Police? Obediently I picked up the receiver and dialled. When I began the explanation, the voice interrupted. 'Your address first, please. Then your name.' Of course. Always give your address first. If you are interrupted, the police at least know where to find the body. When I gave the address the voice sighed. 'We know,' he said. 'There have been several calls. A cruiser is on the way.'

Embarrassment rolled back. My shrieks had roused the entire apartment building. As I replaced the receiver the superintendent asked, 'Did you know him?'

I touched the bump on my head. 'I hope not.'

The apartment bulged with police. Two uniformed officers strode toward the kitchen; another peered into the bathroom; two plainclothesmen plumped down on the chesterfield. One took a notebook from his pocket, poised a ballpoint pen over it, and looked expectantly at the second man. That one scrutinized me with narrow-eyed suspicion.

He began the questioning. My name? Good. I knew that. Did I live alone? Yes. My age? Thirty-three. Did I work somewhere? Yes, at an advertising agency. What did I do there? I was the agency's script editor on a television drama series. I also did publicity for television shows. They looked at each other. Television. Drama series. Publicity. Now about this man I said hit me over the head, did I recognize him? No. He was wearing something over half his face. And just what had happened? That was a bad question. Carefully I told them.

They seemed unimpressed by the pounding which, originally, had

4

awakened me. 'Probably someone saw him enter and tried to warn you,' one said. 'When you didn't answer the door, they figured you were away. Or,' he shrugged, 'unconscious.'

'Someone would walk away, thinking I was unconscious or even,' I gulped, 'dead?'

He shrugged again. 'People don't like to get involved.'

They asked for a description of the prowler. Blond. Medium height. Slender. Very blue eyes. Wearing a blue shirt and jeans. Age? Perhaps eighteen. No, I didn't know how long he'd been in the apartment. No, there had been no communication between us. Had there been an indecent assault? There was a moment of absolute silence. A blow on the head, I decided, is highly indecent. It is also an assault. They were alerted by the pause. Of course. They meant rape. Or attempted rape.

'No,' I said.

They had misunderstood the pause. One leaned forward. 'You're certain?' That was silly. Of course I was certain. Or did they think I was lying, out of embarrassment, or horror, or shock.

'There was no indecent assault,' I repeated.

'He didn't try . . . anything?' one asked delicately.

'He tried to conk me on the head. He succeeded. That's all.'

'Sure he wasn't a boyfriend?'

I tried to imagine being capable, at thirty-three, of rousing a teen-ager to such a frenzy of — what? Jealously? Passion? Frustration? The balance between coherence and hysteria was growing more delicate. 'I'd say I was in more danger from an irate agency client than any teenage boyfriend, which I don't happen to have.'

They were not amused. 'Why didn't he run away after he hit you?'

'I don't know.'

'How long did he stand over you?'

'I don't know that, either.'

A policeman poked his head around the front door. They had picked up a newsboy who answered the description. He had no alibi. Should they bring him in for identification? The detective saw my shiver. 'Take him to headquarters,' he said. 'We'll meet you there.' He turned to me. 'You can come down with us.'

Expectantly they stood up.

'I'd better dress,' I said. They murmured agreement and still stood there. 'Sorry,' I waved helplessly, 'this is a bachelor apartment. I have to dress here, or,' I swallowed, 'in that bathroom.'

They trotted from the apartment.

At the police station we drove into a back lane. Another car rolled into the garage. A blond boy, about sixteen, was motioned from the car, to stand under a bright light. This would be the newsboy. The detective looked at me. 'Well?'

I peered across the dark lane. The boy slouched in exaggerated nonchalance. Short and slight, he looked blindly into the circle of light. I shrugged in helpless indecision. A second boy was pushed under the light. This one was bigger, more defiant, smiling as he held up his head in the light.

The first seemed too small. This one was too powerful. The detectives waited. I felt defensive and irritated. This was unfair. They knew I would be in shock. Couldn't that make me either cautious or overly eager in any identification? What had happened to the traditional line-up?

The detectives matched my shrug. We trailed into headquarters. The room was large and bright and quiet. They gestured to a chair. The bump on my head felt enormous, but there was no pain and the trembling had quieted to spasmodic quivers. A policeman asked if I would like to see a doctor. 'It might be wise,' he said, 'after all, we'd be responsible if anything happened, like — you know.'

That took the edge off what had seemed sympathetic concern. I didn't need a doctor, I said sourly, and I wouldn't hold it against them if I dropped dead on the premises. A policewoman offered coffee and an aspirin.

Twenty minutes later I was ushered into a room on the second floor and the interrogation was repeated. Just how had it all happened? Just who did what to whom?

Finally the detective rolled his report out of the typewriter and handed it over for my signature. Another detective held out a towel and an iron bookend. 'Can you identify these?' he said. 'They were found outside your kitchen window.'

'They're mine,' I said. 'The towel — that's what must have covered his face and — ' I stared at the bookend with new respect. 'You mean he hit me with that?'

'You identify it?' he repeated patiently.

'It's one of a set. It was on the fireplace mantel.'

We had met the official requirements. They offered to drive me home.

The city was awakening in the softly warm summer morning. Cars bunched along Yonge Street. Businessmen and women strode toward buses and subways. Life had not paused so much as a heartbeat. The cruiser pulled up in front of the apartment building. 'A fingerprint man will be around later this morning,' one detective said. 'You won't be going to work, will you?'

I managed a smile. 'You don't think I want to hang around here, do you?' I hesitated. 'Would you like a cup of coffee?' I asked wistfully, trying to stall that moment of being alone in that apartment.

The detective glanced at his watch. 'We'll have to take a raincheck. Thanks anyway.' With a wave, they drove off.

The lobby was empty. I hesitated at the apartment door, opened it and stepped into silence. Violence should leave an imprint. There should be sounds to break the quiet, screams or shouts or cries. There should be waves of shrieking colours, scarlets, purples, yellows, and greens, crackling through the air. Time should be visibly suspended, shocked into stillness at the precise instant of violence. The moment should leave something behind to reflect turmoil to the eye and to the ear.

But the silence was undisturbed. The ashtray on the coffee table held the stub of a detective's cigarette. The bed was as I had left it when I flung back the blanket to assure myself there was no reason for uneasiness. I avoided any glance into the bathroom, wondering if I could ever take a bath in that tub again.

There was one change in the living room. The second bookend was missing from the mantel. Fascinated, I sank into a chair and stared at the four books, standing unguarded by the heavy, old, iron bookends.

'You mean he hit me with that?' And memory slipped the controls. I felt the swift, hard pressure of a hand around my mouth. Twisting from the phantom fingers, I encountered memory's square of blue. Now! Now the blow on the head. Now the fall into the tub. Now the screaming. Now the eyes, round, blazing blue. . . .

The door buzzer spun me right off the chair. The fingerprint man identified himself, glanced at my stricken face, lowered his eyes, and hurried past me into the bathroom.

My head began a dull, protesting ache. I should call the office. I had a spectacular excuse, but I would be late.

Chapter Two

Two days later, at three-thirty in the morning, I surfaced slowly from a drugged sleep. Someone was pounding on the door. I froze. 'It's all right,' a voice shouted cheerfully through the door, 'it's the police.'

I breathed again, but my fingers had trouble buttoning my robe. When I opened the door, the two detectives smiled. 'Sorry,' one apologized, 'we wanted to tell you right away. Your prowler is behind bars.'

Speechless, I waved them into the apartment. They had a boy, picked up an hour earlier. He was carrying a portable radio when a cruiser spotted him. He was a known young offender. They had taken him to headquarters. He confessed to having stolen the radio. He also confessed to being my prowler. 'You don't have to be scared any more,' one detective said.

Relief hit first in my knees. 'You're sure he's the one?' I asked and marvelled at the degree of my relief. Sometime during those two days I had discovered, for the first time, what it was to be completely, irrationally afraid. I didn't seriously expect a return visit from my unknown assailant. I didn't seriously believe, either, that the shadows beyond my apartment were peopled by other threats. Yet fear hovered, a sinister, formless fear of the unknown and the possible.

'Positive,' the detective said. 'He confessed.'

'I'll make coffee,' I murmured, a little embarrassed by the shuddering sigh that went through me. We headed for the kitchen and I was reaching for the percolator when I asked, almost absently, 'How old is he?'

The older detective leaned against the refrigerator. Casually he answered, 'Sixteen.' When, involuntarily, I swung around, he shook his head. 'No,' he said, 'don't feel sorry for him. He's incorrigible. Been up on theft charges before. Spent time in training school. He's on probation now.' He waved a hand dismissively. 'Forget him.'

My sense of relief was oddly shaken. 'Sixteen?' I echoed. 'You're sure he's the one?'

'Absolutely,' the detective said. 'He confessed and he fits your description." He ran down the list of physical characteristics I had given that numbing night. He ended with 'and hazel eyes.'

'Hazel?' That was wrong. 'But my boy had blue eyes. Brilliant, blazing blue. I'll never forget them. Not hazel. This isn't the right one.'

They exchanged a look and smiled. 'Look,' the younger man said, 'he confessed. He fits the description.' I started to protest. 'All right, except for the eyes. But we know this one. He was carrying a radio he had just stolen. What more do you want?'

'I want him to have blue eyes,' I said stubbornly.

'You know anything about these punks?' he sighed. When, silently, I shook my head, he gestured, 'Catching criminals is our business, right?' I nodded, still silent. 'And we do know these punks. Don't get excited about a kid who, after all, might have killed you. He isn't worth it.'

We sat in the kitchen drinking coffee while they talked about young offenders. This one was typical, the younger detective said and ignored the 'but' in my look. Toronto's crime rate was soaring, and Toronto wasn't the only city under seige from youthful criminals. 'The young ones are the worst in some ways,' he said. 'They want to be so tough.'

'Aren't the tough kids usually the scared ones?' I asked, interested despite my prior concern about the miscarriage-of-justice possibility.

'Maybe,' he shook his head, 'but they think it's smart to have a record.'

'Are we talking about delinquents or criminals?'

'Too often the one becomes the other,' he said.

'But that's part of your job, isn't it? I mean the old police emphasis on just catching criminals has shifted, hasn't it? Isn't trying to prevent crime by working with the so-called delinquents part of it now?'

'Working with them?' He waved a hand. 'Lady, when you're taunted and jeered by a bunch of kids who act as if they hate you — and maybe do — well, a cop is also a human being. Yes I know,' he grinned self-consciously. 'I sound sour. Sometimes I want to pack it in.'

'Why don't you, then. Why be a cop?'

He shook his head. 'Sometimes I think you got to be crazy. And if I say because I'm interested and sometimes maybe even because I hope something I do someday will bring some kid back to his senses, I do sound crazy. Or noble. And I'm neither one. I just try to do my job.'

The older man was more emphatic. He favoured the strap. The crime rate was skyrocketing because we coddled young offenders. They were bad and there was only one way to handle a bad boy. You strapped the bad out of him. 'And you won't agree with that,' he said to me.

'No,' I admitted. 'I've never thought much about it, but no, I don't agree. After all that kind of treatment didn't work in the past. I'd think it would have less chance of working now. We're pitching into a whole new era, in every way.'

'Crime is still crime,' he insisted.

'Sure. Polio is still polio, but now we know how to prevent it.'

He glanced at the other detective. 'And when this punk hit you over the head, you yelled for a doctor?'

'I yelled for the police,' I agreed. 'But maybe if that kid, whoever he is, had received the right kind of help sometime, I wouldn't have been yelling for anybody because he wouldn't have been in my bathroom.'

The exchange with these men, whom I liked as individuals and respected as symbols, was friendly and relaxed. It was true that I hadn't thought much about the problems of the young offender and I was a little surprised by the strength of my opposition to their attitudes, primarily, I decided, because a belief in the ultimate rightness of our system was bred in the bone. Months later I thought of that conversation with wonder and a relic of regret.

'Anyway,' I smiled at them, 'we're getting away from the main point. And the main point is I don't believe that the boy you're holding is my prowler.'

They put the empty coffee cups on the counter and stood up. The younger detective grinned down at me. 'You mind a little advice, from a sour cop? You've had a nasty experience. Try to forget it. Get it all out of your mind. It takes time to get over this kind of shock. We got the right one. Catching criminals may be only part of our job,' he added wryly, 'but it's still a big part.'

He was right, I reminded myself. But hazel eyes?

The police station called the next morning officially to report my prowler's capture. He would appear in magistrate court that morning.

Under Canadian law anyone between the ages of seven years and the maximum set by each province is considered a juvenile. In Ontario, Prince Edward Island, Saskatchewan, New Brunswick, and Nova Scotia, the maximum is sixteen. British Columbia, Manitoba, and Quebec set it at eighteen. Alberta selects eighteen for girls and sixteen for boys, and Newfoundland sets seventeen as the maximum. My alleged prowler, whose name they said was David, had reached his sixteenth birthday. He would be tried in adult court.

No one suggested I be in court and I didn't want to go. My mind insisted this wasn't the boy, but emotionally I had no desire to come face to face with anyone who, even remotely, might be my assailant. The police had my signed statement. They needed no verbal testimony.

I called the station that afternoon. The accused had been remanded for one week. Since he was on probation, the Court had requested a report on him. He had not been represented by a lawyer. When I asked why, the officer's voice shrugged. He hadn't asked for one. Did he know he was entitled to one? Probably, the officer said, since he'd been represented 'the other times.' I asked the name of the lawyer from those other times. Everything was moving too quickly. If this boy were to be saved, somebody had to do something. The officer gave me his name and I telephoned him.

He sounded singularly disinterested. The boy was guilty, he said. 'I'd forget it. He's incorrigible.'

'What colour are his eyes?' I asked.

There was a muffled sound. 'What's that got to do with it?'

'The police say they're hazel. My prowler had blue eyes.'

'You believe he's innocent because of the colour of his eyes?'

'Why not? You believe he's guilty because of his past record.'

'Touché,' he laughed. 'All right, if you're convinced, why not call the welfare worker at the Don Jail. She might talk to him and give you an unprejudiced opinion.'

The welfare worker sounded mystified but sympathetic. She agreed to interview David, and she called back the next day. 'I'm sorry,' she said, 'there's no doubt. He's your assailant.' When I murmured, 'But his eyes – ' she broke in. 'You've forgotten,' she said gently, 'hazel eyes turn blue under certain lights.'

I hadn't forgotten. I had never known. I thanked her and slowly hung up the receiver. I should take that repetitive advice and forget it. Yet the figure out of limbo, who had almost literally scared the life out of me, had become a person, a sixteen-year-old labelled 'incorrigible' by too many people. Why would a sixteen-year-old conduct his life in a manner guaranteed to produce imprisonment? Impulsively I called the lawyer again. 'Seems the police were right, you were right, and even the boy was right. I apologize. Now, will you represent him?'

11

'Why?' He sounded wearily bewildered.

'I don't know. Because he has the right to a lawyer. Because he's sixteen. Because he needs help. This business makes no sense.'

'Why not? It happens every day.'

'Not to me. And I'm baffled. What's he like? I mean as a person. He is a person, after all."

'David?' The lawyer paused. 'Quiet. Submissive. Passive. You can't get through to him.'

I touched the bump on my head. 'Yet this quiet, submissive, passive boy smashes me over the head with an iron bookend when he could have escaped out of the living-room windows, or even the kitchen window when my back was turned to him? I wouldn't have seen him.'

'Maybe he panicked, just didn't think clearly.'

'Or maybe,' I said slowly, 'he has a problem. I mean a real emotional problem.'

While he hesitated I got the idea. Did he think a psychiatric examination was in order? He hesitated again. 'I mean of David,' I said and he laughed. Then, astonishingly, he agreed. Perhaps he was curious, too. Or perhaps 'promise her anything – even a psychiatric examination.'

That Friday, when David appeared in court, the magistrate agreed to the lawyer's request.

During the week while we awaited the psychiatric report, my curiosity about the boy began to spill over onto the entire community of young offenders. Everything up to that point had been novel, an experience new in every respect. But for some people this subculture of crime was familiar and young offenders were, professionally, a constant source of concern and possibly frustration. I wanted to talk to these people, preferably those not bogged down in legal thinking.

Someone suggested the priest at the Don Jail. He showed no surprise over my call. 'The main problem,' he said, 'is the public. There's so much we need if we're going to help these young people, but most of all we need the support and understanding and involvement of the public.' He saw them all, he said, the swaggering and the fearful, the young and the veteran. 'But their behaviour is only a symptom. We don't know the cause of this disease we call crime. We're only treating the symptoms.' He added it might be useful, since I was interested, if I talked with a probation officer and he gave me a name and a telephone number.

The probation officer was typical of others I would come to know.

He worked hard with a caseload too heavy for one man; he was sharply critical of government attitudes and of the lack of proper facilities and adequate staff. And he asked not to be quoted. 'If I'm too loud I'll be fired,' he said. 'It might be better for me. This work takes a hell of a lot out of you. But if I go there's one less. And I have my kids to consider.'

Did he think probation was a good thing? 'Certainly,' he said. 'So's parole. Providing you have the right type of supervising officer. It's like being a teacher. Unless you like young people, sympathize with their problems, can remember what it is to be young and take a constant interest in each one, you're nothing but another instrument of authority. And you can forget it.'

And I talked again with David's lawyer. He said David had lost his father the previous year, after an illness of eight years. His mother tried to cope with the bewildering behaviour of her only child. David had held jobs for brief periods of time. One, at an exclusive Toronto club, had ended the day it began. They discovered their new bus boy had a record. No one knew how they found out. The juvenile court is supposed to protect boys and girls from public awareness of misdeeds. Their names are not published in the press. Perhaps, he said, someone recognized David. Or perhaps they had some method of checking. Money wasn't abundant in David's family, he went on, but it wasn't desperately scarce, either. There was nothing so poignant about the boy's story that he should be forgiven everything on the basis of human tragedy.

'But why has he become a . . .' I began, frustration mounting.

'Young punk?' The lawyer finished calmly. 'Who knows. As I told you, he's incorrigible.'

On Friday I telephoned the Don Jail psychiatrist. Yes, he had examined David and yes, he had reached his conclusion.

'Which is?'

'The boy's sane.'

'But does he have any emotional or mental illness?'

'The boy is legally sane,' he repeated. 'That's all we must determine. You do know about the M'Naghten Rule?' The rule, he explained, is still in force in Canada and in most of the United States. It says: 'to establish a defence on the grounds of insanity, it must be clearly proved that, at the time of committing the act, the accused was labouring under such a defect of reason, from a disease of the mind, as not to know the nature and quality' – which means consequences – 'of the act he was doing, or, if he did know, that he must not know what he was doing was wrong.'

'And this boy,' the psychiatrist said patiently, 'is not labouring under any such defect of reason. He is legally sane.'

David was sentenced that morning to eight months in a reformatory.

When I called the lawyer to thank him for his efforts he said, 'The sentence was predictable. Even lenient, considering the circumstances. So,' he sounded thankful, 'it's over. You can get back to normal.'

But the normal had changed. Now it included a stranger who was a question mark, a name on a police blotter, a boy labelled 'incorrigible,' a sixteen-year-old who posed questions about a new and alien world. It wasn't over at all.

Chapter Three

That weekend I decided I had to meet David. It was a startling idea and the instant it became a conviction I began to fight it. I could keep in touch through the authorities. I could meet him later. There was no reason to rush it. The bump on my head wasn't even gone yet. I still took sleeping pills. I still left on the light in the hall. I still had nightmares and I was still scared blue if a floor board creaked.

But if I didn't do it immediately, I might never find the courage. And I was curious. The priest had said, 'What we need most is the understanding and support and involvement of the public.' I was part of the public and I had no idea what it was I was to understand or who needed my support.

Monday morning I telephoned the governor of the Don Jail. He sounded puzzled by the request. 'There are regular visiting hours,' he said. 'You do know that prisoners are permitted visitors?'

'I know.' I felt a little ridiculous. 'But I'd like to talk to him in relative privacy. Although,' I added hastily, 'I'm not anxious to be alone with him.'

'I see.' He was still puzzled. 'I suppose you could meet him in my office. It's irregular, but it could be arranged. Tell me, why do you want to meet him?'

'I haven't the faintest idea,' I said honestly.

The old Don Jail was a huge, sombre building, which threw long, brooding shadows over the area. The afternoon of my appointment I walked nervously toward the massive front door, swung it open and almost backed out again.

Directly in front of the door a guard perched on a high stool beside a desk. To the right was a row of empty benches. Behind the guard was a high, wide, barred door and there were low, rumbling sounds drifting through it. Humans prowling and muttering in unseen cages? The place looked like a great, dismal, indoor zoo.

When I told the guard I had an appointment with the governor, he muttered curtly, slid off the stool and disappeared behind a closed door I hadn't noticed. A few minutes later the governor hurried out. He was short, attractive and energetic, a man with a friendly smile and a natural public-relations manner. But his eyes were appraising. We shook hands and he gestured toward his office.

Inside the office he settled behind a square desk and studied me with shrewd geniality. His job was to make sure the humans here met regulations, were fed and housed, received adequate medical attention, and didn't escape. I decided he would be efficient and practical about that job. I doubted that he was at all philosophical about it.

There was a barred window behind his desk. He followed my startled glance. 'Yes,' he said and swept papers to one side. 'This is your first experience inside a jail?' I nodded and tried to smile. 'I see,' he said. 'And you still want to meet this boy?' I tried to look confident. 'Yes. Please,' I said and my voice cracked a little. He picked up a telephone and asked that David be brought to his office. I flicked dust from my skirt and wondered what on earth I was doing there.

The knock on the door made me jump. When it opened I turned and caught a glimpse of blue, precisely as it had been that first night. I froze. The governor directed the figure to a chair. Feet walked slowly in front of me, stopped, turned, and stopped again.

'Do you recognize this woman?' the governor asked – the public-relations manner had disappeared. I heard a quiet 'yes, sir.' I looked up. He was standing in front of the chair, a thin, pale, blond teenager, gazing steadily at his feet. This, then, was my prowler? This was the stranger who had waited in the darkness? This quiet boy, with the gentle mouth, the thin shoulders, the long sensitive hands, had hit me with an iron bookend? This youngster had waited for me to return to consciousness, had stared down at me while I screamed and struggled?

The governor was saying something. I tried to hear him. 'Miss Beattie wants to talk to you. You will sit down and listen to her.' The boy hesitated.

'You'll have to look at me, David,' I said. And his eyes lifted. Hazel. Expressionless. The governor reached over, flicked on his desk lamp, and immediately the eyes were blue. Blue and familiar in their watchfulness. I felt my skin tighten. Yes, this was my prowler.

He sat down slowly.

'Why did you hit me, David?'

'I was scared,' he said in a low meek voice.

'So was I.'

The blond head went down, the eyes slipping from mine. 'I know. I'm awfully sorry.' He was a very polite young man.

16

The silence moved in again. Outside the rain pelted softly against the barred window. Traffic beyond moved in a busy, preoccupied world. In the real world. This was not real at all, this zoo, this man behind the big desk, this boy sliding down in a chair.

The governor coughed. He told David how kind it was of me to visit him. And I was suddenly appalled. I hadn't considered how this would appear to the boy. The governor caught my eye and halted the monologue.

'David?' I said. The eyes lifted once more, glittering now with defiance. 'I've talked with several people about you. Some of them have tried to help? What's the problem?' It was an idiotic question and an idiotic time to ask it. Even if he knew the answer, why would he tell me?

'I'm no good,' he said dully.

The governor interrupted. He agreed with David. Furthermore, he said, David was a failure even as a criminal. He was capable only of striking defenceless women. David's mouth tightened. Bewildered I felt a new emotion. Unexpectedly, I felt this boy's ally. I was listening with his ears, watching the governor and myself with his eyes, summoning from my own past the young fears and rebellions. I thought of other days when I had stood, shamefaced and stricken, before evidence of my own youthful misdeeds. Now, with this boy, I experienced again the unwelcome, embarrassed shame, the defiance and the peculiar loneliness. It had to be a matter of degree, the degree of the wrong-doing and the degree of the inward damage.

The governor was gathering steam. My own blood was quickening. I should have known better than to put a sixteen-year-old boy through this scene with his victim.

My voice stiff with annoyance, I reminded the governor that I had wanted to talk with David. The boy's eyes swerved to me, showing interest for the first time. The governor stopped his flow of scorn. His eyes were glinting, too. My voice had held chastisement.

'Go ahead,' he said, 'forget I'm here.'

David watched my confusion. Now that I had the platform I didn't know what to do with it. Haltingly I said I was not a Lady Bountiful, or a professional do-gooder. I just wanted to help him, if he wanted help. Then I sat back in the chair, silenced and shaken by this impulsive, unplanned offer.

'I want it,' David said simply. A lot of people had tried to help him, he admitted, and he guessed he just wasn't any good, like – he looked at the governor – everybody said. I searched the young face

17

for sarcasm. None was reflected. His mother, he added, was the best. I hadn't asked about his mother.

When it was time for him to return to his cell, he stood up, walked toward the door, and paused. I held out my hand. He took it in a limp clasp and gave me the first, faint smile. The door closed behind him.

The governor looked inquiringly at me. I shared his question. I had made an offer that lacked definition. It had sprung from what I had learned about David, from a stubborn refusal to accept the word 'incorrigible' and from a sympathetic curiosity, sharpened, I admitted, by the governor's attack.

But I had no idea what the offer entailed, or even how one went about helping a young offender.

'Well,' I sighed, 'that was interesting.'

A smile broke over his face. 'Yes, wasn't it.'

Shaken, I left his office.

Two days later there was a letter from David. He thanked me for visiting him. He apologized for his nervousness. He repeated that he wanted my friendship and he promised to 'do or say anything you want' when he got out. He didn't know when he would be transferred, he went on, or to which reformatory. But he would like me to visit him again. He would try to talk more the next time. He signed it, 'Your friend.'

The letter was written on Don Jail letterhead, with the censor's stamp at the bottom of the page. It looked as grim as the building.

I telephoned the Don to ask when David would be transferred. A voice said he had left that morning for the Ontario Reformatory at Guelph and that his sentence had been lengthened to fourteen months.

'But why?'

'The magistrate didn't know about the breach of probation,' the voice said.

'But he appeared in court three times: the morning after he was charged, the next Friday when his lawyer requested a psychiatric examination, and the following Friday for sentencing. How long does it take to get a report? Or to read it?'

'I guess,' the voice said, 'they were busy.'

I wrote to David that afternoon to ask about visiting regulations. He replied that I could visit him 'as a friend,' and he asked if I would notify him of any impending visit. He wasn't allowed two visitors in

18

the same visiting period and his mother would be coming to visit him, too.

That evening I re-read the letter. He sounded plaintively pleased with our friendship and extraordinarily eager to encourage it. Yet his lawyer had said, 'You can't get through to him.' If David's resistance to adults was so vigorous, why had he relaxed it with me? Because I hadn't criticized? Because my offer to help wasn't qualified? Unlikely. Perhaps he hadn't relaxed it at all. Perhaps he simply regarded me as a mark. I read the letter again, scanning it now for evidence of cunning. It still seemed childishly eager and childishly plaintive.

The reference to his mother was a reminder of my earlier intention to call her. The lawyer had given me her number. I had hesitated, for all the obvious reasons, but if I were going to be her son's friend, we should have some contact.

As I dialled I wondered what I would say if, understandably, she were not too pleased either about this peculiar friendship or about my activities on behalf of her son. But her voice held no surprise or embarrassment or disapproval. She asked no questions. I apologized for being an intruder in her life. She said it was all right. She didn't understand David, she said, and maybe that was a terrible admission for a mother to make about her own son, but I would understand what she meant. He was so . . . quiet. Kind to her, she added quickly, I mustn't get the wrong impression. And she loved him. I should know that, too. So had his father. And she had loved his father, too.

I was choking with questions I couldn't ask: what had David been like as a boy? What had they done the first time he got in trouble? Had they been strict or soft, worried or indifferent? What playmates had he when he was little? A dozen speculations crowded.

She knew from David that I offered friendship. She thought that was generous of me. The nature of the friendship, the reason for it, the reason why I would ask for a psychiatric examination of her son, none of this was put into words. Perhaps those were her unasked questions. We talked politely and she ended, 'I hope he's learned his lesson.'

We promised to keep in touch. We also agreed on the date I would visit David at the reformatory.

The Ontario Reformatory at Guelph, which will accommodate seven hundred male inmates, is set on 945 acres of farm land. It looks like

19

a massive government centre for agricultural research, surprisingly large and gaunt and economical, with windows that seem reluctant to let in the sunlight. The property is devoted largely to farming, with a herd of dairy cattle, since the institution supplies beef, among other things, to hospitals and to other reformatories. The sprawling buildings include the administration building, a school, a chapel, a hospital, a library, and a dental clinic. It is one of the few in Canada to provide facilities to help in the job of prisoner reformation.

For training purposes the industrial complex houses a bakery, a tailor shop, carpenter shop, laundry, motor licence-plate shop, knitting mill, cleaning shop, machine and blacksmith shop, and an iron bed factory.

The inmates, many of them first offenders, serve their time in mixed company. Some are young, between sixteen and twenty-one, others are older, veterans of penitentiaries where they have served sentences for more serious crimes.

Inside the main building, the day of my first visit, uniformed men directed me to a large, bright visitors' room, called the control tower. The room looked like a large recreation centre, with guards at the entrance and barred windows. The guard pointed to one of several long tables. 'Wait there,' he said.

A huge door swung open at the other end of the room and a line of young men, all in drab institutional clothing, walked in. They paraded to a far corner to be searched. Then, with a radiant smile, David joined me at the table.

If he felt strangeness, he didn't show it. He greeted me with the air of someone welcoming a guest to his home. He said wistfully that he had spent his first days 'just sitting' on a cot in his cell, staring at the bars. He couldn't even write letters. The bars, he said, set up a funny kind of barrier. But he decided his attitude was wrong. He had to make the best of this situation.

During the first weeks he had made licence plates. Now he worked in the laundry. He asked about job possibilities when he was released. And he blurted, 'I sure hope I don't let you down.'

At the end of half an hour, his name was called. David stood up. 'That's us,' he said. 'I'll take you back to the desk.' He was still the gracious host. He might have been any sixteen-year-old, whose only concern was the ballgame tomorrow or the exam next week. He talked eagerly as we walked across the room and he waited politely while I signed out. Then, with a broad smile, he went back to the waiting

20

cluster of inmates. At the door I looked back. David was watching, still smiling.

His attitude astonished me. I hadn't been prepared for this self-assurance, this poised friendliness, this air of being at home. Yet he had no responsibilities, except to comply with regulations. He was fed, clothed, and exercised – like an animal – but still cared for. He had no worries about his next meal, or shelter, or even a job. Normal living would be abeyance. Admittedly, confinement in itself would be a pressure and for some temperaments an intolerable one. But if you were afraid of life, uncertain about yourself, passive toward challenges, this might be an answer to your problems.

The advocates of physical punishment would be amused, I thought, by this confused reaction. They could say: 'You see? You find him relaxed. This is what we mean. Put welts on his back. He won't feel so comfortable and smug then.' But suppose, instead of teaching him a lesson, the welts only strengthened his defiance and his resolve to 'get even'? Suppose, instead of kindling remorse, or 'deterring' him, it merely confirmed the suspicion that society had to be outwitted, or repaid for real or imagined insults?

I was abruptly and selfishly grateful for those fourteen months before David would return to Toronto and our 'friendship' would go into practical motion. I wanted to know more about him and his letters would offer some clues. And I wanted to know more about this bewildering, contradictory, controversial world of the offender. Fourteen months would give me plenty of time to read, to talk with probation officers, social workers, law enforcement officers, even government officials. I would use the time carefully.

Chapter Four

But I didn't have fourteen months for a thoughtful, objective exploration of the offender's subculture. Because six months later there was Paul. And Paul belongs in this story because he affected all that was to come.

He came into my life as casually as a letter from a cousin. A friend, my cousin wrote, who was a guard at a training school, had mentioned a boy, due for early release, who wanted to get into radio or television. Since that was my field, could I help the boy find a job?

I didn't need this. My life was brimming over with work at the agency, with reading and talking to people in David's baffling world, and with a hectic personal life. But the guard, I decided, might be interesting as part of my research work, and appeals for help in getting located in showbusiness were so numerous I practically had a set format for assistance. So I telephoned the guard.

Paul, the boy, was eighteen, he said. A reserved kid, but intelligent. It was Paul's first time in a training school. Theft charge. He'd been a model inmate. 'I think this one might make it,' the guard said, 'if he gets a break.'

'What's his interest? Performing? Writing?'

'Nothing like that,' the guard said. 'It's servicing. He's taken courses here and he's pretty good. Fixed my radio once. Yes, I know,' he cut in when I started to speak, 'you're in the production end. But you probably have contacts you don't even know about. He won't know a soul in Toronto. Comes from a small town. And it's tough for a kid, alone in a big city, fresh from training school. Especially' – he threw in the ringer – 'since he'll be on parole.'

'On parole? I thought he was being released?'

'No. Six month's parole. He's earned it. But it makes finding that job a little more urgent. He'll have the extra pressures of parole. I mean emotionally.'

He was coming through clearly. 'And I should meet him,' I said, 'before I start on those contacts I didn't know I had.'

I visited the training school that Saturday. It was a serene and even attractive complex, with none of the starkness of the Don and none of the brooding impregnability of the Guelph Reformatory. I met the guard in the visitors' room. He was a tall, craggy, good-natured man, who shook my hand, said, 'Glad you could make it. I don't think you'll regret this,' and then telephoned for Paul to be brought to us.

We were standing by the window when a dark shadow fell over the doorway. It slipped into the room and hovered, silent and watchful. 'And this,' the guard said heartily, 'is Paul. He's good. Think you can help him get located?'

Medium height. Thin. Pale. Smooth, dark hair. Long lashes fanning down over white cheeks. A disciplined mouth. An air of aloneness. Did they all have to look so alone? He lifted black eyes and searched my face. There was no smile.

'Well,' I said, conscious of the watchful eyes, 'I can try.' I suggested Paul come directly to my office when he arrived in Toronto. I even drew a map for him. 'There you are,' I said, like a master of ceremonies warming up an audience. He refused to be warmed. 'Thank you,' he said, glanced at the guard, received the nod of permission, and put the map in his pocket.

For two weeks I made the inquiries. Everyone was kind and discouraging. One executive said I was doing a fine thing. 'Just what they need,' he said, 'someone to give them a hand. Tough to find a job when you're an ex-con.' When I protested that an eighteen-year-old, who had been in a training school on a first offence, could hardly be classed as an ex-con, be boomed, 'Absolutely right. Shouldn't think of them that way. Keep at it. Great work you're doing.' I thought of David. This would be familiar to him. And perhaps it was a preview for me.

The day Paul arrived there were no job offers and no scheduled interviews. He took the news without comment. 'But we'll find something,' I said brightly, to cover a spurt of guilt.

'Yes.' The word was a block of purpose.

'Now, how about a place to stay?'

'Somebody said the east side would be cheapest.'

'I suppose,' I said doubtfully. 'How's your money situation?' Silence. 'Sorry,' I said, 'I'm not prying. Just being practical.'

'I have twenty dollars,' he said with a trace of defiance. 'What I earned at the training school.'

'Oh.' Twenty dollars? For Toronto? On parole? With no job prospects.

'I got to check in with my parole officer,' he said. 'I got to get going.' His tone chided. I had been no help after all and now I was detaining him.

'Would you like to have dinner with me?' I asked impulsively. At his doubtful look I said: 'When I was a couple of years older than you are now I was rattling around alone in New York. I would have given almost anything to have had dinner with a friend the first day in town.'

'But you don't know me.'

'You don't know me, either,' I laughed. 'If we hate each other, we've only lost a couple of hours. Want to come back around six?'

The dark eyes lingered, full of questions. Then he nodded and, softly, noiselessly, he was gone.

There was no real similarity between David and Paul. Even the quality of their quiet differed. David threw out the impression of a meek acceptance of his lack of worth. Paul had no meekness. His quiet was almost an accusation. And, I realized with surprise, it wasn't hard to believe he would steal, perhaps because he seemed so defiantly self-contained, as if he had decided a long time ago that he could trust no one but himself. Yet he did have a disturbing air of innocence.

He returned promptly at six, appearing in the doorway with a smile flickering like a guttering candle. His parole officer had been out, he reported. He would have to go back tomorrow. And he had found a room. On the east side. He gave that news as if it were an accomplishment he wanted recorded. He mentioned the street and I winced. Under parole regulations he was not permitted to 'fraternize' with former inmates of training schools, reformatories, or prisons. Yet he was released with so little money that the scramble to survive, barring a miracle, would take him into the very areas in which such veterans were most likely to congregate. 'What about the Y?' I asked.

'With twenty bucks?' he countered dryly.

I studied the thin young face and responded to the innocence. 'We might make an arrangement. You could repay me when you're working. Or your parole officer?' A look of surprise flashed across his face, surprise at my ignorance. 'Oh. Money is not part of the aid and comfort?' Silence. 'Well, we'll discuss it later.'

We had dinner in a restaurant that was a showbusiness favourite. A few personal friends stopped at our table. Paul indicated no interest in them, even as names he might recognize. When I apologized for the interruptions, his shoulders lifted. 'I don't mind,' he said. 'When older people are talking, I pretend I'm not there.' I digested that morsel. He looked around. 'But aren't you embarrassed being here with a kid? I mean some of them might, you know, wonder.'

'They might think you're my son.' I had digested the morsel.

'I mean the ones who know you.'

'Then they know me.' He said nothing. 'Oh, I see. You mean they might think you're a . . . boyfriend?' I tried not to laugh. 'Well, if they want to think that, it's their problem, isn't it?' His look was still tentative. 'And you wonder if I'm in the market for a teenage boyfriend? I'm not.' He relaxed slightly. 'Anything else bothering you?'

'I guess,' he said, 'I don't get why you'd want to help me.'

'I haven't, so far,' I reminded him. 'But people do help other people, you know. It isn't that remarkable or questionable. When I was starting out, people helped me. Now,' as he relaxed, 'may I ask a question?' His eyes narrowed. 'Easy,' I smiled, 'I meant where do you come from?'

He named a small town in northern Ontario. He added, almost casually, that he didn't know his parents. 'I was put out when I was a baby. I've lived in twenty-three foster homes.' I swallowed shock. 'My parents didn't want me,' he said in the same even tone. When I murmured, 'that would be hard to know,' he looked up. 'I know,' he said and closed the subject.

We talked of impersonal things: the agency, Toronto, television. And slowly a subtle, almost sophisticated humour poked through his stoic manner. But when, accidentally, we stumbled into a reference to his parole officer, the anger in his voice was startling. 'You don't like parole?' I asked. 'You'd prefer to have served out your time?'

'I'd have gone crazy if I'd been locked up much longer.' His thin fingers tightened around the water glass. 'But I don't like people on my back.'

'You may like him,' I said and thought of the probation officer I had met through David. 'They try to help, you know, not ride you.'

'Sure,' he said, 'he'll be swell. Everybody's been swell.'

'The world isn't that bad,' I said and an Edna St. Vincent Millay line danced mockingly across my mind. 'My dear, my dear, it's not so dreadful here.' What evidence did he have that it wasn't so dreadful here? 'I'm sorry it's been rough for you,' I said and again my voice sounded guilty, as if I were responsible for that rough life. For an instant I felt as if I had been, and I thought: maybe this is what the Don Jail priest was talking about. Ignorance doesn't remove the responsibility.

'Thank you,' he said politely. 'And thanks for dinner, too, but I should explain. I'm not allowed in places that serve liquor. It's a breach of parole. I could be sent back.'

'I'm sorry, Paul. I didn't know. We'll find more appropriate places.' At least he's loaded with responsibility to himself, I thought with a mixture of thankfulness and amusement. But what prompted me to hold out the promise of an association beyond the formal and hopefully brief one of job-hunting help?

He glanced at his watch. He should get back to his room, he said. He wasn't due to be in until eleven but someone had told him it was a good idea to be in early the first night 'in case they check.' He has been well briefed, I thought, and probably by more experienced inmates. I suggested he telephone or call in at the office the next day. 'We have to get busy on the job hunt,' I said cheerfully and his face tightened.

'Yes,' he said. 'I'll come in. Save a dime.'

Paul returned the next afternoon and every afternoon that week. In the Elda Edder of Norse wisdom literature there are two lines: 'The mind knows only/What lies near the heart.' Sympathy was lying near my heart and my mind knew it. David's problems, whatever they were, paled beside the haunting vision of a child, shuttled around twenty-three foster homes, belonging nowhere and carrying with him the conviction that he was unwanted. And no one, it seemed, wanted him professionally, either. Each day he reported no success and each day he left my office with no leads. Each day, too, he showed more strain.

The question of his confinement seldom came up. I didn't question him because I wanted those bruises to fade as swiftly as possible. But it was there. It had to be there when prospective employers asked where he had been trained. He elected to lie, to name a school in

26

another city. That may, or may not, have worked. There were the next-in-line questions about references and diplomas. When I was asked I evaded the question, unless the questioner were a trusted business associate. But a great many people knew now about David. It was a short, logical step from David to Paul. I was receiving practical lessons about the offenders' world, and through those days I trudged emotionally from pity and sympathy, through incredulity, into a kind of quietly raging despair.

I hadn't seen his room, but I could imagine it and I tried to stave off its inevitable depression with dinners, movies, walks through the city, and evenings at my apartment where Paul tried to teach me chess — at which, it turned out, I was excruciatingly bad. Somewhere around the end of the second week he agreed to take a room at the Y. I loaned him the money. And the third weekend, as therapy for his bruised ego, we visited my parents in another city.

That's when he asked if I could become his parole officer, an idea which reduced me to helpless laughter. 'There's no such thing as an Instant Parole Officer,' I choked, 'and anyway I wouldn't know how to go about it.'

'I could teach you,' he grinned laconically. 'I got experience.'

It was a ridiculous idea, but if it weren't impossible, I thought, it might have been valuable as proof that people would go beyond normal limits to help him. And that was looming as an important necessity. He needed desperately to be able to trust someone, to believe that at least one person would unservingly support him. At that moment, with his strenuous resistance to that authority-figure, his parole officer, I seemed the only candidate for the job.

'Couldn't you find out anyway?' he pleaded.

So on Monday I telephoned his parole officer. This was absurd, of course, I said, but I had promised to ask, so just for the record . . . 'Actually,' he broke in, 'it's not a bad idea.' His caseload was heavy and 'this one needs a good deal of personal attention. You have no experience?'

'None,' I said promptly.

'How did you get involved?'

I reviewed the story of David, admitted to sympathy and curiosity, and explained the circumstances of meeting Paul. The parole officer was silent. 'I think,' he said at last, 'it might work. I'd be here if you needed me. You could fill out the report forms, sign them, have him sign them and return them to me. Yes,' he repeated, 'it might work.'

'Don't you want to meet me?' I blurted, panic-stricken.

'You sound responsible,' he said, 'I don't think it's necessary.'

When I hung up I stared aghast at the telephone. I had become an impossibility, an Instant Parole Officer. And I had two resident delinquents. In an effort to remain calm I drew up a list. Paul needed money, a job, a place that gave a greater sense of home, money, friends his own age, money, and most of all insight into his problems. 'I've gone clean out of my mind,' I said aloud.

That evening, when I gave Paul the news, I explained two points. I was not a sergeant-major type. It was too late for me to learn the technique. I would expect co-operation without need to pull rank, or I'd resign. Secondly, while I agreed that some of the rules appeared unnecessary with him, they would all be followed. If he hoped for a more flexible arrangement under this plan, he was mistaken.

'I understand.' He put out a hand. 'Shake on it.'

And so it began; that incredible, six-month journey through the anxious, grey land called 'rehabilitation,' my partner a teenager who was a shaft of darkness, an accusing shadow falling over the days, a boy bristling with defiance and antagonism, who could chill gaiety with a glance and instil guilt and defensiveness with a word, a teenager who seemed as fragile as crystal and as indestructible as man's demand to survive. And about him always the aura of waiting. Or was it I who waited?

I had envisioned my role as a six-month companion in his efforts to find a job, fashion a new life, and, hopefully, develop that insight. It was an ambitious vision and an unrealistic one. I had no experience in the routine of helping a job hunter who carried the emotional and practical stigma of a record. I had no experience in being the target, as every parole and probation officer must be, for the disappointments, the frustrations, the angers, and the bitterness. Most of all, I was unprepared for the depth of my own sense of responsibility to this stranger – not only for immediate help, but in an unfathomable fashion, for easing the misery of the past. I didn't know then, either, that this unconscious emotion is another hazard for everyone who becomes involved with the troubled young.

The end of the first jobless month Paul said his girlfriend was coming to Toronto from his hometown. I joyfully envisioned evenings when I could read a book, wash my hair, think a thought and stop smiling. But she had barely arrived, this quiet, pretty girl, older than

Paul and full of questions about my involvement, before she was gone again. Perhaps they quarrelled. Perhaps she had come to tell him their relationship was over. Paul gave no explanation. And I went back to smiling.

The fifth week, when the situation was reaching Red Alert both financially and emotionally, I called his official parole officer for help. He suggested the John Howard Society and thankfully I called them. As an organization set up to help ex-convicts I assumed they would be eager to help a first-timer. Perhaps they were. Perhaps Paul, with his boundless air of unco-operation, put them off. Or perhaps my participation distorted the picture. But during the interview Paul remained a silent wall against which the man bounced geniality and practicality. When it was apparent he would never be Paul's friend, father-image or mentor, he turned us over to another man who tried just as valiantly. Unfortunately he leaned heavily on the difficulties-of-getting-a-job-when-you-have-a-record. Maybe he intended it as a challenge. It wasn't. It merely underlined Paul's dependency on that hated, necessary enemy – society. We parted with no job leads, no offers of concrete help and hearty reminders it would be tough. I could have brained them. I didn't know what they should or could have done, but, whatever it was, they hadn't done it.

The end of the second month, in desperation, I yielded to the temptation to unload part of my responsibility on a personal friend who was an executive in a department store. 'There's this boy,' I told him, 'fresh from training school. If he doesn't get a job soon he may go back and if my bank manager has his way, I may go with him.'

My friend laughed. 'Your approach is original. You're suppose to say this is a reformed boy who deserves a break and that some day, when he's a contributing member of society, he'll bring his kids into my office and we'll all cry because I made it possible.'

'That too,' I agreed wearily, 'but will you please give him a job? I'll be responsible, for what that's worth.'

I heard him sigh. 'Buy me lunch,' he said, 'and don't let this become a habit.' I thought of David.

Paul wasn't delighted with the new job. His training had equipped him for a position higher than that of an apprentice. He was being cheated. Again. But, realistically, it meant a paycheque and a home for him. He found a basement studio in a private home, and gratefully, even happily, I checked two items off the list.

29

But they were the practical items, the average goals of an average young job hunter. And Paul wasn't an average young job hunter. He had a record and behind that record were the problems that had put him in the training school. Moreover he was on parole, facing what the guard had termed the pressures of parole.

Persuasions that he try to find friends his own age seemed doomed. He had no hobbies except chess, and chess players are seldom teenagers. He wasn't interested in study groups, dances, church groups, political groups or any other kind of group. His good reason for resistance to every suggestion was relentless disinterest. The real reason was his record. And parole. And his past.

'What do I have in common with the average teenage crowd?' he would demand.

'Being eighteen?'

'Sure,' the dark eyes would flash accusingly, 'plus a record. And I'm out somewhere and suddenly it's ten-thirty. What do I say? Sorry, I got to go because I'm Cinderella and I turn into a pumpkin at eleven o'clock? Or' – bitterly – 'into an ex-con?'

'It's only three more months,' I would point out.

'And then it's all wiped clean? Then I don't have a record?'

And what do you say, I wonder. But you were the one who stole, Paul? Now you must take the consequences? Did you tell this starved eighteen-year-old that society wasn't to blame for that? Did you say that society had done its best? After all, society found shelter for you, Paul. Twenty-three shelters. Society fed and clothed and housed you: filled the cavities in your teeth – if not in your emotions; took care of you when you were sick – physically; exposed you to an education – of sorts? Did you tell him that society cared when a child was uprooted and relocated when, for some reason, the last home, the last shelter, hadn't worked out? Did you tell him society honestly cared when an unwanted child cried in the night? And did you tell him that society even had a category for him in the clinical, textbook analysis of delinquency? Broken-home child, that's you, Paul. The set-adrift child. All the books list you as the 'potential delinquent.' And did you explain, as society was eager to explain – out of guilt – that lots of kids had 'gone through bad times' and had become 'contributing members of society' – which meant contributing to the society that did so much for you, Paul. Most significantly, did you remind him that, while society would cheer – if it noticed – when you made it, society would also lock you up as an incorrigible if you didn't?

30

The thousand deforming demons – the guilt, which comes from feeling unwanted and therefore inexplicably inadequate, the revenge and hate, which are the fruits of guilt, the terror and loneliness and ruthless needs – they all danced and jabbed in him. And once they burst through the stern guard he had thrown up against further pain. Once there were tears, pouring from him in great racking sobs like the cries of all the lost and lonely in life. And when they died, he wrenched from the last shudder and turned to me, black eyes filled with cold, hard resentment. I had witnessed the inner misery and plunder. I had glimpsed the needs. And my comfort, my caring, was another shame.

Perhaps it was then, in that instant, that I caught a glimpse, too, of the further damage I could inflict, despite the sympathy, despite the passionate determination to try to wipe out some of that inner torment. Because my instinct was to remove the shame, to reassure him, to offer an even greater measure of security. And so deeply troubled, so lonely and confused a boy could never understand that this was intended as a springboard into life, not a refuge, an escape, from it. And I wasn't equipped, through training or experience, to help him to understand.

When it was time for the fourth monthly report, I took inventory. Emotional inventory. He showed signs of more self-confidence. He moved with greater ease through the city. But he was digging deeper into this unit which, unknowingly, I had fashioned and which satisfied his longing to belong. He was making no effort to make a life of his own, apart from that false and potentially wounding unit.

In fright – and that is the only way to describe it – I called a psychiatrist with whom I had worked on a radio series. He agreed Paul probably needed psychiatric therapy, but it would be futile, even dangerous, to suggest it. 'He'll think you consider him a sick freak,' the psychiatrist said. 'You can't undo the damage of eighteen years in a few months and yes, you can make things worse. I'd recommend you begin to discourage this constant association. He's growing too dependent on it. Unless you intend to adopt him which,' his voice held a rueful laugh, 'I gather isn't the case, it is unrealistic and bad for him. Try to get things on a more practical level.'

I did try. I began by slowly being less available, less yielding, less pampering. But panic over the hurt I might inflict and a sense of frustrated helplessness in attempting a task which, as the psychiatrist said, was really one for a 'qualified' person were constant influences.

I was trying too hard, too nervously, and Paul, confused by the subtle and persistent change, began his own slow withdrawal, shoring up against still another rejection. The careful comments, the encouragement that he seek the world of his peers, the 'practical' conversations about his problems, they all went through the filter of past experience, past hurt, and a solid expectation of inevitable abandonment. I wasn't conscious of it all then. I knew only that he was developing a new and worrying brand of resistance.

The parole rules became points of sarcasm. The eleven o'clock deadline was absurd, unless I expected him 'to go berserk and kill somebody.' When we dined in restaurants without liquor licences, he would remark dryly that he was glad I wouldn't let him near the drinking troughs, since he might 'contaminate the drunks.' And the fraternization rule became an issue. One evening he mentioned a training-school friend he met accidentally on the street. 'We're gonna get a bottle and have ourselves a time,' he announced.

'It's up to you, of course,' I said, grabbing anxiety, 'but if you're caught, you know the possible results.' And he left the apartment. To meet his friend? I didn't know.

Then one afternoon he tramped angrily into the office to say he had been picked up for questioning. When, startled, I asked why, he shrugged derisively, 'Because I'm on the list. I got a record, remember? Every time someone pulls a job in my specialty, which happens to be stealing, I'll be hauled in for questioning. They're gonna be on my back until I die. And you talk about a fresh start!'

'I think you're overreacting,' I said mildly, but the next day I called one of the detectives. I told him about Paul.

'That bang on the head really got to you,' he sighed. 'And you don't know these punks.'

'Maybe not and I'm not asking for special favours. But I do know something about this kid. Could you please take it a little easy?'

'Tell you what,' he said, 'we'll take it easy, but if we find your faith is misplaced, he's inside in a flash. Incidentally,' he added with a chuckle, 'what's with the other one?'

'David? Still in Guelph, thank goodness. I can think of few things I need less right now than another troubled teenager.'

'Shame,' he scolded mockingly. 'You're supposed to be bleeding from every pore because he's locked up. What happens when he gets out? And he will get out, you know. He wasn't hanged.'

'I hope I know more. I hope I've learned something from all this that will be useful — to both of us.'

'Sorry you got into it?' he asked softly.

Was I sorry? 'In a way. I think I'm too appalled by what we do to kids to be sorry or glad. I just wish I knew more.'

'Welcome to the club,' he said. 'Welcome to the club.'

I fished out the memory of David, friendly and laughing in the control tower at the reformatory. It was unfair to compare him with Paul, but I had to admit that he sounded less exhausting. At least in his letters.

Our correspondence had been regular, despite Paul, although there had been one letter from him in which he said worriedly that he had not heard from me in almost a month. Had he done or said something wrong? Guiltily I had written that my silence was solely the result of frenzied activity at the agency and an effort to help a young friend, newly released from training school. David took that news without comment. In his reply he was more eager to report that his mother had remarried. 'As long as she's happy,' he wrote, with only a hint of martyrdom, 'that's all that matters.'

I had put that letter aside, thankful that at least one of my resident delinquents was, apparently, under a measure of emotional control.

Chapter Five

Was it Thoreau who said, 'We are punished for our suspicions by finding what we suspected?' I did have occasional, flickering suspicions, especially about the now-resisting Paul. I must have. I found them one afternoon. And it happened because I did an article for *Maclean's Magazine*.

When Pierre Berton, the editor of that era, asked for a story on David, I refused. David might interpret it as exploitation. Pierre argued that I could be more useful to boys like David if I told this story in print. People were not deliberately uncaring, he said, they were only innocent of facts. 'Tell them this story, show them this one boy, and some will become interested in all boys like him.'

I agreed with the theory, but I questioned David's capacity to understand it. Pierre threw in the clincher. If I didn't write the story, he would assign another writer to it. And that was too risky. David would emerge from official reports and the comments of observers who were not exactly overwhelmed with sympathy for him. It was not inconceivable that I would emerge either as the heroine, the female David armed with a sequined slingshot, fighting the mighty Goliath of indifference, innocence, hostility toward offenders and even our system, or else a do-gooder who, however you sliced it, was still a blind idealist. Either image would prejudice a reader.

And, equally, if not more important, any of it could be damaging to David personally and to our relationship.

So I wrote the story and sent a letter to David, telling him that he would be protected by a fictitious name and that I hoped he agreed it could be helpful to other people. His reply was predictable. 'I'm very glad you're writing it,' he wrote. 'And I'll be proud to read it.'

I hadn't told Paul about David. I was afraid he might think I collected young offenders as a hobby. Now, when I explained, he tilted an eyebrow. 'Aren't you afraid people will think you're a nut? I mean, offering to help some creep who hits you over the head?' He paused. 'Yeah,' he grinned, 'I remember. That's their problem.'

The only surprise – and maybe shock describes it more accurately – was an unexpected and enlightening confrontation with the Department of Reform Institutions. The magazine wanted pictures inside the Ontario Reformatory. The routine request was passed from government hand to government hand until it reached the then deputy minister. He refused. Spiritedly. I assured him the story was merely a personal experience, not an 'exposé' of anything. He still refused. The denial of the right of the public to see inside a reform institution, supported by public funds, through the pages of a reputable magazine, seemed unreasonable and absurd. With growing irritation I announced his refusal would be included in the story. The reader would be left to ask the reason. The deputy minister reversed his decision. The magazine's photographer would be permitted inside, but only to take pictures in the control tower – where the public was free to visit.

When the story came out, entitled 'I Made Friends with My Burglar,' a new world opened up. At a cocktail party a man intoned, 'When I read it, I said to myself, that's easy. She fell in love with the bloke. I was right, wasn't I?' I couldn't reply. I had already spilled half my drink. Another man slapped me on the back when we were introduced. 'My God!' he shouted. 'You don't fit the image! I thought you were a frustrated old maid, all flat heels and good works!' And another asked what kind of trouble I had been in as a teenager. 'Fascinating case of identification,' he prodded. 'Just proves you can never escape your subconscious.'

There were countless others eager to speculate on my psychological hang-ups. And only a few were genuinely interested in the problems of young offenders.

On the other side of society's wall, I discovered how many wanted a friend. Some looked for jobs. Some wanted money. Some wanted whatever 'friendship' entailed. And there were the sad parents, convinced of their sons' innocence, tracking every lead to possible assistance. A week after the story came out it was clear I could become the busiest unpaid social worker in the country.

Then a nineteen-year-old telephoned for an interview. He was newly released from prison. He wanted to talk it over. When he arrived he was refreshingly honest. He needed work; if he didn't find it in the legitimate market place, he would return to his old profession. Stealing.

When we explored the situation we agreed there was a good chance he would pick up his thief's tools once more. He wouldn't inspire sympathy in most prospective employers and his job training was nil. But he took the list of names and assured me he would try to be more humble.

At the door he paused. 'Look,' he said, 'this ain't none of my business, but you seem straight. I wasn't gonna say nothin', but this guy you're helpin' – not the one in Guelph, the other one, the one who's makin' an idiot of you.' Warning bells crashed. 'I heard what he's sayin' and my advice is smarten up. He thinks he's got a great thing goin'.' He rolled his eyes. 'He's boastin' about his conquest.'

My voice was chilled. 'You must be mistaken.'

'Okay,' he waved a hand, 'if that's the way you want it, but I tell you, this guy's laughin' at you.' Memory threw up a dozen frozen images of Paul. 'He tell you anythin' about himself? Anythin' true?'

'I thought all he told me was true.'

'Sure. Okay. He tell you he visited his father one weekend when you was tied up? He tell you he knows him?' At my blank stare he nodded. 'No, huh. You got the poor-little-orphan routine. Okay, so part of that's true, but not all. And did he tell you he stole from the last family that took him in? Did he tell you that's why he went to jail, because they got fed up? Other families got fed up, too.' He looked sorrowfully at me. 'You really trusted him, right?'

'Yes.' Anger crackled. 'I trusted him. Aren't people who don't rob or cheat or lie supposed to trust?'

'Not bandits,' he said promptly. 'Not thieves, hoods, punks. And don't never forget that. We got our code. It don't cover squares. Why don't you write him off?'

I straightened in the chair. 'Thanks. Let me know what happens to you. And if I can help, you know where to find the easiest mark in town.'

He flipped a finger against his forehead and went out the door. I turned to face the window. Every memory pranced between my eyes and the view from the sixteenth floor. And raw, hurt rage exploded. I would splatter Paul all over the walls. I rehearsed the scene of my denunciation. He would never know what hit him.

The fury lasted several minutes. Deflated I slumped back. He had asked only for help in finding a job. Even that request had not originated with him. If I had chosen to ladle out anything else, that was my responsibility. I had known he was a damaged, emotionally twisted boy. This anger was wounded pride and the pain of being betrayed in a faith. And people who tried to help young offenders couldn't afford the luxury of either emotion.

It struck me then that I had accepted this story almost without question. Why? Because I knew the hurt take their revenge and I knew I had hurt Paul? I couldn't be sure of that. Paul's informer hadn't said when he had heard the story. And what if he were mistaken, or lying for some reason. It was pointless to ask Paul. If the story were true, he would deny it. If it were untrue, my doubt could dynamite any good in our relationship.

The next meeting with Paul was an exercise in restraint. When he appeared in the office door the ghost of his informer stood beside him. There had to be an explanation. Perhaps Paul had said something that had been repeated, exaggerated, or completely misunderstood. But to whom would he talk? The boy from the training school? He was seeing him? And perhaps others?

'What's the matter?' Paul asked abruptly.

'I was thinking about your training-school friend. How is he making out?'

His eyes widened in surprise. 'How would I know. I'm not supposed to have those unhealthy associations. And how come you thought of him?'

'The magazine article,' I said vaguely. 'It's taken me down some strange paths.'

Over dinner he was unusually quiet. Finally he took a deep breath. 'I've decided to buy a car,' he said. 'I need one. The dealer wants a signature. He says yours will do.'

Here we go again, I thought. 'I'm afraid not, Paul. It's your decision, of course, but I would recommend that you wait. Second-hand cars aren't cheap. Repairs, general maintenance,' I waved a hand.

'I don't want a lecture,' he cut in sharply. 'I just want your signature.'

'And my money if you can't meet the payments,' I inserted gently. 'These are the responsibility items we've discussed.'

'Forget it,' he said flatly, angrily. 'I'll get the signature. And the money.' He paused. 'Somehow,' he added significantly and I ignored the insinuation, the jab of emotional blackmail which had become part of his new approach.

'Up to you,' I repeated and surprise flashed across his face.

I was busy during the next few weeks, busier to Paul than to anyone. He telephoned regularly, the first time to say triumphantly that he had his car. And we met infrequently for dinner. Some of the tension had gone from him. He appeared even to be accepting our new relationship without resentment. And sometimes, when we talked, the informer's story seemed impossible. But the question persisted, the awkward question that would not be banished. If the story were true, and if Paul had, indeed, been 'playing me for a sucker' over the months, would I have acted the same way if it had been David? I was thankful David was still in Guelph. I had a patch of time to sort things out – again – before that would change.

So the letter from David, one October morning, announcing his imminent arrival in Toronto, was a dreadful shock. He would come directly to the office, he wrote, and he was awfully excited. Marvelous. I circled the date on my desk calendar, prayed for a reprieve and, ironically, went to meet Paul for a dinner to celebrate the end of his parole. During it he said, his eyes watching me, that he did thank me 'for everything.' Then he put out his hand. 'We made it,' he said. 'Shake on it.' We shook on it.

For ten days I told myself something would happen to prevent what privately I thought of as another bout with a delinquent. And I tried to find one valid excuse to renounce my pledge of help, one justification for withdrawing that idiotic offer. It was unfair and unreasonable to David, but the journey with Paul had put me on a strange, unwelcome, self-revealing rack. I wasn't anxious to plunge in again and I thought of the probation officer's remark, during our first conversation: 'Working with these kids takes a hell of a lot out of you.'

But one morning I walked into my office, sank into a chair and stared at the calendar. It had to be a mistake. Or I was hallucinating. This could not be the day of David's return to Toronto.

David was prompt that afternoon. He had said he would be in my office by three o'clock and precisely at three the desk telephone rang. I didn't answer it. Nothing in the world, I decided frantically, could make me answer it. I simply wasn't programmed for this kind of work. It rang again.

The receptionist said a gentleman was waiting to see me. 'Will you ask him to come up, please?' I said and took a compact from my bag. My face looked composed. It should not look composed.

David was smiling in the doorway. 'David!' I cried shrilly. 'How wonderful to see you!' He stepped into the office. 'Close the door,' I waved urgently. 'Take off your coat. Sit down.' And drop dead, I added silently.

He closed the door and stopped, confused by the commands. He started to take off his coat and paused, one arm still in the sleeve, to look for a peg. The coat dropped to the floor. Slowly he turned, looking like a puppy anxious to please and uncertain about the way. I fell back in the chair. 'Want to start again?' I giggled.

His grin widened. He picked up the coat, folded it and put it on the filing cabinet. Then he lowered himself cautiously into a chair. 'Hello' he said.

I looked at the thin, pale, young face, the child's mouth, the wide, hazel eyes, free of wariness. 'How are you?' I asked, with a creeping shyness. We were on neutral ground now. The first meeting shouldn't count. The second had been on my ground, where the victim receives proof of revenge. At the Guelph Reformatory it had been his ground. He was at home there. But this time we met as equals. He had paid his debt. As the vicitm I had received my satisfaction.

'Fine,' he said. He looked through the office window at Toronto spreading north. 'A little scared. That is scary, at first.'

'Of course,' I said comfortingly. 'It's bound to be.' He did look nervous. 'How's your mother?'

'She's fine. She'd like to meet you.'

'I'd like to meet her,' I said politely and thought what a ridiculous conversation. 'What about her husband?' David looked confused. 'I mean how is he? And do you like him?'

'He's okay.'

A topic not to be pursued, I thought. 'You've been home, of course. I mean today.'

'Sure,' he nodded, leaning back in the chair. 'I got in this morning. I was going to come straight here, but I wanted to get sort of, well,' he grinned, a little shyly, 'cleaned up first. I don't mean just from the bus trip. I mean,' he looked out the window again, 'you always feel kind of grimy when you come out of . . . that place.'

'Yes,' I said. 'And have you any plans? Are you going to take a holiday?'

'I've had my holiday,' he said dryly. 'I got to find a job.'

'Of course.' This is the boy from the Don Jail, I told myself. This is the teenager at the reformatory. This is my pen pal. This is also the cool young man, my mind snapped, who conked you on the head. 'I haven't done any job hunting for you,' I said firmly. 'I didn't know what might interest you and anyway I think it's better for you to find a job yourself.'

A chuckle, friendly and understanding, from David. He thinks I'm nervous because he is newly released from a reformatory. 'Sorry,' I said to sympathetic eyes, 'I'm a little disjointed. We've been busy around here. And that boy I mentioned turned out to be more of a problem than I had anticipated.' That is the other problem, I realized. I'm conscious of the possibility that he's heard the story.

'I'm sorry,' he said. 'You have bad luck with us.'

'Do I?' I smiled at him, a cool, adult smile. 'That remains to be seen, doesn't it?' He said nothing. 'Well now,' my voice took on a business-like briskness, as if I were trying to control the conversation through rank of years. 'Have you decided on the kind of work you'd like?'

He slid down in the chair and abruptly the boy at the Don was back. The transformation was startling. His eyes were downcast, his mouth thin, his hands as tense as the rest of him. He is responding to the tone of my voice, I thought, that kindly but superior tone, the one adults use when they feel threatened by the young.

'Sure,' he mumbled, 'but I'm not qualified.'

'Could you become qualified?' I said encouragingly.

'I guess. But I can't afford to take the courses.'

And I stiffened. Not again. The bank dried up. If you want to be a doctor, or lawyer, or scientist, I told the face silently, you're on your own. He caught my change of expression. 'I want a job and then I'll think about it,' he said quickly. 'Right now anything will do. I want to leave home, too. Mom and her new husband won't want me around.'

'They told you that?'

'No. But that's how I feel.' He tapped his shoe. 'I'll get a room. When I'm working.'

'Does your mother live at the same address?' I asked, trying to ease the conversation back to a friendlier, more relaxed level.

A strand of blond hair fell over his forehead. He took a comb from his pocket and lovingly manoeuvred the hair back into the ducktail style. 'Sure,' he said, 'near where you live.'

'I'm thinking of moving.'

'You should,' he said gravely. 'That place has bad memories.' He

40

might have been referring to something with which he had no connection. 'Well,' he stirred in the chair, 'you're busy and I got to see the guys.'

'Would you like to have dinner with me?'

'Mom wants me home tonight.'

'Of course. Then, tomorrow night?'

A widening grin. 'Okay. You want to meet somewhere?'

'Why don't you come here about seven. We'll decide then where to eat?'

'Sure.' He stood up, reached for his coat and opened the door. 'See you then.' And, with a grin, he waved goodbye. I watched his silhouette pass the glass wall of my office and I was amused by my earlier apprehension. He was really quite likeable. This was different from Paul. In every way. I swung to look through the window. And certainly I had served my painful, illuminating apprenticeship.

Chapter Six

It was cool, that evening of our first dinner together, with a rosy dusk that deepened slowly into lavender. We took the Yonge Street subway and rattled through the deepening twilight to a restaurant near my apartment. David said it would be more convenient for me.

While the other diners talked and laughed around us, David explained that he had been to Parkdale the previous evening. Did I know the area? No? It was in the west end of the city. He knew a lot of guys there. They had been glad to see him. They hadn't changed at all, he said, with surprise that his absence would make no difference. 'You'd like these guys,' he said, as if he knew my taste in people.

'Do they . . .' I was about to ask if they worked in the area, but David anticipated another question.

'Steal?' he supplied calmly. 'Yeah. Some. Not all.'

'As a profession?' I held back a laugh. He said it as one might explain that his friends were mostly doctors or salesmen.

'I guess. They don't work at it all the time. But they don't work much at anything else.' And he grinned. His hazel eyes glittered under the lights. When he turned his head they were blue, but I felt no leap of remembrance.

'You're putting me on,' I accused.

'I'm not,' he said indignantly.

'So how's business?'

'Pretty good for some,' and he grinned again, 'not for others.'

'When business isn't good,' I felt a stirring of curiosity, 'how do they live?'

'Unemployment insurance. Welfare. Most of them got families. When they're living at home they don't have any eating problems. When they aren't . . .'

'They don't live at home all the time?'

He shook his blond head. 'Course not. If everything's okay, they stay home. When they're not making it too good there, they move out.'

'For what reason?'

'You know, folks beefing or boozing or something. Then they move.'

42

'To where?'

His eyes widened. I was more innocent than he had assumed. 'They get a room, of course. Or sleep in the restaurant. Or shack up,' he glanced up quickly from his veal cutlet, 'I mean with another guy. Share, like.'

'Sometimes they sleep in restaurants?'

'Sure,' the grin again, 'cheapest rent in town. A coke a night.'

'The restaurant people permit this?'

'They ain't . . . aren't crazy about it. But when they get mad, there is always another restaurant.'

David's swift correction of grammar was endearing. He was careful in conversations with me to have every 'g' in place, too. Words might slur, or be transposed, but he was trying. In one of his letters he had said he thought he might like to be a writer. As a bid for my interest it wasn't subtle, but at least he was trying to 'do or say anything you want.'

'It's interesting,' I said now, 'but is it a satisfactory way of living?'

His slim shoulders lifted. 'Not the greatest, but what are you gonna do?'

What indeed? And amusement died. 'You're still planning to go into a different line of work?'

David put down his fork. 'Yes,' he said earnestly. 'Like I told you at first up there I was gonna go back to a life of crime.' He made it sound like a choice between law and medicine. 'But I got to thinking. You offering to help and everything. I decided not to. Go back to crime I mean. I'm gonna try. It's gonna be hard,' and he shivered.

'Why would you consider returning to a life of crime when you were in a reformatory? Wasn't the fact that you were behind bars an indication of something?'

'It indicated I got caught,' he laughed. Then his face changed to meet my unbidden frown. 'I know,' he said seriously, 'you don't understand my world.'

'True,' I agreed. 'What does it give you, except stretches behind bars? I'm not talking now about right and wrong,' I added, 'I think stealing is wrong and I think you agree. Yet you steal. What's so absorbing about it? You make it sound like an addiction.'

He looked down at his plate. 'Maybe you're right. It's like being hooked, in a way. I can be all right,' he glanced up. 'You know, no stealing. Never think about it. Then I get the feeling. I can't tell you what it's like, but I know I'm gonna do something. I don't know what, but it's gonna happen. And it does.' His voice was tense, his eyes looking steadily into mine, his shoulders hunched as if to communicate his intensity of concern. And Paul was abruptly at the table, a phantom between us. Maybe David was genuinely trying to explain how it was with him. Or maybe, I thought, he's setting me up for kill.

'You mean you can't help it?' And my voice was neutral.

'That's it,' he paced the words. 'Like you said, an addiction.' Like you said. Not a bad mind. Swift. Alert. Aware.

David straighted in the chair and took an audibly deep breath. 'I got something to tell you,' he said. 'Maybe you'll feel different about me when I tell you, but I got to.' He paused. 'You remember the night in your apartment.'

'Vaguely,' I murmured and wished he hadn't mentioned it.

'Well, first, I got to ask something. Who was at your door?'

'I don't know. The police thought it was someone trying to warn me about you.' Reminiscing with your attacker is an intriguing experience. I could feel my eyelids twitching. 'By the way,' I tried to look poised, 'where is my other bookend? They found the one you . . . used. But the other one hasn't shown up.'

'It's at the bottom of your garden,' he grinned self-consciously. 'I dropped the one I hit you with outside the window. When I went over that courtyard wall it seemed dumb to have evidence on me, so I buried it. I guess,' he said pensively, 'it's still there.'

'Wait a minute,' I was backtracking, 'you asked about the door pounding. How did you know about it?'

'I was there. Right behind your bed. When you sat up, you scared the hell out of me.'

'Sorry about that.' Memory jumped. 'Behind the bed?'

'Sure. When you lay down again I didn't know what to do. I started around the side of the bed, but I figured you could see me, so I got back again.'

'Then it was you!' The words rushed out. 'The blanket! You . . . it didn't move when I turned over. It was you.'

'My leg,' he said calmly. 'I was standing there. My leg was holding the blanket. When you tugged, I got back.'

And I was back in that moment, full of uneasy surprise, pulling the blanket, puzzled by the resistance. 'I see.' I was trying to breathe evenly. 'That's what you wanted to tell me?'

44

'No,' he hesitated, 'I mean, well, I'd been in your apartment the weekend before. I thought you had stuff I could pawn,' he looked almost accusingly, 'but there wasn't that much, so I figured if I came back when you were there, I might get money.' He waited again. 'But that's not what I want to tell you either.' He looked at me. 'You remember when I hit you?'

'Vividly.'

'I didn't mean to hit you with that bookend. I mean, when I got my hand around your mouth, I reached into my back pocket with my other hand.'

'The bookend was in your back pocket?'

'Yeah. One in each. So,' the hazel eyes darkened, 'so I reach around, see. I was kinda excited. And my hand grabs the bookend first.'

'First?'

'I was reaching for a knife. A switchblade. It was in my pocket, too.'

The room, quite suddenly, was too bright. People gestured, their lips moved, but I could hear nothing. A shudder rocked through me. 'You intended to kill me?' My tone sounded politely inquiring.

'I guess so.' His voice was soft.

'Why?' The question was an arrow of ice.

'I don't know. That's what scares me. Maybe I shouldn't have told you.' His eyes searched my face. 'You look kinda funny.'

'Do I? It's a curious experience,' I swallowed, 'listening to someone explain that he intended to kill you.'

'I know.' He bit his lip. 'I'm terribly sorry.' The apology was so monstrously inadequate, so incredible, that I laughed. The laughter was pitched too high. David twisted a cigarette between his long fingers. 'I wanted you to know,' he said, 'so things could be straight between us.' It was a simple statement, the plea of a child.

I tried to lift the coffee cup. 'You've given me a bit of a start,' I said, holding tight to the longing to scream and be done with discipline. 'Please,' as he started to speak, 'don't say anything. I suppose I should try to help you find out why you would want to kill me,' I added more to myself than to the watching teenager.

'It does scare me,' he repeated.

'Yes. Well, unfortunately, I don't know that much about . . . psychological problems.' His eyes darkened. 'I'm sorry,' I went on hastily, 'I'm not suggesting that you're crazy. I guess almost everyone could kill under some circumstances. You could be that afraid, or that angry, or that protective of someone, or that something.' If he were being honest and therefore frightened by a murder intention it wouldn't help to indicate my own fright. And if he were lying – I tried to see behind the eyes – I was damned if I'd let him know he had succeeded once again in scaring the wits out of me. 'I think,' I straightened determinedly in the chair, 'under the circumstances, it would be better if we pretended that we had met more – more normally. Unless,' I hesitated again, 'you want to talk about this to someone who could help you professionally, like a psychiatrist, or a priest who knows something about psychology. You are Roman Catholic, aren't you?' He looked surprised by my information. 'Your lawyer happened to mention it.' I said and his head ducked again.

'Yes,' he muttered. 'But I don't think right now . . .'

'Then,' I said, 'let's forget it.' And I thought: who are you and what are you? 'And I think we should get going. I have a pile of manuscripts to read tonight.' And if I don't get out of here, I thought, I'm going to start screaming.

'I'll start the job hunt tomorrow,' he said, shifting his mood gears, 'and I'll report regularly to you.'

'I'm not your parole officer,' I said sharply and the hazel eyes darkened again. 'I mean,' softening my tone, 'you don't have to report.'

'Oh,' he said, 'sure.'

At the restaurant door he offered to walk home with me, 'It's just around the corner, David,' I said quickly. 'Thanks, but I'll be fine.'

'Well, I'm – '

'I know,' I interrupted, 'you're sorry.' And I walked with haunted strides back to the apartment.

At the apartment door my key chattered in the lock. In the hall the light switch clicked under an unsteady finger. I looked helplessly around the apartment. Now what did I do? I had to do something. I didn't want to think about that conversation.

I stared at the still-empty place where the bookends had stood. Even if David were lying, he had intended to frighten me. Why? And if he were telling the truth, what did it mean? Why would he tell me something guaranteed to stop me cold in my emotional tracks? To ease his conscience? A kind of test? A cry for help?

The wind beyond the windows sounded like a moan. Nervously I pulled the drapes. He had been in the apartment when the pounding

46

started. He was behind that bed. And a half hour later he was still there? His leg had imprisoned the blanket when I turned over. I pushed aside the vision of my hand, pulling at the blanket in the dark and encountering that leg. He didn't have to press against the bed to get out and anyway, why was he there? He had stayed in this room, ignoring the easy escape through the windows. Why? When I tumbled, unconscious, into the tub he had waited. For what? To find out if he'd killed me? Yet when I came to he still waited. For my reaction? Everyone within a two-block radius had that in those ear-splitting screams. Yet he had not moved. He could have killed me then, but he had not moved.

'Was there any indecent assault?' The detective's voice whispered in memory. One hand around my mouth; the other reaching for a knife. For death. Not rape. Death. Why?

I didn't know what any of it meant. But I was deeply, disturbingly aware of one fact. David's confession, true or false, had planted a new sense of apprehension to me. I didn't want to admit that I was afraid of him – or of some facet of this incomprehensible personality – but I was.

So what now? I had bungled the attempt to help Paul. Now this teenager had a problem I hadn't counted on, one which skewered me to alien fear. Yet no one had begged me to assume this responsibility. If it turned out to be more complex, more disturbing than the first sight of the vulnerable victim in a jail had suggested, that was no justifiable excuse for retreat. I thought again of the priest at the Don Jail. And the probation officer. And the welfare workers. Nobody had said it was easy. Nobody had said, 'it's a real fun thing, helping these kids.' If I turned my back on this boy, he would haunt me for the rest of my life.

Chapter Seven

For a month David was the epitome of a self-defeating, troubled teenager, apprehensive about the future, disinclined to assume any responsibility for it, but anxious to 'do or say' anything I wanted. He was a striking contrast to Paul, whom I saw once or twice a month and who, it seemed, had taken a full and firm hold on his life.

David reported by telephone daily, and he visited the office two or three times a week. He stayed with the job hunt. Or so he said. We stayed clear of any reference to the 'mistake' which had saved my life.

But sometimes a phrase or a look would throw me back and an edge of remembered fright would go through me. In the quiet times, with the lights burning in the apartment and early snow falling beyond the windows I reminded myself that one isolated act of violence did not indicate a brutal nature or even a serious emotional disturbance. But I had no intention of triggering another attack. David and I met in public places. That was my one concession to my nervous system. We did not meet alone in my apartment.

It was close to ten o'clock one evening when I unlocked the front door to find all the apartment lights burning. David sat in one of the armchairs, a book in his hand. My eyebrows shot to my hairline.

'Hi,' he ground out a cigarette. 'I wanted to talk. You weren't home, so I waited. Hope you don't mind.'

'How did you get in?'

He grinned and pointed to the window. 'You know me.'

I was tempted to laugh and let it pass. That was easier. And less dangerous? The lack of ground rules with Paul had not advanced criminal psychology one inch. I went to a chair at the far end of the room. 'You're welcome here any time,' I said, lying in my teeth, 'but we have to set rules.' His head went down, as a puppy will hang its head, hoping to prevent scolding by acknowledgement of the misdeed. 'My friends come through the front door. This may seem a novel idea to you, but it is quite common. And when my friends are here, either I'm here, too, or they have my permission to be here in my absence. If you can't cope with these rules, we're in trouble.'

'I'm sorry,' he mumbled.

'Now,' I cleared my throat, 'what's up?'

He twisted in the chair. He was worried, he said, because he had 'that feeling' again. I stiffened. If he were going to have 'that feeling' I would prefer he have it elsewhere than in my apartment. 'I'm afraid,' he went on, 'I'm gonna do something. I don't know what, but I got that feeling.'

Wouldn't it be wonderful, I thought desperately, if I could tell the difference between a genuine reflection of this boy's thinking and feeling, and comments designed to make him more interesting to me, or to himself. Maybe he was deeply concerned about some 'compulsion,' or something he regarded as a compulsion, which drove him to commit acts against society and himself. David's voice droned softly behind my thoughts. Then it halted. He leaned forward. 'And then,' he said quietly, 'there's this.' His hand went into his pocket, came out holding something, a small, black something, which bulged at one end and had a tiny round hole in the other.

A roaring fright went up my back. My God! That's a gun! That gun is pointing at me! That gun is pointing at me because he is pointing it at me! He's come to finish the job.

For thirty seconds we stared at each other. It seemed like ten years. Without conscious decision I held out my hand. 'You'd better give that thing to me,' I said.

David sat motionless, steadily pointing the ugly black thing at me. Fright turned into disbelief. This really was too much. 'Give that thing to me.' Anger sharpened my voice.

David stood up, the gun steady, and started toward me. The anger had done nothing for the rest of me. I debated about standing, if only to shorten the suspense of his walk, but a weakness in my knees hinted I could easily fall flat on my face. I settled for an impatient wave of my hand and my fingers curled around the gun barrel.

I stared at the gun.

'Sure,' David said softly, 'it's a starter pistol. Like a toy. But I could use it. It does look real. I could use it – like in a holdup.'

It did look real. He could use it. In a holdup.

'You see what I mean,' he said and went back to the chair.

I didn't see at all. 'But of course,' I tucked the gun down the side of my chair, 'you don't have to use it.'

'I don't know.' His voice was vague. 'I'm scared. That feeling. Will you keep it for me, so's I won't have it to use?'

I hadn't reached the 'for me' part, but I knew David would retrieve that gun over my dead body. 'Of course,' I said, as if someone had asked me to hold a bag of groceries.

The silence was thick. I rearranged my nerve ends. David was smiling in pure satisfaction. Because I had removed temptation? Or – ?

'Well,' he said easily, 'I'd better go. Thanks a lot.' He headed for the windows. I pointed to the door. "My friends,' I said, 'also leave by the front door. Another common practice.'

He flashed that great friendly grin. 'Yeah,' he said. 'You know me.'

Which was the problem. I didn't know him. When the front door had closed behind him, I went back to the chair and lifted out the gun. It lay small and black on my palm. Impulsively I opened the clothes closet and shoved it under a pile of blankets.

In the week that followed neither David nor I referred to the gun. We didn't discuss 'that feeling' either. Maybe we should have discussed it.

At four-thirty one morning I jumped awake at a sharp rap on the apartment door. I grabbed a robe, put an ear against the door, and called, 'Who is it, please?' A voice bawled 'police' like someone summoning hogs from a far pasture.

When I opened the door, two police officers strode inside. They scrutinized the living room. One asked if I knew David and when I said yes, the other officer stared at me. 'You his girlfriend?' he prompted, while the lights burned down on my naked thirty-five-year-old face. Now that, I thought, is the kind of comment that gives the human race a bad name. 'Actually,' I began, ready to announce that my passion for David knew no bounds. But they didn't look as if they would be receptive to that brand of humour. 'No,' I amended, 'I'm just a friend.' They weren't satisfied. I reviewed the circumstances of the friendship. They looked at each other. 'So,' I said, encouragingly, 'what's happened?'

David had been picked up, with another teenager, on a residential street, at two-thirty in the morning. He had no job; he would give no home address; he offered no reasonable explanation for the nocturnal stroll. Since one officer thought he recognized David, they were taken to headquarters. David was charged with vagrancy. They were exploring the possibilities of other charges.

'Like what?' I asked and thought of Paul. They exchanged a glance. 'You mean there's been a robbery in that neighbourhood?'

Another silent glance between them. 'We're not here to discuss that,' one said.

'We are if he's to be charged,' I said shortly.

'You a lawyer?' the officer asked.

'No.'

'Well, right now he's charged with vagrancy,' the officer said, 'and he'll appear tomorrow morning.' He gave the address of the court and added that David had asked them to contact me.

'Do you always notify in person?' I asked.

'Not always,' the officer said.

'You mean I was just lucky?' They didn't answer. 'Well, thanks anyway. Telephones do jangle the nerves.'

A mute smile from one of them. 'And please tell David I'll be in court. Who's the Crown Attorney?' I knew Crown Attorneys rotated in the various courts and somewhere I had picked up the information that talking to the Crown, before the court appearance, if the accused had no defence lawyer, was a good idea. You filled, in part, the function of the defence lawyer, presenting the facts, offering a defence and preventing assembly-line justice.

They assumed it would be Mr. Stanton Hogg.

When they left I turned off the lights and went back to bed. David's misadventure didn't seem too serious, although there was always the possibility that 'that feeling' had struck again and something more than walking a residential street was involved.

The magistrate's court, where David was scheduled to appear, was a mellowing yellow brick building set tastefully on a tidy lawn. It looked like a new school.

Inside, I followed the directions of a stony-faced officer and walked up two flights of clean, white steps. To the left was the courtroom. To the right was a long bench, polished by countless waiting bodies, lining the wall and facing three officers, one labelled Crown Attorney.

By nine-twenty the corridors were filled with the unmistakable sight and smell of justice: the mixture of briefcases, expensive clothing – the lawyers; inexpensive clothing – the defendants; cleaning agents and suffering. People clustered; lawyers exchanged views and gossip; police officers strode by with that solid tread which has no sound to equal it, and knots of families and friends gathered like survivors of a disaster.

At nine-thirty a tall man, surrounded by a whispering, hurrying band of police officers and lawyers, walked with quick, certain steps up the stair, past the bench on which I sat, and into the office marked Crown Attorney. The door clicked behind him. I scrambled off the bench, knocked on the door and told the officer who opened it that I wanted to speak with the Crown. He frowned. 'He's busy,' he said. 'In a minute.' And he closed the door.

The Crown continued to be busy for another ten minutes. By nine-forty-five I knew my defence had to be condensed. What would Clarence Darrow do? He'd create the opportunity. I knocked on the door again. A man with a briefcase opened it this time. When I repeated my request he gestured into the room.

It was a long, narrow office, with a window facing the door. Several officers and lawyers congregated in low-voiced groups. A desk was directly in front of the window and seated behind it was the young man I had watched hurry past me. He lifted his head and gave me the impact of a pair of alert and questioning eyes. I knew immediately that I wouldn't want to be prosecuted by this man if I were guilty and pleading innocent. 'Yes?' he said, politely impatient.

'I'm sorry to intrude,' I began and stopped. It was imperative to say the right thing. This man would deal in facts, not emotions. He would make his recommendations to the magistrate and magistrates are inclined to accept the recommendations of respected Crowns.

'Yes?' he repeated and pointedly glanced at his watch. Ten minutes to ten. In a rush of words I told him about David. 'Who are you?' he interrupted. I told him my name and his eyes narrowed slightly, as if he were looking inward at a mental file. 'You wrote a story in a magazine about a prowler,' he said. 'This the one?' I nodded and silently blessed the magazine. He had the background facts; he wouldn't ask 'you his girlfriend?' – unless, of course, he thought I'd 'fallen in love with the bloke.' But he didn't appear that breed of mentality, either. He rose and picked up his briefcase. 'He can be released on bail,' he said. 'If he has a job by next Friday, I think the Court might see fit to suspend sentence or even dismiss.' We hurried to the door. He paused. 'How much bail can you afford?' he asked, matter-of-factly. I hadn't considered that. 'A hundred dollars?' he prodded. I winced inwardly.

'Yes, of course,' I said, trying to communicate faith in David and my own affluent state in the same breath. 'I'll have to bring it down, of course,' I added. Rich people didn't carry money with them. I had read that somewhere.

A smile twitched his face. We went into the courtroom. It looked like a bright schoolroom. Rows of spectator pews were clean and shiny and hard. The winter sun sent yellow beams of light through long windows. People sat expectantly on the solid benches, whispering among themselves.

I slipped into a rear pew and the doors closed. The clerk declared we were to stand. The magistrate climbed laboriously to his perch. He looked like a principal called in to mediate between a teacher and a troublesome student. He sat with a rustle of his black gown and obediently we followed his example.

David sat with other prisoners in the prisoners' box. Stanton Hogg bent over papers at a long table. Other young men busied themselves with briefcases. Obviously some prisoners had defence counsel. David caught my eye and grinned, hopefully and apologetically. There was no fear on his face.

The clerk rose to read out the charge against the first accused, a short, worried-looking, middle-aged man. His lawyer looked young and a little nervous. There was no majesty and no drama in this confrontation between a citizen and the law. We had the chanting, the rising and sitting, the open reading of the charge, the 'swear to tell the truth, the whole truth and nothing but the truth' – as if anyone could, in fact, ever do that – and all the hallowed, comforting formalities. But the trial seemed a debate. The learned counsels met politely to debate the issue, which happened to be a man's guilt or innocence.

The accused was convicted. While he listened stricken to a sentence of six months in the reformatory, I wondered if, by chance, he might be innocent, or, if he were guilty, if confinement would 'reform' him. Didn't Confucius believe that if you regulate people by law and law enforcement 'people will try to keep out of jail, but will have no sense of honour,' and if you regulate them through morals and moral teachings 'people will have a sense of honour and will reach out toward the good?'

The clerk was rising again, this time to read out the charge against David. My resident delinquent glanced over his shoulder before he, too, faced the Bar of Justice. The clerk's voice stopped. Mr. Hogg stood. He recommended, he said, that this case be laid over for one week. He also recommended that the accused be released on his own recognizance. He turned slightly and our eyes met. I didn't have to put up any bail money.

When court recessed we met in the corridor. 'He . . . you . . . both of you have until next Friday,' Mr. Hogg said, brushing aside my thanks, 'and you tell him for me that if he skips I'll get him if I have to walk every inch of the way to Vancouver.' And he strode toward his office.

David walked up cheerfully. 'Hi,' he said.

'You . . . we,' I echoed Mr. Hogg, 'have one week to get a job. Mr. Hogg says if you skip he'll get you if he has to walk every inch of the way to Vancouver.'

'He would, too.' David grimaced. 'He's tough.'

'I'll drive you home. We have things to discuss.'

David stoutly maintained his innocence. He had been walking with another teenager. They were minding their own business when the cruiser pulled up. He had said 'no fixed address' because he didn't want them to notify his mother. He knew, he assured me, that I would answer his call for help.

'Probably there was a b. and e. in the neighbourhood,' he said, 'and they were rounding up everybody. That's breaking and entering,' he explained, 'like what I did to you. Almost.'

'Yes,' I murmured and thought of Paul.

He slouched in the car seat, his thin body folded, with an air of weariness. He could be telling the truth. I couldn't ration belief for reasons unclear to either of us. I pulled up in front of a restaurant. 'Want a coffee?' Pale eyebrows moved languidly up. Without speaking he opened the door and spilled out into the sunshine.

In the restaurant he collapsed in a booth. He asked no questions about the conversation between the Crown Attorney and me. When the waitress put the coffee down before us, David picked up a spoon and aimlessly stirred milk into his cup. He avoided any direct look when I broached the subject of a job. He'd shown no genuine interest in a job since he left Guelph. He went through the ritual of hunting – and I had only his word that he did, in fact, hunt – because it was expected of him. I studied the withdrawn face, the mouth which said so much and so little. Maybe he did feel defeated, and defeatism destroyed interest, put everything beyond reach. But now the situation was urgent.

We worked out a job-hunting schedule and when we returned to the car his mood had changed. Now he could joke with the humour that was one of his most engaging qualities.

Until the fourth day of the hunt, David's telephone reports were recitals of failure. But on Thursday his voice crackled with excitement 'I got a job,' he shouted. 'Not much. Hoisting boxes in a factory, but I got it. They wanted me to start Friday. I told them' – a buoyant laugh – 'that I had an unbreakable appointment. So I start Monday.'

I arrived at the courthouse at nine-fifteen Friday morning. David was not there. At nine-thirty Mr. Hogg, surrounded by his faithful entourage, climbed the stair. He lifted an inquiring eyebrow. I smiled and he disappeared into his office.

Time inched forward. David did not appear. At ten to ten I went downstairs and pushed open the outside door. No sign of him. Dismally I climbed the stair. Perhaps he was ill. But surely he would get a message to me.

At five to ten Stanton Hogg came out of his office and headed straight for me. 'Where is he?' he demanded.

I swallowed a tennis ball which, unaccountably, lodged in my throat. David would not have skipped. There was no reason to skip. Unless, my mind twitched, he had lied about that job. 'He isn't here yet,' I hoped for a miracle, but the stair was empty. Mr. Hogg looked at his watch. 'He'll show,' I said desperately. 'He has a job. He got it himself,' I added, as if that compensated for David's absence.

'Did you tell him what I said?'

'I told him. He'll be here.' I looked at the clock, gravely ticking on the wall. 'Does he have to be here when Court convenes?'

David's name would be called three times – three times the cock will crow, I thought wildly – and it was possible to delay calling him until after the first recess. But, Mr. Hogg's face darkened, he had only three chances to respond to the call to Justice.

Court was convening. We walked inside.

David's absence was almost tangible during the next hour. I made so many trips out to peer down that flight of stairs that a police officer, standing in the corridor, began to peer down with me without knowing the reason for my anxiety. Court recessed. Court reconvened. David's name was called twice. I started seriously to peel off my nail polish.

Five minutes later I crept out into the corridor again. David was bounding up the stair. 'Hi,' he called. 'I slept in.' I fell against the wall. 'Sorry,' he said breathlessly, 'we celebrated last night.' He looked from me to the closed courtroom door. 'Don't you think we should be in there?' he asked.

Mr. Hogg turned as we opened the door. I rolled up my eyes and his mouth tightened. David's name was being called. For the third time.

And David received his freedom.

When we returned to the corridor I grabbed David's arm. 'Don't ever do that to me again. You took ten years off my life and I haven't that many good ones left.' He laughed, protesting that I should know he would never intentionally 'let me down.'

'I'm not talking on so lofty a plane,' I sighed. 'I'm talking about not sleeping in.'

Mr. Hogg walked toward us. I explained why David had been late. He looked speculatively at David and back to me. 'I'd like to talk to you about all this sometime,' he said.

'Yes.' I met the penetrating look. 'I'd like that.'

The next week we had lunch together. Stanton Hogg started off bluntly, studying me with the intensity of someone trained to find the hidden in people. 'That article of yours,' he said, 'I was interested in your reactions. You appear to disagree with our system. Do you have any alternatives in mind?' The smile in his slowly paced words softened the challenge.

'Nothing that will stand the legal fraternity on its ear,' I admitted. 'I'm new to this market place, but right now I have the impression that it isn't enough to judge someone guilty of a crime and just punish him. Take David. He's been judged, and punished, three times. The last vote isn't in yet, but the repetition of activity does suggest that, at least for him and for his type, the system doesn't work. I think we must find the 'why' of the crime. We must treat the cause,' and I thought again of the Don Jail priest, 'not merely the symptoms. Which,' I admitted, 'is not a profound or new idea.'

Stanton Hogg's eyes moved lazily toward the dining room door. 'See that man?' He gestured a thick-set man hurrying into the room. 'If he pulled a gun right this minute and pointed it at you, are you telling me that I would not have the moral right to take the gun from him, even if it meant killing him, to protect you and others in this room? And to do it before I invited him to sit down and explain his problem?'

'You mean remove the threat first. Of course. But that doesn't cancel out the need to find the "why" later.'

'But it is the function of our system to remove the threat,' he said, 'to protect society. And the lawbreaker is a threat, even a menace, whether he's that man pointing a gun, or David breaking into your apartment. The law is not a therapeutic organization.'

'But surely our legal system must include prevention,' I objected. 'And asking "why" is the first step toward that prevention. If you don't get at the cause of any . . . disease, you never find the cure.'

'Isn't that the responsibility of science?' he asked slowly.

'You mean the psychologists and sociologists and criminologists? The specialists?' When he nodded, I plunged on. 'Sure. If they could get together and agree, which they don't seem to do at the moment. But anyway the results, the findings, must somehow be incorporated into our legal system.'

'The operative word is "somehow,"' he pointed out. 'The question is "how." Example: you asked for a psychiatric examination of David. Why?'

'Because I thought there must be something wrong, some emotional disturbance. Yes,' I said to his look, 'I know. We aren't interested, legally, in emotional disturbances. The M'Naghten Rule. Maybe we start there. Maybe we must turn our thinking, as a society, upside down.'

'You think all offenders are emotionally disturbed?' he asked with a smile.

'Not in the general sense of the phrase, no. But I think there is a reason, or maybe a lot of reasons, why someone, especially the young, deliberately choose to commit antisocial acts – criminally antisocial, I mean.'

He began a cross-examination that proved conclusively that I didn't know, really, what I believed. But he also had that rare gift you find in brilliant teachers, the ability to expand a question or a comment that, basically, is simple into so interesting an answer or theory that the questioner marvels at his own profundity.

And that lunch had three important results: it made me less defensive about my involvement in the world of the young offender; it made me realize how much there was to learn, and it launched a friendship that was to have a major influence much later.

Chapter Eight

Over the weeks David had referred frequently to his friends in Park-dale. When I asked their reaction to his decision to leave the life of crime, he pursed his lips. 'They know how tough it is,' he said.

'To kick the habit?' Don't fight it, I thought. 'And you can't per-suade them to join the withdrawal?'

'Some don't steal all the time,' he objected. 'And all of them want to go straight.' And he agreed solemnly when I chanted that the long-est journey begins with the first step.

Two weeks after our courtroom appearance, David called with big news. His friends, he said, had decided to form a club. He wanted to talk about it.

He was bristling with excitement when he arrived at my office. These friends, he said, talked together all the time. 'I guess that's how it started,' he said. 'Anyway, they want to do something about delinquency. To prevent it,' he added, catching my smile. 'So we've formed a club called the Saints.' He ignored my choking spell. 'And they've elected me president.'

When I recovered, I repeated, 'They've elected you president of a club called the Saints?'

'There used to be a gang called the Saints in North Toronto,' he went on, missing or ignoring the irony, 'but they disbanded. They were a street gang. You know, black leather jackets, bicycle chains, motorcycles, stuff like that. I guess,' he grinned again, 'they did something about delinquency too. Like increase it. But we're gonna be a club.'

'You mean your club will be more benevolent, like the Lions or the Rotarians?' I tried to match his seriousness, but visions of Rotarians in black jackets, carrying bicycle chains, got in the way. 'How do you propose to fight delinquency?'

He hunched forward. 'We figure one reason guys get in trouble is just sitting around. Or hanging around street corners with nothing to do. You get bored and you pull a caper for kicks. Okay. If the guys had a club, some place to go, something going on, like weekly dances and sports and a meeting place and stuff like that,' he gestured, 'that would make the difference.'

Now where did he read that, I wondered, or had I underestimated this teenager. 'And how do you plan, concretely, to go about it?'

'Well, there are about twenty guys now and there's this church in Parkdale, St. Mark's. It's got a big meeting room upstairs, and Father Orr, he's the priest, says we can use another big room downstairs for dances. We're getting the dances organized now. So we can use the money for other things.' He grinned at my lifting eyebrows. 'I mean like charity work. Loans to guys who ain't . . . I mean haven't got any money. Stuff like that.'

'How many could attend the dances?'

He squinted, meditating. 'I'd say the hall could hold three or four hundred. We'll probably get a couple of hundred at the beginning and if we charge a quarter a couple – '

'I wasn't thinking about profits. I meant the purpose. You intend to fill up their time, twice a week, so they won't fill it with trouble?' I thought of Paul. 'And what about the rest of the time?'

'You mean how do we show them they don't have to lead a life of crime,' he said gravely. 'You don't understand what it's like for us.'

'True. That's why I'm asking questions. I think the idea is great. But I'm asking how you intend to develop it.'

'For one thing, we'll have each other.'

'You have each other now.'

'This will be different. We get guys off the streets. We hold meetings and talk things over. We show them they don't have to steal.'

'I see.' I didn't, but as David said, I didn't know what it was like for them. 'Do you rent the hall from St. Mark's?'

'Father Orr says we can use it free if we keep it clean. We'll be responsible for any damage. We don't expect any, but you never know. And we rent music equipment. We'll have our own combo eventually.'

'What do you plan to do with the money, apart from charity work?'

'Put on other activities,' he said as if he had anticipated that question.

'Well, as I said, I think the idea is great.'

'And you'll help?' he asked eagerly.

That word again. 'Why, yes,' I began slowly, 'but I don't know

60

about right now. I mean we're busy and I wouldn't want to say yes and find I haven't the time. Anyway, how could I help?'

'With the organizing, like.'

'Is Father Orr helping? Or does he just provide the hall?'

'He sits in on the meetings and he'll be at the dances. He said he'd help in any way.' His eyes were accusing.

'Well,' I said heartily, 'you get things underway and when the smoke clears around here, I'll see what I can do.'

If a group of young people had decided 'to do something about delinquency,' I thought, they did deserve help. I thought of Paul, smiling and satisfied at our last meeting. And now David, excited about a new idea, maybe a new life style. Maybe, I sighed, things did work out for the best in this best of all possible worlds. If you just hung on.

Chapter Nine

The first week in December there was another knock on my apartment
door at four-thirty in the morning. I bounded off the bed, alarm muted
by memory. David had been walking those residential streets again?
A voice growled 'police' to my query and when I opened the door
two police officers strode inside. One asked abruptly if I knew Paul.
Surprise. Drops of shock. 'Yes, of course. Why?'

'He's in trouble. Bad trouble,' he said. 'He asked us to contact you.
He shot the lock off an apartment building door. He claims it was all
a mistake, a drunken spree with a friend. A friend,' he added cynically,
'who got away.'

The city was in the throes of an epidemic of armed robberies. The
courts were making examples of gun-carrying offenders. Paul could face
a possible five to seven years in prison. 'Has he identified the friend?' I
asked when I could speak.

'No,' the officer said and they began the interrogation. This was no
minor vagrancy charge. How long had I known Paul? Had I received
any gifts from him? Why would I receive gifts, I asked and one shrugged. 'You his girlfriend?' They looked baffled when I sighed. I wasn't
his girlfriend, I said and tried to explain.

'Do you have a gun?' the officer asked abruptly. I started to say 'of
course not' when I remembered David's starter pistol. They looked at
each other as I went to the clothes closet, pulled it from under the
blankets and handed it to one of them. 'Where did you get this?' he
asked.

'A young man asked me to keep it for him,' I said airily. 'He was
afraid he might be tempted to use it.'

'What young man?'

I shook my head. 'I'm sorry. He has nothing to do with this.' They
exchanged another look while I wondered how many years I could get.
'When may I have it back?' I asked innocently, as the officer shoved it
into his pocket.

'You can't. It's illegal for you to have it.'

'But I promised to keep it for him.'

'We'll keep it for him,' he said dryly.

When they left I stood a long time, staring blankly out of the window. Foolish and irresponsible though the act had been, I told the darkness, Paul was incapable of violence. Perhaps his companion had pulled the trigger. But why was he with a man who had a gun? And I met the real question. To what degree had I contributed to this? The silent, lonely, starved, closed-in boy I met, the one whose barriers I seemed to crash, the one who became dependent on the unit I established, the one from whom I had withdrawn – what had happened inside that boy? What interpretation had he given the well-intentioned withdrawal? And later, when the withdrawal became more solidly selfish – what had he thought then? He had been rejected again? Had he, and his trust, been betrayed once more?

The next morning, after a hurried call to the office, I pushed open the heavy door of the Don Jail. Involuntarily I glanced toward the governor's office. But there was nothing this time to warrant official consideration. The guard climbed off his high stool, offered a book to sign, pushed a buzzer and turned me over to another guard, who led the way to the visitors' area.

A heavy wire mesh screen divided the prisoners and visitors. It is a zoo, I thought, and saw Paul walk in. He stopped well back from the wire. His hands were shoved into his pockets. His eyes dared me to speak. 'What happened?' I asked.

'Didn't they tell you?'

'You tell me.'

In a dull monotone he told his story. He had spent the evening with a friend. They got drunk. They were driving in Paul's car when they saw a display of guns in a Yonge Street store window. They got out to look at them more closely. Paul's shoulders lifted. 'So we were drunk. It seemed a great idea to go inside for a closer look. We didn't intend to steal anything.' His eyes challenged again. 'We went to the side of the building. It was close to another building.' His hands dug deeper into the pockets. 'My friend had a gun, so we shot the lock off the door. Somebody heard us. They called the police. We ran when the cruiser came. My friend got away. I didn't. That's all.'

There were questions to be asked. Why was he with a man who had a gun? Had he known about the gun? I looked around. This wasn't the time or place for questions. And maybe I wasn't the one to ask them.

'You chose a bad time for this, Paul. You'll need a good lawyer.' His dark head dipped in agreement. 'I don't know about bail. I'll have to find out.' Another silent nod. I looked around. 'Well, I'd better get busy. I'll see you later.'

He turned swiftly and walked away. I left the Don and telephoned Stanton Hogg. He didn't waste time. 'Don't fool with this one,' he urged. 'Get — ' and he named one of the better-known young criminal defence lawyers.

When a human being faces the Bar of Justice in our society, I thought, even the professional reputation of his lawyer counted? 'All right,' I agreed. 'And bail?'

'It will be stiff. The gun. You'll need property bail.'

And bail was arranged through another friend, willing to take the gamble. Paul was released and we went to the young lawyer.

When we emerged from that interview, a slender, young, dark-haired girl was waiting. Paul mumbled her name. This was his new girlfriend. She resembled the other girl in her quiet manner, but there was a sensed intensity about her that was both moving and attractive. Paul went for cigarettes and she burst into a torrent of confidences. What Paul needed, she said, was psychiatric therapy. He was a good boy, but he was mixed up. I took another look at her. 'Does Paul agree?'

'Goodness, I haven't said that to him.' She seemed surprised by my insensitivity. 'But it's true, isn't it?' When I agreed she took a deep breath. 'Anyway, the first thing is to get him off.'

I heard the answering silent appeal within myself: yes, please God, get him off, give both of us another chance. But there was another inner hesitation. Get him off at any cost? Maybe to deny truth? If we got him off not because he was innocent, but because he had a good lawyer, what would that prove to him? Yet what would five to seven years in prison prove to him?

The morning of the trial I met Paul and his lawyer outside the courtroom. I was to be a character witness and someone Paul could depend on for future help. 'One thing,' the lawyer cautioned, 'this magistrate isn't enthusiastic about women who try to act like social workers. He may be rough on you. Don't get angry. Just answer any question yes or no. Understood?' Understood, I agreed, and we went into the courtroom. The lawyer paused and looked at Paul. 'You still refuse to identify the man who was with you? It might help.'

'I refuse,' Paul said.

'And everything you've told me is the truth?'

Paul met the look. 'Yes,' he said firmly.

The cautioning about the magistrate was valid. Before I left the stand, he swivelled and glared down at me. 'Perhaps,' he rumbled,' since you are so successful in this work, you should go into it professionally.'

I caught the warning look from Paul's lawyer. And I tried to crush back embarrassment and a spurt of anger. This world of the young offender was tough enough, I thought furiously, without receiving scorn from the authorities. The magistrate waited. He expected a response. 'Thank you,' I said evenly. Let him decide if I were returning sarcasm or merely stupid.

Back in my seat I was gathering up shredded dignity when I realized something was going on. The Crown had called a woman as a witness for the prosecution. I didn't know this Crown, but he looked satisfied. Even triumphant. The woman lived across the street. She had been sitting at her window and she had seen everything. Paul had been alone. There was no other man. He might have been drunk, but he was alone.

Paul straightened in the prisoners' box and I stared at his stiff shoulders. Why lie to me and to his lawyer? Fear of being denied help if he told the truth? Or projecting the image again of the poor little kid who gets into trouble through no fault of his own? The Crown was introducing another witness. A detective. A search of Paul's apartment, he said in a flat voice, had uncovered a television set and other stolen items. They had been identified by the department store where Paul worked. In the swirling confusion I heard the echo of my friend's voice: 'And some day, when he's a contributing member of society – we'll cry.'

The magistrate was rumbling again. I didn't hear a word. He finished his lecture. Paul's hands were clasped tightly behind his back as he stood before the court. The magistrate found him guilty. And he pronounced sentence. Perhaps he did understand the problems of troubled youth. Or perhaps my disturbing premonition about the significance of a 'brilliant defence lawyer' was true. The sentence was six months in the reformatory.

Paul's girlfriend grabbed my hand in relief. Had she known the truth, I wondered. Paul turned and walked away without looking back. Numbed, I agreed with the girl that it was very fortunate. She said he had learned his lesson; he had been terrified; and six months wasn't 'that long.' 'He'll need us more than ever when he gets out,' she said. She was busy already with the future.

'Don't you think this time he needs someone who knows what he – or she – is doing?' I asked. She frowned. 'We'll see,' she said. And together we left the courtroom.

Throughout January I tried to understand it. Somewhere I had made dreadful mistakes with Paul. My theory of teaching trust may have been basically sound, but as an amateur in a highly professional field I had blundered badly. It was true, as a psychiatrist had said once, 'You can't undo the damage of years in a few months.' And now I didn't know what to do.

I made one trip to Paul's former training school to talk with the school's psychiatrist. He knew Paul, but their association had been spasmodic. 'He needs a lot of help,' he said. 'You got through, obviously. And then,' he smiled gently, 'you didn't know what to do with it.' He said his own time and energy limitations prevented the concentrated therapy boys like Paul needed desperately. 'What are you going to do,' he asked with a sigh, 'when you see a kid a few times and you know he needs all the help you can give him, and there is a line-up waiting behind him for the same kind of help. That's my problem.'

Should I get in touch with him? 'That depends,' he said thoughtfully. 'Maybe it would be better to wait a while. I doubt if you'd know how to handle this right now anyway.'

So I returned to Toronto, to apologize to everyone and to face still another damaged teenager, because David was constantly there, asking when I would attend a meeting of his Saints' club. My excuses ranged from a cold I certainly didn't want to inflict on his friends to the exhausting pressure of work. I wondered sometimes if he knew the real reason, if he knew about Paul and sensed, perhaps, that I didn't want to meet any more young offenders.

But one afternoon a man who identified himself as the manager of a Parkdale clothing store telephoned. I had been given as a reference, he said, by teenagers who claimed to be members of the Young Men's Saints' Club. They wanted jackets, he said, scarlet jackets. The word 'Saints' was to be emblazoned on the backs of the jackets. And they wanted credit.

I told the grave voice that I knew about the club and that, as far as I knew, it was genuine. Its members wanted to do something about delinquency.

'What?' he asked pointedly.

'I think they're against it.' And how was I involved? 'If you're asking if I'll be responsible for their account,' I said, 'the answer is no. I've no reason to doubt that you'll get your money, but I can't find it in me to go on the line for forty jackets, even if they do have 'The Saints' emblazoned on the backs.'

He thanked me. He guessed he would let them have their jackets.

If they were prepared to invest money in jackets – and idly I wondered where they planned to get the money (from the dances?) – they had to be sincere. It was wrong to refuse to attend even one meeting. I was David's friend and I was letting him down. If the whole thing seemed beyond me, I could tell David they were a grand bunch and let it go at that.

The next time David telephoned I told him my cold was better, work had lightened, and I was ready to attend a meeting. We agreed on the following Wednesday night. 'I'll tell the guys,' he said excitedly, 'and I'll pick you up at the office. You might not be able to find the church. Okay?'

'Okay,' I said and made another circle on my desk calendar.

Book Two

Chapter Ten

At seven o'clock that cold February evening David arrived at the office, accompanied by a young man whom he introduced as Tom, and, together, we chattered noisily onto the streetcar. A half hour later we arrived in Parkdale.

The streetcar stopped in front of a restaurant, one of the boundaries of the lives of the Saints. Down the street was another boundary, the pool hall. Facing us, across the street, was the most important boundary, the stern, grey building, Number Six Police Station. A few yards from the opposite corner, half-hidden in the twilight, loomed St. Mark's Anglican Church.

The area had the feel of unacknowledged defeat. In the air was an apathy, an unnatural, withdrawn, joyless quality, as if people waited for the return of that other, better time, when Parkdale had been a charming, relatively wealthy area of Toronto.

We walked toward the rosy brick church building, silhouetted in the dimness. David was talking rapidly, nervously. A bright light, like a beacon, shone over the door to the church hall. Inside, beyond the entrance hall, a bigger room was lined with lockers. To the left, a flight of steps. To the right of the locker room, the main hall where the dances were held. We went up the steps toward the sound of young voices.

They were crowded on the landing, these young men who made the headlines. You couldn't mistake them, a fierce, restless vitality, an arrogant tilt of the head, grins which didn't cancel out a thoughtful scrutiny and an air of goal-less rebellion. They were wearing scarlet jackets and jeans.

David mumbled my name to a short, thin, intense teenager. This was Aaron, the chairman of the meetings. He welcomed me with unexpected poise. Several Saints appeared older, bigger, more aggressive, but they turned immediately when Aaron said, 'Okay, let's get going.'

A tall, muscular young man, attractive, with dark hair, glinting grey eyes and a sharp deep voice, cupped his hand under my elbow and guided me through the crush of members to a table, facing rows of chairs. His name, he said politely, was Ron.

A blond, who looked about twenty, watched with such cynicism that I moved uncomfortably under his gaze. Ron introduced him as Bruce, the club's vice-president. Another dark-haired teenager, introduced as Topper, pulled out a chair for me. A short, eager boy, with a delightfully pushed-in face, hopped forward to save a book from a tumble off a windowsill. This was Mike. And another one, called Tony, asked if he could hang up my coat.

David melted into the crowd, while fifty pairs of eyes studied me. There was a quality in their appraisal which suggested that, whatever the private hostilities, they were direct in their reactions. They would sense the false or the faked. They seemed even to wait for it.

I reached nervously for a cigarette and four matches flamed from four different directions. Someone pushed an ashtray toward me. Another adjusted my coat on the chair back.

Aaron called the meeting to order. He introduced me as 'a friend of David's, who wants to help us.' David, at the other end of the table, smiled tentatively and looked at his friends, as if seeking their reaction.

The meeting opened with roll call and the collection of dues. Some hadn't paid their dues. Their names were written into a book and a check was made of their total debt. A couple were warned that they had been moved from 'acceptable' to 'questionable.' And all the time the noise swirled and bounced and bubbled through the room. I caught fragments of conversation. Someone referred to 'the fuzz.' I glanced at Tony. 'Police' he translated. Another phrase: 'a bale of weed.' 'Package of cigarettes,' said Tony. Gossip was exchanged. Someone was 'on the street.' 'Out of jail,' my translator volunteered. 'Don't worry,' he grinned, 'you'll catch on.'

The chairman announced the next item of business. Three members, he said, had been charged with armed robbery. I almost swallowed my cigarette. According to the club rules, Aaron went on gravely, any member who got into 'serious trouble' with the police was expelled from the club. They debated and reached their conclusion. Armed robbery was 'serious trouble.' I nodded in furious agreement. A Saint moved that the offending trio be expelled. Notice of their expulsion would be mailed to their new address, Kingston Penitentiary.

Aaron paused to explain to me that minor charges, such as vagrancy, disturbance of the peace and even certain b. and e.'s were tried by the

70

Saints' club court, irrespective of the decision handed down in the adult magistrate court. I thought of my question to David about delinquency-deterrent methods within the club. Apparently loss of membership was one and judgement by their peers another. Aaron listed the Saints' club court officials. When he reached 'Crown Attorney' he slapped a hand over his mouth. 'We don't have a Crown now,' he gasped in open consternation.

'And we won't have one for seven years,' someone shouted. The meeting roared with laughter. The club's Crown Attorney was one of the trio convicted of armed robbery.

Hurriedly Aaron moved to the next item on the agenda. The treasurer, who doubled as secretary and was absent that evening, had 'borrowed' from the club funds without returning the money. The discussion was heated. The decision was typical of the Saints' practicality. He would be relieved of his treasurer's responsibilities, but he would continue as secretary. 'That way,' Ron explained, 'he'll have to face us every week.'

They discussed the Saturday night dances, attended, as David had predicted, by roughly two hundred teenagers. The dances produced revenue and they also kept the guys off the streets. Unfortunately they also kept members who acted as bouncers, soft-drink-stand attendants and music supervisors off the dance floor. The bouncers said, too, they were getting fed up with having to grapple weekly with the same troublemakers. Couldn't regular disturbers be barred from the dances?

Ron stood again. He was beginning to impress me with his influence in the club and with his apparent capacity to deal reasonably with the problems. Barring troublemakers wasn't practical, he announced. The club needed the money and you never knew when these guys might 'cool it.' But more importantly, 'We don't want to stir up any feelin'' against us.' He reminded the members of the rumour that a commercial company was watching the dances to judge potential revenue. If a lot of guys were barred, Ron explained, the competitor might decide he could open up successfully.

I silently debated that logic. Surely no commercial outfit would be eager for troublemakers either. But I had missed the point. The dances had to be known as 'fun affairs,' at which you weren't going to be beaten up or 'hacked.' They had to be free of overbearing authority. And the club had to be known as a strong group, fully capable of handling problems.

So, under Ron's persuasion, the membership agreed to establish specific breaks during the evenings and alternate weeks off for the working members. The 'music guys' could work it out among themselves.

Then it was time to interview membership applicants. They lined up to give names, addresses, ages, and, where possible, telephone numbers. Some were nonchalant, slouching against the wall to indicate supreme unconcern over the judgement of their peers. Others looked openly anxious to be accepted. I wondered idly why a club with the announced purpose of fighting delinquency would attract young men who, by their manner, indicated pride in their – I thought of David – profession.

Once the vital statistics were recorded in the black notebook, the applicants were invited to wait outside the meeting room. Then they were summoned individually for intense quizzing. Questions were direct. Had he been in trouble in the past year? Six months? One month? A no brought the cautioning, 'remember we check with Number Six.' A yes meant closer questioning. Was he keeping straight? Did he have any beefs against anyone in the club?

As each applicant left the room again, the meeting was questioned. Did anyone know him? Did anyone have a beef against him? No secret blackballing here. I thought gleefully of the riotous results in adult clubs if this procedure were adopted.

One boy didn't make it that night. They didn't trust him. Another was put on probation, which meant he could attend the meetings but had no vote.

Throughout the meeting a man in a clerical collar sat at the back of the room, suggesting by his manner that he was completely at ease and even participating, although I don't recall if he said a word.

This was Father Orr, the young rector of St. Mark's. He was not tall, but he gave an impression of height. In repose his face was impassive, except for eyebrows which were dark and heavy and, by the degree of lift, could communicate interest, cautioning, or wry astonishment. At one point I caught his smile and its radiance was surprising. His hair was straight and black, combed meticulously from a high forehead. His eyes, large and dark and heavily-lashed behind glasses, were thoughtful. He wasn't as I had mentally envisioned him. Probably, I thought with self-amusement, I've seen too many of the 'Boys' Town' movies. I had expected a genial 'one-of-the-boys' attitude, firm and kindly, but zestfully eager for the next ballgame. This man gave the impression of a certain aristocracy of spirit, a sensitive and highly developed sense of taste in all things. I wondered what he was doing in this violent world of the young offender, which, I suspected, was totally alien to him. But then, I thought with renewed amusement, he is probably secretly querying my presence in it, too.

After the meeting Aaron introduced us. Father Orr acknowledged the introduction with a silent smile and led me into the study which was his home. He lived in a jumble which gave the impression of orderliness. A table in the centre of the room was a mass of books and papers. A piano was covered with sheet music. A desk, in front of one windowed wall, looked as if it had been vacated only moments earlier. Even the studio couch was littered with books and magazines. And a low bookcase was jammed. To the right of the front door was a small kitchen and, tucked in one corner, was a tiny bathroom.

Father Orr swept a book off a chair, motioned me to sit down and closed the door. He lifted those eloquent eyebrows. 'Well?'

'Whee!' I replied. And our friendship was born of that inarticulate exchange.

He said he had read the magazine article on David, which apparently had satisfied some of his curiosity about my involvement. 'And you wonder about me?' he said with the perception I came to understand as an essential ingredient in this man. He had been born in London, Ontario. His background was academic: Ridley College in St. Catharines; Trinity College; Harvard University and the Anglican Seminary in New York. He was doing advanced academic work, studying music and studying languages. And the Saints? 'The club isn't an official parish project. On the contrary,' the smile flashed, 'I'm not winning any popularity contests because of it among the parishioners. They aren't enthusiastic at the prospect of what some call young hoodlums swarming over church property.' The Saints had come to him, he said, they had asked for the use of the hall. And since he believed the church should be involved with young people like the Saints, he had given permission. But it was a self-governing club. He participated only on request. The Saints' religious backgrounds varied and he wasn't on a religious crusade. 'I'll be pleased if they become interested,' he said, 'but I won't pressure them.'

When I left that evening he said he would be glad to have my moral support at the Saints' dance that Saturday night. I thanked him for the invitation, but I made no commitment.

The street was dark and empty and quiet. I walked slowly to the streetcar, my mind conscious of the sensations of the evening, but unready yet to try to find meaning in them. The evening had a mystic sense of being complete in itself. The experience was unrelated to anything else in my life and it had, in itself, a sense of climax.

When I settled on the streetcar, my mind began to hook onto some of the sensations, letting them spin and twirl against the backdrop of experience and interest. I knew, as one might touch another's pain, without comprehension but with sympathy, that I welcomed this sense of immunity. I wanted to keep a safe distance from the harshness of the world of the Saints.

Yet they were not as I had expected. They were friendlier, more sensitive to my nervousness, more willing to offer at least polite reassurance. They had sharper senses of humour than I had anticipated and they were well mannered. I hadn't expected to be dodging knives, but I wasn't prepared, either, for the politeness. I shouldn't have been surprised. Neither Paul nor David – except for the initial unpleasantness with David – had acted like an ill-mannered, humourless savage. Had I considered them to be exceptional? Or had I set them apart because they appeared anxious to change their lives?

That thought jolted into another. These Saints apparently were anxious to change their lives, too. All fifty of them? It was remarkable that all of them had experienced simultaneous maturity and emotional rehabilitation. Actually it was highly unlikely. I thought of the cynical gaiety, the eager contempt for authority, the flamboyance that simmered in the meeting. If they had all decided to shift into a new life, I had news for them: they were trailing remnants of the old one. Sensibly it was probable that a core within the club had made the decision, for any one of several good reasons, and organized the club. The others would be attracted out of curiosity or for kicks or, as David had said, for something to do. Those would be the challenges to the club and to any adults associated with it. The ones who were unconvinced yet available.

Idly I wondered who belonged to the core and who were the . . . the unconverted. Aaron would be a core member; David had to be and that Ron, the one who seemed to exert consistently persuasive influence, and of course the vice-president, Bruce. Probably Mike and Tony and Topper and – my mind halted. I was labelling the members who had shown particular friendliness and courtesy as the 'good guys.' Anyway, it wasn't that important. With the failure that was Paul riding beside me and the question mark that was David apologizing for wanting to kill me, I had no intention of pitching headlong into any challenge, however intriguing.

74

For two days I went through alternating and conflicting reactions. Thursday morning I decided the meeting had been a provocative experience and yes, I liked them and I wished them well, but I would not become involved. Thursday evening I knew I couldn't refuse to become involved. Friday morning I was convinced that if I became involved, somebody should lock me up and throw away the key.

Friday afternoon the probation officer called to ask how things were going. I explained my quandry and he laughed. 'You'll get into it. You're hooked.'

'Maybe if I could be objective – '

'Lots of luck,' he interrupted. 'Granted, too much emotional involvement is a bad thing, as you've learned. But they've had the clinical, textbook approach. I guess there's a line that's appropriate,' he said. 'Can't remember who said it. "Don't munch whipped cream as if it were venison." In other words, relax. It's not all venison.' His tone changed, as if the question of my involvement were settled. 'It's interesting that they'd choose a church as headquarters. Anglican church, you say? The priest is called Father? Maybe they want a father-figure. Or,' he paused, thoughtfully, 'respectability?'

'I don't know what you're talking about.'

'I don't either,' he laughed. 'Go to the dance. And let me know what happens. But remember that whipped cream.'

And that Saturday night I went to my first Saints' dance. A blare of music saturated the night air outside the hall, its beat so furious and primitive that it hinted of activities inside that could swamp Father Orr in trouble. The entrance hall was crowded with teenagers. There were no Saints' jackets. I recognized a few club members, some in suits, others in clean, white, neatly pressed shirts and pants. The girls were astonishing in their variety; extravagantly formal cocktail gowns mixed with sweaters and skirts; young faces almost hidden under layers of make-up, others clean and somehow defenceless.

Aaron and Tom were at the ticket desk. When I put down a quarter Aaron shoved it back. 'On the house,' he said.

'Nothing doing,' I protested. 'We need the money.' We, I thought, we.

Aaron scooped it up. 'Thanks. It's goin' pretty good tonight,' he went on, marking the amount in a book, 'about two hundred so far.'

A soft-drink dispenser was set up in a corner of the second room and a Saint busily supplied bottles from a stacked array of cases behind him. Beyond, in the large hall, were the jerking, writhing, gyrating bodies. At the back, on the permanent stage, the club musicians were preparing for their number while another Saint hovered over the record player. He was master of ceremonies. In the centre of the stage, like a small flagpole, was a floor microphone and stretched across the back was a huge, glittering sign, YOUNG MEN'S SAINTS' CLUB DANCE.

It looked very professional. It also looked like any typical teenage gathering in North America. Hugging the walls were the non-dancers, gathered in groups to talk conspiratorially, or stand, silently in twos, holding hands and watching the bobbing crowd.

'You want to go in?' Father Orr shouted. And we edged into the main hall. The dancers were familiar in their solemnity and their air of isolation. No one smiled. No one held another warmly against himself. Together, they danced alone. Yet the air shivered with an almost hostile sexuality. When the music ended and the ritual was completed, they permitted brief smiles to flicker, hands to touch, fingers to interlace. Then they turned again waiting toward the stage.

Aaron sidled along the edge of the crowd toward us. 'Got time off,' he explained. 'Everything okay?'

'Fine,' I yelled as the music erupted.

A pretty, round-faced girl in a white tulle dress stood beside him. Confidently she slipped her hand into his. Shyly she murmured 'hello' when Aaron introduced her as Veda. They acted as if they had recently celebrated their fiftieth wedding anniversary.

Through the crowd I caught sight of Ron. Of all the Saints he was the one that night to rivet my attention. He seemed that particular breed of person to whom things happen, or who make things happen. His vitality was almost rude. His zest for life – I watched him gather up a girl in a great expansive hug and roar with laughter – seemed enormous. But his eyes were shrewd and strangely penetrating for so young a man. He looked out at you. You had no impression of looking in at him. A number of the teenagers seemed to watch him, almost as if he were some barometer. And I wondered again if he were somehow, for some reason, the real force behind this club.

He intercepted my scrutiny, waved and jostled through the crowd, holding the hand of a tall, vivid brunette. This, he said, was Lillian – dark, moist eyes, beneath heavy dark brows, a wide, smiling mouth and a well-rounded body that wore blue satin like another skin. Her head bobbed as Ron introduced us. 'Hi,' she said, 'I've heard about you.'

It looked as if most of the dancers had 'heard about' me. As they jerked past several waved, murmuring to their partners, and, occasionally, a girl would join in the welcoming, accepting wave.

Father Orr pointed to a row of empty chairs. We started toward them when a tall teenager pushed toward us. 'You wanna dance, Jeann?' he asked, as the rock 'n roll reverberated.

'You must be kidding,' I gasped.

The young man turned away in confusion. I caught his arm. 'I'm sorry,' I said, 'that was dreadfully rude. Thank you for the compliment, but I meant this is beyond me. I'm sorry.'

'Sure.' The smile broadened and he disappeared.

Three minutes later the master of ceremonies made an announcement. 'The next number,' he said, 'will be a slow one, so Jeann can dance.' And the dancers watched as David walked toward me, one hand held out and a shy smile on his face. I have never danced so badly in my life. As I tromped over David's feet, my mind was not on dancing or on the watching young people. It was eighteen months since David and I had met in my bathroom. The hand that now held mine had swept out of nowhere to encircle my mouth. The other one, the one pressed lightly against my back, had reached for an iron bookend. Or a knife.

The music ended. David murmured 'Thank you,' escorted me back to Father Orr and limped away.

Father Orr started to speak and, abruptly, he stopped. 'Wait here a minute, please,' he said.

Two men stood in the doorway, their eyes sweeping over the dancers. I don't know how I recognized them as detectives. Perhaps it was the intensity of their scrutiny or the unsmiling, set faces. They exchanged a few words with Father Orr and walked into the hall.

No one appeared to notice them. Everyone was aware of them. They moved like a grey chill over the room. The dancers continued their musical ritual. Groups along the wall barely glanced as the men patrolled inexorably past them. Beside the stage, the men paused. One reached out and opened a door. Both peered inside. Satisfied, they closed the door and walked in front of the stage to pause at another door. Once more the quick thrust of the door opening, the look inside, the door closing. And they resumed that steady patrol past teenagers who ignored them with tension, past solitary silent figures, toward the corner where I stood. They stopped. Without speaking they studied the crowd. One nodded to the other and the silent walk resumed. As they passed me, our eyes met. I tried to smile to break the accusing coldness.

They looked away and walked out of the hall, to pause and murmur to Father Orr, tip their grey hats to him and then shove through teenagers into the entrance hall beyond our vision.

Father Orr returned to me. 'Those were detectives from Number Six,' he said. 'And you wonder why they come? Surveillance. I'm not sure what they expect to find, but so far they've not found it.'

'How do they feel about it,' I gestured toward the teenagers.

'They resent it, of course, but they aren't surprised. I think they accept it as another reminder of their social status.'

'Can't you stop it? Call the mayor for example?'

'Not a good idea, I'm afraid,' Father Orr smiled. 'The Inspector at Number Six is not our greatest supporter. A call to the mayor would only heighten his antagonism and we can't afford that. Not with him right across the street.'

'But I thought there was co-operation between the club and Number Six – ' remembering the meeting and the warning to applicants that they 'check with Number Six.'

'An exaggeration,' Father Orr murmured. He stopped as Ron hurried up. The Saints' combo was ready to play. If we wanted to hear them, we should go immediately into the big hall.

'I imagine,' Father Orr observed, 'we'd have no difficulty hearing them if we were a block away.'

The combo exploded. They had a raw, undisciplined sound, but while I wondered absently about irreparable damage to ear drums, I couldn't shake the chill of that official walk. What had they expected to find? Drugs? Fugitives? Gambling? In a church hall, with the priest on duty? And what did the surveillance accomplish, except to heighten the hostility of these teenagers toward the police. Certainly that patrol had no characteristics of a friendly stroll.

Dr. Ashley Montagu, the anthropologist, once wrote that 'a human being is a problem in search of a solution.' What kind of a solution was this police attitude to the two hundred problems in this hall?

When I left the dance that night I carried a jumble of questions and a single, clear decision. I liked these young people. Their problems, visible like the tips of icebergs, appalled me. As the probation officer said, I was hooked. But a sense of self-preservation begged to be heard.

That cold tour had triggered an emotion, just as the governor's ridicule of a defenceless teenager, David, had triggered one. I would become involved all right. But this time I would be sensible. I would be objective and I would do my best not to see behind those young faces.

Chapter Eleven

The next Wednesday night I took my place at the table and looked
around at the crimson jackets and the mystery faces with that feeling
of relaxed interest that comes from having made a sensible decision.
There was less restraint this week. The Saints shuffled into the room,
scraping chairs into position, a few scowling, some laughing, everyone
talking.

'Okay, you guys, settle down.' Aaron ordered.

Ron's voice topped the tumult. 'The man says knock it off!'

'What's his beef?' a Saint muttered and grabbed a chair.

'You gonna sit there?' His friend looked astonished. 'I'm gonna sit on
the windowsill.'

'What clown thinks he's gonna sit on the windowsill?' Ron wheeled.
'Go sit on a chair. This is a meetin', not a kindergarten.'

'I can't hear nothin',' someone yelled from the back of the room.
'How come I always got to sit here, for crissake!' He looked around.
'You there, Father? Sorry.'

'Okay,' a shout came from the back, 'so who swiped my bale of weed?
Okay, who's the wise guy?'

'Holy Geez, we got a thief in the crowd!' someone roared.

'How come you can put your f – ' pause, 'sorry, Father. I mean,' glar-
ing at another Saint, 'how come you can put your coat on my chair? I
don't want your – I didn't say it, Father – coat on my chair!'

A whisper from a black-eyed teenager. 'This place spooks me, you
know that? All churchs spook me. Let's get goin'. I got another date.'
He turned to a disbeliever. 'No, not with the f –,' a glance, 'sorry,
Jeann. Not with my probation officer. You're a real howl. I got a date
with a broad. We're gonna – ' and the voices dropped, both faces lit up
and they collapsed in mirth.

'Who left a lighted cigarette on the windowsill?' Topper demanded.
'You wanna burn the place down? You a firebug or somethin'?' A Saint
shoved through the crowd to snatch up the cigarette. 'I'm sorry. I will
kill myself immediately,' he said humbly.

'If you guys don't shut up,' Bruce growled, 'I'll knock your brains
out.'

'We ain't got none to knock out,' someone yelled. 'Don't you know that, big man?'

And Ron, leaping to his feet, 'You guys! Everybody! Settle down! Now!' The noise dimmed. And they were quiet.

Halfway through the meeting, Ron stood up, his face serious. 'There's somebody here who's willin' to help us,' he began, and enlarged on the advantages of the help. 'And I think,' he concluded, 'that somebody should be made an honorary member of the club.' I glanced at Father Orr — Ron had to mean him — and back to Ron. He was pointing at me. The motion was seconded and everyone applauded.

I was moved and flattered by so apparently rapid an acceptance. Ron stood again. Father Orr was to be made an honorary member, too. The meeting noisily endorsed the motion. Aaron filled out the membership cards, delicately questioning the line marked 'age' on mine, while the Saints giggled and clapped. Then Ron stood once more. 'And I think,' he said gravely, 'that Jeann should have official club protection. I move that I be appointed her bodyguard.'

'Where were you when I needed you,' I muttered. Nearby Saints chuckled knowingly. David didn't hear and I didn't repeat it. But of course Ron was joking. Wasn't he? Someone seconded the motion. The meeting passed it. I thanked Ron and the Saints. I said I hoped he wouldn't be kept too busy and everyone applauded. We moved on to the interviewing of membership applicants.

The next morning I delivered the bulletin to my probation officer friend. 'A bodyguard,' he laughed. 'You're moving up fast. I'd say that gesture has a message: "lay off, fellas, or meet me in the alley." '

'Or it's a joke,' I said. 'Or maybe a dramatic bit to impress me, and themselves.'

'You mean with the physical dangers in their world?' He sounded doubtful. 'I'd say the threat isn't to your body, probably to your trust. Or your reputation.'

'You mean he knows the "unconverted," the ones most likely to try to take advantage, whatever that means? It makes sense,' I agreed. 'He certainly knows how to handle the rowdy ones at meetings.'

'With brains or brawn?'

'When the brain — which seems a particularly good one — doesn't convince, there's plenty of brawn to back it up. He's one of the most powerful young men I've encountered in a long time. Gives a girl a warm, secure feeling,' I added with amusement. 'I wonder if he'd work overtime — on irate agency clients?'

'Has he a record?' he asked suddenly.

'A record? I don't know. I doubt it. He seems too scornful of the ones who do.'

'Because they got caught, or because they committed crimes?'

'You ask good questions. I guess the answers will come eventually. Right now I don't want to ask too many questions of them. Is that wrong?'

'Let sleeping records lie?' And he laughed again. 'Probably wise. They'll be sensitive to your curiosities, especially the ones who're making the dramatic fresh start. The so-called delinquent feels pretty guilty,' he said reflectively, 'even before he commits a crime. That's part of what it's all about, of course. Anyway, I'm glad you have a bodyguard. You may need him.'

'Cool, calm, and bodyguarded. That's me,' I said cheerfully and he mumbled, 'Good luck.'

But the following Wednesday my planned role as the spectator-apprentice ended. When I opened the church hall door a gale of voice sounds, shrill with agitation, rushed to meet me. I grabbed a passing Saint. 'What's going on?' He grimaced. 'Come on in. You'll see.'

As I walked into the main hall someone yelled, 'Who the hell do they think we are?' And Bruce fired back, 'A bunch of hoods. And they're right!'

'Who is "they" and what have they done?' I asked.

The Saints turned, faces angry or indignant or worried. 'Number Six,' Tony volunteered, his eyes shining. 'They've been raidin' us. Some guys been picked up three, four times since Monday.'

'But why? What's happened?'

'That's it,' another Saint pounced. 'They won't tell us. They haul us in, start yellin', make the god –' he stopped, 'make accusations and throw us around and they say we know all about it. All about what?' he demanded of no one in particular.

'I'm gettin' the hell out of this club,' one declared. 'If they're gonna be on our backs just because we belong to this club, I'm gettin' the hell out. And fast. I got enough trouble.'

'They even trail us in the cruisers,' a round-eyed Saint confided. 'I'm walkin' on the street, mindin' my own business and I look around and there it is, creepin' along behind me.' He shuddered.

'Even when they let us go – and they gotta 'cause we're clean – they pick us up again,' one growled. 'I been picked up five times in the last seventy-two hours. And I got stopped a dozen times.'

'Wait a minute,' I interrupted the barrage. 'Where's Father Orr?'

'Out,' someone supplied. 'Had a parish meetin'. He said you'd be here.'

'Oh.' Great. I was elected to handle this emergency. 'Okay, first, have you gentlemen done anything to upset Number Six?' They looked at each other. No one spoke. 'No details. Just yes or no.' A chorus of 'No!' Predictable. 'And they gave no reason for the questioning?' Another chorus of 'No!' 'And how long were you held?'

'Depends,' someone volunteered. 'Different lengths of time.'

'Were you advised of your rights?'

'What rights?' someone asked and they looked bewildered.

'You do have rights, you know.' Their eyes were intent. 'For instance, there's a limit to the time you can be held without being charged. I don't know the limit, but I'll find out. And you can make a telephone call.' I groped for the rights of any citizen. 'You can refuse to answer questions until you're represented by a lawyer. It's a free society, you know, and you're supposed to be advised of your rights.' This seemed news to most of them and I realized the depth of my own ignorance. I had taken for granted not only the rights of any citizen, but the explanation of them to anyone questioned by the police – whatever his age.

'Who'd we call?' someone asked. 'You said we could make a telephone call.'

'Father Orr. A lawyer. Me.'

They looked at each other. One Saint, a tall, attractive blond, pulled a pen from his pocket. 'Hey,' he called with friendly insolence, 'what's your telephone number.'

'All of you write it down,' I ignored the giggles. 'If you get into trouble and you can't reach Father Orr, call me. I don't know what I'll be able to do, but I can learn.' One by one they marked it down. 'Now,' I said, 'let's find out what's going on.' When someone yelled, 'How?' I said, 'By asking, of course.' 'Who?' the shout came. 'Number Six. Maybe the Inspector.' A chorus of 'the Inspector' came from fifty young throats. The two words conveyed anger and distaste. 'He can't be that bad,' I objected.

Ron ground out a cigarette, shoving the stub into a corner. He glanced at me, and, with a grin, picked it up again. 'Wait until you meet him,' he said.

'Fine,' I nodded. 'Let's make it now.'

It occurred to me that we should check our legal standing before we hurled into Number Six. The Saints agreed. I called Stanton Hogg. His reaction was calm. There was a detective at Number Six, he said, who was interested in youth problems. It might be wise to talk with him. 'And Jeann,' he said gently, 'I wouldn't storm in.'

I reported back to the Saints. We headed for the door and, breathing heavily, surged across the street. I thought of Stan's admonition. Fifty young men and a resolute woman did give the impression of a storm.

'Perhaps,' I suggested, 'we should cut this to committee size.' While they conferred in a circle around Aaron, I dealt with the sensible question. What if some of the 'unconverted' had been mixed up in something. Yet that wasn't the point. The point was this – harrassment, this – the only word was bullying.

A committee of four, representing the executive, was selected. We walked into Number Six. A desk sergeant looked up startled from his newspaper. I outlined our problem. Detective x wasn't on duty. His eyes swept the scarlet jackets. 'I think you should talk to the Inspector,' he said, amusement in his eyes. 'Maybe tomorrow.' We thanked him, the Saints mumbling their disappointment. When you're primed to charge the enemy, delay is frustrating. Feet lagging, we returned to the waiting Saints.

Father Orr was in the hall when we pushed open the door. 'Number Six,' I said to the querying glance. 'They've been raiding us.'

'Oh?' He covered the Saints with a look. 'What have we done?'

'We plead innocent to unknown charges. But we intend to beard the Inspector in his den tomorrow. Will you be free?'

His eyes rolled. 'To beard the Inspector. Yes, I'll be free. But I think we should talk. Now.' And he motioned me up the stairs.

Father Orr was scrupulously fair about the Inspector's opposition, but it made no sense to me. A band of previous offenders located immediately across the street from a police station would give any police officer reason to ponder. And the Saints were not ideal neighbours.

But the club's announced purpose was anti-delinquency. It was within easy surveillance range. It was supervised by a priest and housed in a church hall. The Inspector might have suspicions about the sincerity of some of the Saints. He might question the likelihood of 'reformation.' But surely he would agree that the experiment was worth a try.

The next afternoon I left the office early for the summit meeting. When I arrived at St. Mark's, the Saints had congregated. We trailed across the street. At the police station door Father Orr made a practical suggestion. The bearding committee should be composed of only the adults. That had a major advantage. We could talk about the Saints adults-to-adults. They agreed. They stood grouped about the door, faces sombre, hands shoved into pockets, the laughter gone.

The Inspector's office was pleasant, looking out over Queen Street and centred by an impressively large desk. Behind the desk sat the Inspector. The moment I saw him I knew I was in trouble. He sat stiffly, his eyes devoid of friendliness. A handsome man, with military bearing, he greeted us with an icy politeness that set my teeth on edge. It was immediately apparent that we would never be pals.

He stood slowly in acknowledgement of Father Orr's introduction of me. His eyes lingered on me. I managed a careful smile and we sat down. Father Orr asked delicately about the recent raids. The Inspector said they had not been improperly conducted; this was police business; he was not obliged to take us into his confidence. I fixed my attention on a spot on the wall. Silence would be best. Otherwise I might turn this confrontation into a calamity.

The Inspector went to the crux of the matter. He did not agree with the idea of the the club. He did not believe it would work. He believed it would produce nothing but trouble, especially for Number Six. He knew more about these young punks than we did. Our approach was totally wrong.

Father Orr listened intently. Then he cleared his throat. What approach, precisely, did the Inspector recommend?

'Convert them!' The Inspector snapped the phrase so fiercely I thought for an instant he had said 'shoot them!' He said he had been converted seventeen years earlier. It had changed his whole life. 'Get them to your altar,' he thundered.

'Faith is hardly an act of force,' Father Orr protested.

'Nothing else will solve their problems,' the Inspector insisted.

'But surely faith is an act of love,' Father Orr persisted, 'and if you have had no experience of real love, it would be impossible to understand the love of God.'

'Convert them, or your church will be an arsenal,' the Inspector declared.

'It's a small church,' Father Orr smiled, 'if they had an arsenal – of guns, I presume you mean – I'm sure I would stumble over it.'

I went on staring at the wall. The Inspector warned he would regard the club as an unfavourable influence; he would watch closely all its activities; he would put opposition on active duty. We could expect no

84

assistance, no support, and no understanding. Father Orr stirred in his chair. We would take his advice into serious consideration, he said. Perhaps if the Inspector attended a meeting, saw the membership in action?

'I've seen them in action,' the Inspector said. And he bowed us out of his office. He didn't say what a great pleasure it had been to meet me. I didn't say what a great pleasure it had been to meet him. At least we were both honest.

The Saints were waiting in the uncertain sunshine. Ron shot one look at Father Orr and muttered, 'Yeah.' Aaron asked anxiously, 'What did he say?'

'I wouldn't call him our greatest fan,' Father Orr remarked mildly, 'but I suppose we haven't given him much reason. Yet.'

We walked mournfully across the quiet street. The afternoon had mellowed into one of those spring days when warmth is a whisper and the shafts of pale sunlight find leftover traces of winter's grime. The street looked as depressed as we felt. David said nothing, his eyes down, hands in his pockets. Tony hopped closer to Father Orr. 'But what did he say?' he urged.

'Primarily that he isn't convinced we are sincere about the club's purpose of fighting delinquency.'

'So what's he gonna do?' Ron scowled.

'Keep an eye on us,' Father Orr reached to open the church hall door. David got there first. We streamed inside. 'We don't have a sympathizer,' Father Orr told the silent Saints, 'but let's not be carried away by that. Everyone likes to feel the martyr sometimes, but I'd prefer we regard this as a challenge.'

The Saints were painfully eager to discuss it. For once in their young lives the opposition of authority was unwarranted and they knew it. The knowledge was sweet. They had no intention of diluting that sweetness by admitting that the police could be justified in their suspicions.

'Is he gonna close us down?' David asked.

'He would have no right to do that,' Father Orr said, 'unless we became some sort of' – the radiant grin again – 'crime syndicate. All he can do is say "show me." '

'I'll show him,' Ron growled, while another Saint faked a blow at the wall. 'Pow! I could clock him so fast – '

'That's childish,' Father Orr shook his head. 'And I assume we aren't going to be childish.'

The Saints walked around the hall, muttering among themselves.

Members who had not been with the waiting committee wandered in and everybody told everybody what had happened. Everybody scowled at everybody.

'Well,' Father Orr said cheerfully, 'now that we understand the situation, I think we shouldn't dwell on it. Number Six isn't going to be the only sceptical group. Keep that in mind. As for the recent raids, I think they will end. The Inspector didn't say so, but I think they will end.' He turned to me. 'Will you come up for a few minutes?'

In his study he closed the door. 'And how did you like him?'

'A real charmer,' I sighed.

He pushed books to one side and sat down on the armchair. 'Of course,' he said, 'neither of us appeared too willing to look at it from his viewpoint. And he does have the responsibility of keeping law and order in this community.'

'But he also has a magnificent opportunity to prove to a bunch of teenagers that the police are not out to get them. Even if he can't see himself as the friend of youth, or a worker among delinquents he's certainly intelligent enough to know that his hostility will only heighten theirs. And he isn't exactly overwhelmed with admiration for our intelligence,' I added indignantly. 'That arsenal crack, now really!'

'I think we can safely assume that the Inspector is of the "stern discipline" school of law enforcement officers,' Father Orr murmured.

An unsettling thought crept into my mind. 'Of course there is a difference between your position and mine in all this, isn't there,' I said. 'I mean, if I make a fool of myself at least I don't involve the whole church.'

'It would be most unfortunate,' Father Orr agreed with exaggerated gravity, 'if at some point I were charged with – what's the phrase – contributing to delinquency? But,' he sobered, 'I do have a responsibility to these young people, as well as to this parish.' His hands fanned. 'No heroism. Just fact. So I guess we should try not to make fools of ourselves.'

Chapter Twelve

If the crime rate did go up immediately in Parkdale, as the Inspector predicted, and if any of our Saints were responsible, we weren't aware of it.

But the next week there was a jump in the number of membership applications. News of the club might have gained a coincidental momentum, but there was also the splendid possibility that word had travelled about a couple of adults who were willing to run interference for them. And that was a two-sided coin.

If the club were to achieve any part of its purpose as a delinquency deterrent and a rehabilitation aid, the teenagers had to have faith in the advantage of membership. The grumble of the Saints the night of the raiding discussion that 'if they're gonna be after us just because we belong to this club, I'm gettin' out fast' clung to memory.

On the other hand, without a unanimous conviction within the club that, as David said, they didn't have to 'lead a life of crime,' we had to make it clear that our interference constituted a protection against possible police bullying, an honest attempt to understand and to help, but in no way did it sanction lawbreaking. That was the tricky part and it was something they would come to understand only through demonstration.

'I think we can call this the mutual getting-to-know-you time,' Father Orr said, 'and there'll be surprises. On both sides.'

I fell over one at the next meeting. That afternoon a Toronto newspaper had headlined the story of two teenagers, charged and convicted of armed robbery, who were packing for Kingston Penitentiary when the genuinely guilty teenagers were apprehended. I was excited about the story on two accounts; the incident itself and the opportunity it gave to offer the Saints an example of the role the club might play in future.

During the meeting the members launched into a discussion of the club's future and Aaron invited comments from the adults. I had the newspaper with me and, with cherishable passion, I made a speech.

In essence I said that the club, properly organized, could become a force sufficiently strong and respected to undertake a form of watch-dogging, so that this – and I held up the paper – would be less likely to occur.

It struck me that my passion wasn't igniting any fire. They were listening almost in stunned silence. They had to begin to think of themselves as members of society, I intoned, to understand the responsibilities as well as the privileges of social membership. There were flaws and injustices in our system, but they had to be fought from within society not attacked from without. Their silence, relentless and even a little embarrassed, began to suck vitality from my enthusiasm. While I wavered to a conclusion I scolded myself for throwing so ambitious an idea at them so soon. The sincere Saints were newcomers to the role of being straight. The unconverted might find the idea only ironic.

Finally I sat down. Aaron coughed. David fingered a cigarette. Bruce ducked his head, a peculiar smile on his face. Ron stared at the ceiling. The others looked at the floor, each other, the windows, and their fingernails. Aaron coughed again. 'Thank you, Jeann,' he said. 'Would anyone want to comment?' He paused. 'Or,' brightening, 'shall we go on to the membership applicants.' They moved on.

When the meeting adjourned, Father Orr left for another meeting. Ron tapped my arm. 'You goin' home?' he asked, while the Saints shuffled past, their eyes avoiding me.

'Expect so. Why?'

His powerful shoulders lifted and dropped again. 'Just thought I'd walk you to the streetcar.'

Ron was smiling as we strolled the moon-splashed street, as if he were amused by some hilarious secret. 'All right,' I said at last. 'What's so funny and what did I say tonight to put them into near coma?'

He crumpled with laughter. 'You don't know,' he gurgled, 'and you were so damned earnest. Those guys, the ones you called' – laughter rolled over him – 'the genuinely guilty teenagers, the ones who were gonna let those poor innocent kids take the rap, those guys were the Saints who got seven years for armed robbery.' He collaspsed in mirth. 'And one of them,' he howled, 'was our Crown Attorney!'

My mind did an instant replay of my speech and I stared at him before I lost my own struggle against outraged laughter.

The incident did slow me down, but only briefly. With my track record

88

so far in delinquencyland, I was learning to take the bad with the worse and to cut my losses. And at the Saturday night dance the Saints appeared to have recovered, and even forgiven me for my earnest innocence.

But the highlight of the evening was my attempt to bridge the viewpoint gap with the detectives. I decided, as Father Orr said, that we should try to see it from their side. They were acting under orders. It was even possible that they found this surveillance duty as distasteful as the rest of us. If we indicated some understanding friendliness, it might be a first small step toward each other.

When they entered the hall I tried to replace the sight of these stern-faced men with the one of the protective giants of my childhood, the police I had been taught to trust and to respect. Idly I wondered, too, how many of the Saints' parents had used the police as a childhood threat, the too-familiar and deadly 'If you don't obey, I'll get a policeman to lock you up.'

They walked slowly through the crowd, these key figures in the fight for the future of the teenagers. When their scrutiny turned to me, I dredged up my warmest smile, my most friendly 'good evening.' Their look wasn't churlish, but it did leave me with the distinct impression of having been flicked across the face with a wet haddock. Frustrated and irritated I watched them leave.

Later that evening Father Orr and I talked about the practicalities of helping the Saints organize their club. They needed a constitution. They needed to be taught proper meeting procedure. And the meetings needed a highlight. The obvious one would be guest speakers.

Father Orr introduced the idea at the next meeting. The members didn't appear overjoyed, but they were impressed, if only by the possibility that adults in various professions would consent to 'address' them.

'Like who?' someone called out.

They knew of my involvement with showbusiness and their minds moved quickly. Guest speakers could be celebrities, preferably girl celebrities. Shirley Harmer, for example, who co-starred with Robert Goulet on one show; the girl dancers on *The Wayne and Shuster Show*; the actresses on the drama series.

That wasn't quite what we had in mind. The speakers should contribute without distracting. And we hoped to find people interested in the Saints as human beings, rather than social freaks or genetic jokes. They should also represent areas of life new to the Saints. Privately Father Orr and I discussed the possibility of Alex Barris, a Toronto newspaper columnist, who was scheduled to host a television series that summer – which gave him added glamour for the Saints – and who was a man of intelligence and sensitivity and humour. Father Orr tossed his name into the noisy exchange. Ron nodded thoughtfully. The Saints followed and David made one of his rare verbal contributions. 'Since Jeann knows him, I move she invite him for us.' The motion passed.

The Barris appearance was a success and both the Saints and the adults were encouraged by it. They considered future possibilities more seriously. Someone made a suggestion I thought, at first, was a joke. 'How about the Inspector?' The members shouted with laughter. But Ron stood up. 'Not a bad idea. It makes sense.' The laughter faded. Father Orr was assigned the privilege, or responsibility, of issuing the invitation.

Later, in his study, I asked: 'You really think this is a good idea?'

'Splendid,' he said, 'but of course he won't come.'

And, of course, he didn't. The Saints' reactions varied from Bruce's growling 'so who's surprised?' to Tony's 'I don't get it? Why's he fightin' people who are fightin' delinquency?' While they considered that question, Father Orr broke in with marked casualness.

'Perhaps you'd find Stanton Hogg of interest.'

Momentary silence. Then: 'Depends on how you serve him,' one shouted, 'roasted or broiled.'

Father Orr ignored the shout. 'He's an interesting man,' he observed. 'You might find him worthwhile.'

'I never did,' a Saint called out, 'unless you figure fourteen months at Guelph is worthwhile. That's what the – ' he paused, 'the gentleman gave me.'

Ron waved a hand. 'Okay, stop clownin'. I think it's a good idea.' The motion passed. I was to invite him on behalf of the club.

Stanton Hogg's initial reaction wavered between incredulity and amusement. 'You may be right,' he said finally, 'I would meet them on a more informal basis. I could give them a better picture of my job. And maybe,' he smiled, 'they could give me a better picture of themselves.'

The night of his appearance we arrived precisely at meeting time. Yet the meeting had been called to order. We could hear the rumble of male voices behind the closed door. Aaron opened the door to my knock. 'Hi,' he said, barely glancing at their speaker, 'we'll be ready in a minute,' and he closed the door again.

I was amused. They had matters to discuss that weren't for the ears of a guest speaker. Or, amusement fleeing, for the ears of a Crown Attorney? I tried to smile casually at Stan, but as we waited panic mounted. I didn't know if Father Orr were inside and I didn't know what they could be doing. Lighting a fuse? Putting a bucket of water over the door? Setting up a machine gun?

'You're quite certain,' Stan said quizzically, 'that I'm welcome?'

'Of course,' I said heartily. 'They're just –' Just what? I thought. 'Just finishing up something.'

Five minutes later we were summoned inside. Fifty-five pairs of eyes watched our progress to the head table. I checked the chair before Stan sat down, glanced under the table and crossed my fingers.

With a politeness which now seemed ominous, Aaron introduced their guest. He said Mr. Hogg was 'well known to the members.' Stan stood up and a hush fell over the room. Then the Saints erupted in loud, intense, prolonged booing. I measured the distance to the door. Stan waited, his face expressionless. Abruptly the booing stopped and faces cracked in wide, delighted grins. Laughter filled the room and applause replaced the booing. The 'tough Crown' was their captive guest.

Stan moved easily into his informal talk about the functions of a Crown Attorney. He didn't recognize by a word or a look that his audience was something other than average. He might be addressing the Rotary Club, I thought with a secret giggle. When he finished the Saints applauded furiously and Aaron, with only a trace of hesitation, invited questions.

They had a good many questions and only a few were stained with antagonism. Stan ignored the antagonism. He answered each seriously and reasonably. For the first fifteen minutes the Saints prefaced their questions with a polite 'Mr. Hogg.' Ron disposed of the formality. With buoyant friendliness he called, 'Hey, Stan,' and the members adopted the salutation. For the remainder of the question period their deadly enemy was 'Hey, Stan.'

As we left the meeting I overheard one Saint's evaluation. 'You know,' he muttered to a neighbour, 'he ain't a bad guy, when you get to know him.'

But the seed of this new idea, that a representative of authority might be a good guy, wasn't left long enough to take root. With exquisitely ironic timing, the Inspector struck again. He delivered his bombshell bulletin through Father Orr.

The Saints' club charged admission to their dances. That made them a commercial business. Commercial businesses required licences. No one had to debate this club's chances of being granted that licence. The Inspector had taken his reasoning straight to the inevitable. Without the dances, there was a good chance the club would fold.

The meeting writhed in rage. Aaron asked for ideas. They all had ideas. Violent ones. 'You can't run the club from behind bars,' Father Orr remarked and Ron sprang to his feet. 'Father Orr's right. We gotta be practical. We gotta find a way around this.' He stopped and attention swung to him.

His eyes narrowed in concentration. His chin buried in the collar of the crimson jacket, his expression was so intense that I was seized by a surprising excitement. While the meeting hummed expectantly I waited, as eagerly as the rest, for him to pull the answer from that shrewd, inventive mind. What is it about him, I wondered. Ron snapped his fingers. 'Got it,' he said. 'No law says we can't take up a collection for charity. Right?' He looked at Father Orr.

'You mean hold the dances as benefits?' Father Orr frowned. 'You may be among Toronto's one hundred neediest cases,' he said wryly, 'but I don't think that's what the Inspector has in mind.'

'We know what he has in mind,' Ron said while the members growled. 'But I mean real charity. I know somebody right now who could use a handout.'

'So do I,' someone shouted. 'Me.'

Ron rapped for silence. 'This is serious. It isn't illegal to hold back enough for expenses. Every club does that. Right, Father?'

'Providing the expenses are legitimate,' Father Orr agreed, 'but you must remember this is a church hall. The donations must be genuine.'

'Sure,' Ron nodded, 'no cheatin'. We don't need a profit. We need those dances. Right, guys?' Everyone clapped. 'So all they can do is nail us for makin' a mistake if we're wrong and that ain't no crime. Yet. So let's try it.'

They tried it Saturday night. A sign was posted in the entrance hall, next to a wicker basket. It said all proceeds would go to charity. The grapevine had the story. Couples smiled knowingly and dropped in the usual admission price. If anyone hesitated, Ron stepped up with a friendly slap on the shoulder. He was the club's built-in insurance.

There was no serious resistance until a member of a north Toronto gang read the sign, grimaced to friends, and dropped in a nickel. Ron's hand folded over his shoulder. 'That will be two dollars,' he said. 'Two dollars!' The teenager twisted under Ron's hand and pointed to the sign. 'A donation. That's what it says, fella. I made it. One nickel.'

'Two dollars,' Ron repeated, fingers digging deeper into the shoulder. 'If you hadn't tried to get smart – fella – it woulda been a quarter. Now, two bucks or you don't get in. Maybe you'd like to discuss it outside? Fella.' And he twisted the shoulder.

Still muttering the teenager pulled out a two-dollar bill and dropped it into the basket. Instantly Ron's hand released him. 'Thank you,' Ron bowed mockingly. 'Pleasure to have your company.'

When the receipts were counted, the revenue was a new high. When I mentioned it to Ron he laughed. 'So we got a lot more charity-minded folk than you thought. Really,' he patted my shoulder, 'there's a lot of sweet guys in Parkdale.'

But the Inspector's attempt to torpedo the club with a technicality solidified hostility toward Number Six, even among Saints who, earlier, had seemed only bewildered by his opposition. And that hostility was emerging as a major problem. Now, if we passed an officer on the street the Saints delighted in projecting images of themselves they knew to be distasteful, even repellent; a burst of boisterous laughter after a whispered, pointed comment, an exaggerated slouching walk that, invariably almost collided with the officer, and glances loaded with challenge.

The first time I witnessed the open taunting I suspected the incident was also a test of me. We had been walking to the restaurant when they spotted an officer. Glances, knowing and bright, passed between them. Swifty, deftly, one Saint slipped my handbag from my arm. Another yelled 'Stop, thief!' and two peeled off after the fleeing Saint. The officer spun to give chase. I had a horrified vision of a 'capture' that would throw the Saints into paroxysms of mirth at the officer's expense. I halted. And the others in the group halted too in expectant silence. The officer had taken the first rapid stride when I yelled, 'All right, Jim. You win. I'm not in racing form.' And I laughed. The officer stopped and turned an official, questioning look at me. I tried to telegraph an apology that wasn't a betrayal of my young friends. The Saints returned. Aaron slid his hand cheerfully under my arm. We closed ranks and, giggling, we passed the officer. The little joke was the prank of children. The officer was justified in his obvious impatience, but his look held, as well, a cold dislike and contempt.

Somehow this antagonism – on both sides – had to be diluted, if the Saints weren't to explode in some disastrous confrontation. Somehow we had to find someone at Number Six who understood the needs of these wilful teenagers. I remembered Stanton Hogg's reference to the detective at Number Six who was interested in the problems of young people. He might be the answer, this Detective x. The most appealing idea would be an incident, during which the Saints, individually or as a club, received undeniably fair treatment.

One night, late in March, I thought I had found the ideal opportunity.

We had gone to the restaurant after a meeting and we were wedged together in a booth, David, Bruce, Ron and another Saint who had become interesting because of his ambition. Peter was seventeen, quiet, good looking, intense, and oddly out of place among these strident young people.

He had confided that he wanted to become a professional musician and we were talking about the cbc when Tony rushed up. 'Hey, Pete,' he said, excitement bouncing in his voice, 'didja know they have a warrant out for you?'

The identity of 'they' was instantly and mutually understood. My surprise was double edged. It was still hard to associate any of these young men with actual crimes, but with Peter it verged on the impossible. His eyes were wide. 'I haven't done a thing,' he gasped.

'Do you know of some . . . caper?' I asked.

'Honest! No!'

Father Orr and I agreed that the Saints might not always tell us the truth in matters of innocence or guilt. It was frustrating, but we had to be realistic. They weren't conditioned to telling the truth to adults. Yet Peter sounded honest. So it had to be a mistake. And if Number Six acknowledged the mistake, which seemed logical and inevitable, the Saints would have their proof that the police not only were fallible, but willing to admit it. 'Well,' I said cheerfully, 'let's find out what it's all about.'

'How?' Peter stared at me and the other Saints stopped talking.

'By asking,' I said patiently.

'You mean give myself up?' He sounded horrified.

'It isn't giving yourself up if you haven't done anything and you don't know about anything. It's probably a mistake, and it's only sensible to straighten it out. Okay?'

94

'Will you come with me?' he asked, still stunned.

'Of course,' I slid off the booth seat. 'Come on.'

We went out into the misty night, trailed by Saints clearly fascinated by this new approach to an old problem. As we walked toward Number Six I thought if Detective x were on duty, this would be a triumph.

He was on duty. The sergeant directed us up a flight of stairs to his office. At the office door Peter's hand slid unexpectedly into mine. He looked like a student called into the principal's office. When I knocked on the door frame, Detective x looked up in fastidious boredom from behind a big desk. 'Yes?'

'Excuse me,' I said, 'but this young man has heard you have a warrant out for him. He thought he should come in and find out what it's all about.' I smiled, an adult-to-adult, aren't-these-kids-something smile. But Detective x had strangely frosty eyes for such a good guy. They slid over my smile and fastened on Peter.

'Name?' he asked briskly. Peter mumbled his name in a low, frightened voice. The detective rummaged through papers, found a file, and looked again at Peter. The look suggested he knew that he and Peter belonged to the same genus, but that they were of a different species and that members of Peter's species should be despatched somewhere – immediately. Peter threw me a look of mute appeal that we forget this madness and make a dash for it. I shook my head and we walked toward the desk. There were two chairs beside it. We didn't sit. We hadn't been invited to sit.

Detective x opened a desk drawer and pulled out a set of glossy pictures. He threw one at Peter. 'You know them,' he said.

Peter scrutinized the print. 'No, I don't,' he said. I looked apprehensively at him. If he were lying. . . . 'I don't,' he repeated to me.

Detective x threw me an iced glance and returned to Peter. He repeated that Peter could identify the boys in the picture. He didn't explain why he believed this, or why it mattered, but it was clear Peter better not know them. Peter's repeated denials roused him to more emphatic and equally mysterious accusations. The police 'knew about' Peter. They knew 'his real name.' Peter looked bewildered and Detective x had lost me, too. The accusations continued, cold and steady. Peter grew more frightened and more flustered.

'Detective x,' My voice had its own chill now. 'Is Peter charged with something? And if so, what?'

The detective pointed a blunt finger at Peter and flipped it back at me. 'You tell her,' he commanded.

'No,' I jumped him angrily. 'You tell me.'

He swivelled in the chair. 'And just who are you?'

'A friend,' I said and waited.

'What kind of friend,' he asked, eyebrows tilting.

Anger blazed to a dangerous heat. 'I beg your pardon?'

'I asked,' his voice dripped insinuation and sarcasm, 'what kind of friend?'

Peter was watching, interested now in the exchange between the detective and me. 'The kind I assume you are to any friends you might have,' I said, a little surprised by my calmness.

And it no longer mattered if Peter were innocent or guilty. Here it was. Again. The same attitude. That destructive attitude. That – yes, bullying. 'This has been most interesting,' I said evenly. 'I had looked forward to meeting you. Stanton Hogg spoke so glowingly of you.' I twisted the knife. 'Actually he was the one who recommended we talk to you any time we had problems.'

Detective x frowned. 'You know Stanton Hogg? The Crown Attorney?'

'He's a friend of mine,' I said and understood, for the first time, the satisfaction of the Saints in defeating this enemy. Detective x picked up the prints. Primly he opened his desk drawer and shoved them inside. Then he leaned back to include Peter and me in an expansive smile. 'Well now,' he said, 'isn't that interesting. I'm afraid I didn't catch your name?'

I told him my name; told him crisply about the Saints; told him I had assured Peter that the authorities would welcome the opportunity to clear up any misunderstanding, or get the facts. With the tide of malice flowing, I added, 'After Stan's comments about you and your interest in helping young people, I was delighted when the sergeant said you were on duty.'

His smile didn't waver. 'Absolutely right.' He turned to Peter. 'And it is a good idea to get these things cleared up. Son.'

Merriment shone on Peter's young face. I had felled the bad guy. I might not be a fast draw, but I had deadly ammunition. And distaste crawled through me. The change in Detective x had been degrading, to himself and to all police. Despite the petty satisfaction I wished he had greeted my glacier announcement with supreme indifference. Now the incident would reinforce the Saints' belief that the police were 'out to get them.' And it would strengthen their suspicions that knowing the right people and the right approach was better than being right, or being honest, or being innocent.

Detective x ushered us from his office, invited us to drop in anytime
– an invitation greeted by both of us with a queer little silence – and
sent his best regards to our mutual friend, Stan. We went back out into
the night so Peter could tell the Saints of our victory.

Chapter Thirteen

I don't know if the incident went down in Saint history as 'the night Jeann bagged a cop,' but I do know it strengthened my allegiance to these young dispossessed.

The question of the identity of the 'sincere' Saints and the 'unconverted' lingered, but its importance diminished. One reason was the lack of indication that there were any 'unconverted.' No police officer tramped into my apartment or Father Orr's study at four in the morning to report a Saint in trouble. No hint of criminal activity came to our attention. Sometimes I wondered if David had been right, if the club itself, providing the companionship and a place to go, both fervently needed by all the dispossessed, had been the answer.

The other reason was my deepening involvement. Affection was growing for these twitchy teenagers, affection and respect. The inviolability of friendship, the unshakeable respect for the rights of members – including the right to expect support whatever the emergency – their bluntness, their gusty rebellions, their laughter and excited, aimless talk, even their lust for experience, any experience that happened swiftly, consumed them totally, and satisfied mysterious appetites, all of it was fascinating and absorbing.

We still had no real clues to the reasons for their past activities. None of the textbook theories on delinquency seemed applicable. None of the Saints were from wealthy homes, but none, as far as we knew, were products of genuine poverty. We knew no Saint, either, who was 'the victim of a broken home.' They were all school dropouts, but that was a symptom, not a cause.

Sometimes it seemed that their indifference to more average social values and conduct was a 'silent scream' to find or to develop values that were deeply personal, even spiritual – however scornfully they might dismiss the articulated idea. But they were human beings and human beings want to be taken into account. And I wanted to know them, as they were – whatever that meant. That desire left little room for suspicious speculations.

Perhaps they sensed the honesty of that desire, as the wounded are more sensitive to the true responses in others. As the weeks passed we became ingredients in each other's lives.

They talked more freely when Father Orr and I joined them in after-meeting sessions. They dropped in at the study more frequently to visit Father Orr. They tramped into my office and a few came regularly to my apartment. The invitation to call 'when in trouble' was also enthusiastically accepted.

It seemed to have varying significance for them. One Saint said he tacked my number beside the telephone, 'So's Mom will know someone to call if I disappear' – presumably into Number Six. Another said he kept the number handy because 'It makes me feel safer.' And another told me he carried it in his wallet, 'So's I won't be so alone.' But their definition of trouble differed from mine. It could be a fight with a girlfriend, a job hunt, a disagreement with parents, or simply a mood of nocturnal depression that had to be shared. And all troubles became more acute after midnight. By April, I no longer leaped into the air when the telephone rang at one, or two, or even three in the morning.

The only question mark was David. Our tenuous relationship was changing. He visited the office less frequently. His telephone calls dwindled. He didn't drop in at the apartment and we didn't have intimate dinners. Part of the subtle new remoteness was my fault and I knew it. Yet he was working; he was cheerful; he appeared to be living a reasonably ordered existence. We talked at the meetings and dances, although the exchanges were usually limited to 'How are you?' 'Fine' – David was always fine – and a footnote on a current event. But he knew I was there if he needed me.

Sometimes the memory of his 'confession' jabbed and I would think, 'there's something wrong with that boy. He needs the trained help of a specialist.' Yet, remembering the psychiatrist's remark about Paul, I worried that if I suggested it, David might think I considered him 'a sick freak.' And it would do little if any good, unless he wanted the help. And anyway where were the specialists, beyond professional psychiatrists who were too busy or too expensive?

Occasionally, too, I wondered if my growing friendships among the Saints had put a damper on our relationship. He had encouraged, even urged, that association, but maybe it wasn't working out as he had anticipated. We were not the 'twosome' in the club. The Saints knew and respected David's prior claim, but they accepted that as blandly as they accepted him as president. That was another puzzle. He volunteered little leadership and exercised virtually no control. He was treated with due seriousness when he made a suggestion, but no one, it seemed, expected him to lead them. Yet he was the president – despite mounting evidence that Ron was the real force in the club.

And Ron and I were rapidly becoming genuine friends. He was the first to accept the invitation to call, and initially the calls did have the premise of a problem, or at least a question. He'd had a fight with Lillian, his girlfriend, and could I tell him something – anything – about women? He'd seen a horse he wished he could buy. He'd read that a friend had been sentenced to five years in Kingston and would I like to go with him to visit the friend sometime – as an experience? Some of his questions may have been clues about his side of our friendship. One evening he asked what the word 'milquetoast' meant. I had used it as a description of myself in some situation. When I said 'timid' he snorted. 'You were never afraid of anything in your life,' he said and that – however untrue it was – seemed immensely satisfying to him.

He possessed a remarkably adaptive and a surprisingly non-young, rather than mature, mind. He seemed to understand what he termed, with adult amusement, 'that crazy world of advertising' without need of explanation. And he urged constantly that I stop being stupid, working such 'dumb hours.' He also slid inoffensively into the area of my personal life, asking bluntly about my love life and satisfied when I assured him that I had one.

Most significantly he assumed the role of mentor, as well as body guard, about the club. When members resisted an idea, it was Ron who, privately, explained. 'You gotta understand. These guys don't think that way.' Or when a Saint appealed for financial help it was Ron, unaccountably knowing of the appeal, who would make the recommendation: 'He's okay. You'll get it back.' Or 'Don't be stupid. He's playing you for a sucker. Say no.' And I learned to trust his judgement.

He had set the ground rules for those club discussions immediately. He would offer advice and insight, but he wouldn't talk about individual members. 'They're friends. You don't talk about friends behind their backs.'

'I don't mean gossip,' I protested, 'but if we're going to help, Father Orr and I must know some things about them.'

'You'll learn. Just don't be stupid.' That advice became the recurring theme. And he meant it, just as he meant it when he said I was on his loyalty list. He would not betray my confidences and 'I'll never lie to you.' He added a postscript that was to govern our relationship. 'I'll always give you an honest answer to any question. But I won't volunteer anythin'. That means you got to know the right questions.' It seemed an odd thing to say, even then.

He didn't talk too frequently about himself. He did mention one night that he wasn't living at home 'just now,' and I assumed he shared with another Saint, eating off the unemployment insurance which appeared the financial mainstay of most Saints. He wasn't working 'at the moment' and he indicated no interest in his future, another Saint characteristic. And, again like most Saints, he seemed to spend most of his time in the restaurant, the poolhall, the movies, 'with the guys,' or on the street corners.

Silently, sometimes, I questioned his participation in the club at all. It seemed increasingly doubtful that he had a record and I wondered if, through some inexplicable involvement with young offenders, something had happened to make him pursue this anti-delinquency route, even if it did contain a rousing hostility toward authority and a flat contempt for most – not all, but most – police. But I didn't ask. When he wanted me to know he would tell me. And in the meantime he was teaching me about the subculture of the Saints.

The end of April he provided a practical, unforgettable lesson. He called at three-thirty one morning. 'I'm sick,' he said. My cousin, who was staying overnight, had rocketed off the bed when the telephone rang. At my 'how sick?' she fell back, mumbling about the wild life I led.

'I don't know. I feel awful. I'm at Dan's Chili Place. I just wondered if you had a doctor.'

I told him I'd get back to him. My doctor was away. I was referred to the 'on call' physician. I told him I was calling for a teenage friend, sick in a Parkdale restaurant. 'Could I bring him to you? Or could you possibly go to him?' Silence. 'He sounds very ill.' Silence. 'Doctor? Are you still there?'

'I'm here.' He sounded bewildered. 'Why doesn't he call his own doctor? Or go home? Is he unconscious?'

At three-fifty in the morning I told the story of the Saints to silence. 'Either he's sleeping in the restaurant – they do that – or he's too sick to get to his room. He wouldn't have cab fare.' That stopped me, too. 'I'll be responsible for your bill,' I said hurriedly.

'I think you should call Medical Services,' he said. 'If you can't get anyone, call back. I'll see what I can do.' And he hung up.

The Medical Services girl repeated the questions. Why was he in a restaurant? How did I know he was sick? Was he, perhaps, drunk? Why had he called me? Why didn't he go home? Why didn't he have a personal physician? What was his address when he was home? Who was I, again? 'I think,' she said finally, 'a hospital emergency would be best. You could call an ambulance, or drive him there yourself, if you have a car.'

'Providing I can lift him, if he's passed out by now. Thanks.'

I called the restaurant and told Ron's weak voice that I would be there in twenty minutes. The agency stationwagon, borrowed for a business trip, was parked outside. When I pulled up, Ron was leaning against the restaurant door, his face grey, his eyes glittering with fever. We drove to the nearest hospital emergency.

The waiting room was presided over by a sharp-eyed woman in her fifties. Ron sank into a chair. I explained. She glanced at him. What was his name? His home address? Ron shook his head. Did he have insurance? Another shake of Ron's head. I would pay the bill, I told her and her voice lifted, 'Doesn't he have a home?'

'He has a home,' I confirmed, 'and I'll pay the bill.' Her look was eloquent. Deliberately she poised a pen over the next question, 'relation to patient.' 'I'm a friend,' I said sharply and her eyebrows went up. 'Will you please get a doctor?'

'Follow me,' she demanded and rustled down a corridor. At a cubicle she swept aside a curtain with the air of someone unveiling a monument. She gestured to Ron. 'You wait in there.' Ron disappeared. 'And you,' she looked at me, 'wait in there,' she pointed to an adjoining cubicle and marched away.

I dropped into a chair. It was four-thirty. Silence settled. A half hour later I went into the corridor. Ron's cubicle was silent. I rapped gently on the door frame. No response. I pulled back the curtain. He was sprawled, face down, on the white examining table, his head cradled in his arms. I listened. He was breathing.

Another half hour. I pushed through the curtain again. The corridor was empty and silent. Determinedly I strode to the nurse. How soon, I asked, would someone be around to administer to my friend?

'We're busy,' she said sternly. 'We have sick patients here.'

'What do you think he is?' Her face changed. 'Fine,' I said angrily, 'if you'll guarantee he'll live until you're no longer busy, I'll go back.'

Ten minutes later my cubicle's curtain was flung back. A man in a white jacket glanced in. 'Sorry,' he said, 'must be next door.' I heard the low rumble of male voices. My curtain was flung back again. 'He's sick,' the young man announced. He sounded surprised.

'I knew that an hour ago,' I snapped. 'How sick?'

The doctor ran a hand through thick, black hair. 'Sick enough to be kept in bed. I'll give you a couple of prescriptions,' he wrote on a pad. 'Make sure he gets these immediately.' When I gasped, 'He's not staying here?' the doctor shook his head. 'No beds. Anyway he's not sick enough. But keep him in bed.'

'Hold it,' I halted the professional instructions. 'You have the wrong picture, probably from that angel of mercy at the desk.' His smile was faint. 'This boy is a friend. He is also a member of a church club.' I laid emphasis on the 'church' and his eyes flickered, 'with which I am associated. We do not share an apartment. And he has no home at the moment.' My voice was rising.

'Then you'll have to get him a room, won't you.' He handed me the prescriptions. 'He should have these at once."

'Thanks a lot,' I stuffed them in my bag. Ron appeared, his eyes swollen and his face white. 'Drop me off at the restaurant,' he said. 'I'll sleep there.'

'We'll discuss it. Let's get out of here,' I glared at the doctor, 'all this humanitarianism is smothering.'

In the car Ron went back to sleep. Where now? My apartment? My cousin wouldn't care for that. The church hall? Father Orr had only a studio couch. The only solution was a room. But – I looked at my watch – at six-thirty in the morning?

I drove to an all-night drug store. Ron was sitting up when I came out. I handed him three pills and he threw them, wordlessly, into his mouth and swallowed. 'How much?' he asked worriedly. 'I got to pay you.'

'I don't remember. I'm in shock.'

His smile was slow. 'Different world to you, isn't it?'

'I don't expect them to call a specialist for a hangnail," I started the car, 'but . . .'

'You don't get it,' he said gently. 'I don't have an address, or a doctor, or anythin' socially acceptable.'

'The medical profession was not established on the premise that you had to have references to receive medical treatment,' I glowered.

'But if I'd been the mayor, or Father Orr, or' – he grinned – 'you.'

'I don't want to discuss it. Now, practicalities. My cousin is at the apartment. She'd have a fit if a strange young man walked in and found her in her nightgown. Anyway there's only one bed. It would be crowded with three of us in it. So we'll make a bed here in the wagon — I'll get the pillows and blankets from the apartment — and you can sleep here until I go to the office. Then we'll find a room.'

An hour and a half later I drove the sleeping Ron to the agency. When we found a room and telephoned to make certain it was available, Ron insisted he could find his way there and he promised to take his medicine.

Before noon he telephoned. 'Thought you'd be worryin',' he said. 'I got the room. It's fine. There's a telephone downstairs,' he gave me the number. 'I'm feelin' better already. You humanitarians sure give great service,' he chuckled. 'But,' his voice sobered, 'don't take it so hard. I mean, you just got to learn the way it is.'

Chapter Fourteen

Ron was right, of course. I did have to learn the way it was, and that meant, among other things, learning that many aspects of daily life, which were routine to Father Orr and me were not so at all for the Saints.

But in a different way when I met Bill I thought I had learned the way it was with Ron. I thought I had the answer to my question about him.

I saw Bill first at a Saints' dance. He sat on a chair against the wall, lean, unsmiling, perhaps twenty-five. Even in that relaxed pose, with one leg over the other, he had an air of alertness, a disturbing tension as if he were constantly on guard. And there was a quality about him, a strangely haunted look, at once melancholy and wild.

I edged through the crowd, prepared to offer a welcome to a stranger. He stood up. 'You're Jeann,' he said and a smile touched the corners of his mouth. 'I'm Bill. Ron's brother. I've heard about you from him.'

He didn't look like Ron, apart from an impression of physical strength and his eyes. His gaze was just as penetrating. Probably, I decided, he's come to inspect the adults with whom his brother has become involved. Maybe Ron's parents had asked him to check us out. That thought was hugely satisfying. The Saints' parents were mystery people. None had indicated any interest in the club.

'I didn't know Ron had a brother,' I said and sat down beside him.

'Sure,' he slid back into his chair. 'He has three. I'm the oldest. Bob is between Ron and me. We have a younger brother and two sisters.' He looked at me. "How did you get involved in all this?"

He was getting down to it. 'You know about David,' I said. He doesn't want a recital of events, I told myself, he's interested in motive. 'David asked me to attend a meeting. He thought I might help the club.'

'How?'

'I ask myself the same question,' I smiled.

'But you came back to another meeting. Why?'

He's like his brother, I thought, he gets to the heart of the question.

'Because I like them. Because they're interesting. Because I'm curious. Because,' I gestured helplessly, 'I hope I can help.'

'What's your angle?' It wasn't rude, the way he asked it. It was almost impersonal, as if he knew everyone had an angle and he was merely curious about mine.

'I don't know what you mean,' I said, a little defensively.

'I've been curious.' His voice flattened out. 'I heard about you before. In Kingston Penitentiary.' He didn't say he worked there. He didn't say 'I'm a lawyer,' or 'I'm a social worker.' He had to mean he had been a prisoner. He was watching me. 'I just got out,' he said, his voice soft. 'I spent five years there. With my brother Bob. It wasn't the first time, either. But we got a nine-year sentence.'

'Five years?' I repeated. This attractive, soft spoken, well-mannered intelligent young man? 'For what?'

'Armed robbery,' he said calmly.

My body settled inside my skin with a thud. From the moment that David's hand had gone around my mouth, I had done little but reel back in shock and surprise. He didn't look like someone who would commit armed robbery. I didn't know what an armed robber should look like, but this wasn't it. And he didn't look like someone who had spent five years in prison, either. 'That's ridiculous,' I said aloud.

'Ridiculous it wasn't,' he laughed ruefully. 'I spent two years in solitary, too.'

The music bounced through the hall. I could see Ron in a corner his head bent toward Bruce, and my mind leaped. Of course. There it was, the answer to my question of his involvement with an anti-delinquency club. Or rather, here it was, sitting beside me. With another reason at home. Two brothers. Armed robbers. Two reasons, two good reasons to get into the battle against the destructive disease of crime. Ron was almost twenty. He would have been fourteen or fifteen when his brothers were sent to prison. 'Not the first time' echoed. They had been behind bars before. He had grown up in the dark confusion with two brothers who were criminals. He knew what it had meant, to them, to his family, to himself. No wonder he was so familiar with this world. Bitterly familiar. Painfully aware of social reactions; searingly aware of personal damage. It even explained his cold resentment toward the attitudes of Number Six.

I sat back. 'Your brother got nine years, too?'

Bill rubbed a speck of dust from his shoe. 'We pulled over a hundred armed robbery jobs,' he said steadily. 'They made examples of us.' The grey eyes looked at me. 'I'm supposed to be incorrigible, you see.'

'Who says?'

'The magistrate. I'm. . .' he tilted his head, as if he were hunting the exact quotation, 'the most incorrigible man in Canada.'

'Incorrigible is a stupid word,' I snapped. 'And it's used with wicked recklessness. Even by magistrates.'

'You think I could be saved?' His voice softened sarcasm.

'Let's say I think there's an answer for people who are inclined toward criminal activities. I don't believe anyone is "incorrigible." I don't even believe the phrase "juvenile delinquent." It's stupid too. Delinquency, after all, comes from the Latin word, "delinquere," which means to fail and somebody has to explain to me how a juvenile can be judged a failure.'

'I've wanted to meet you,' he said again. 'A lot of guys in Kingston and Collins Bay Penitentiary wonder. I was there, too,' he added. 'And we all read that magazine article.'

'So I gathered. From the mail pull. Was it the title, "I Made Friends with my Burglar"?' And I laughed. 'It does kind of grab you.'

'It grabs,' he agreed with a grin. 'So does the fact that a victim wants to help her attacker. You got to admit it sounds screwy.'

A Saint threaded through the crowd. 'Hey, Jeann,' he called, 'you got a quarter I can borrow?' When I handed it to him he saluted. 'Thanks a lot. Pay you back next week.'

As he walked away Bill said: 'He won't, you know.'

'Pay me back? Probably not. Some do. Some don't.'

'You always give it to them?'

'When I have it.'

'Why be a sucker?'

I shrugged, self-conscious under his scrutiny. 'Maybe because I have a good memory. Of the Depression. When people knocked on doors for handouts. One day I found the sidewalk in front of our house marked with white chalk. I asked my father about it. He said someone had put it there as a sign to others that we were good for a handout. I was highly indignant, even then. Even a little girl knows the word 'sucker.' But my father said it was better to give to a hundred who didn't need it than to miss one who did. He's a . . . square, too. But it made sense.' I caught a signal across the room from Father Orr. 'I'm needed,' I said. 'I hope you come back again.'

107

He stood up. Five years in prison. And not the first time. 'Thanks,' he said, 'I will.'

Ron shouldered through the teenagers. 'You meet Bill?' he asked. When I nodded he said, 'He tell you he just got out?'

'Yes,' I paused. 'He told me. I like him.' And I waited again. I didn't know what to say. Now I understand? I'm sorry?

'He took part in the Kingston riot,' Ron went on and pride swelled his voice. 'He got two years in solitary for it. And six months in the psychiatric ward after.'

Surprised horror this time crawled through me. 'Real solitary?'

'Sure. You think it's a health resort?' Ron fumbled for his wallet. 'I got the clippings here,' he said.

I put a hand on his arm. This loyalty was no surprise, either. 'Father Orr's getting anxious. I'll see them later.' And I left him standing there, holding the wallet with his brother's press reviews.

We were getting to know them. Or know about them. And Timmy was another surprise. A different kind of surprise, and if anyone had asked about my keen interest in him, my answer would have been prompt and obvious. It became automatic to produce answers for my involvement with any of the Saints. There were so many questions by this time; some squinty-eyed in their search for those psychological hang-ups; some honestly bewildered 'what are you doing with a bunch of kids like that?' and some, as I learned with astonishment and sorrow, essentially hostile. I didn't understand then that the hostility, bred largely by guilt – and maybe concern for public images – made for viciousness sometimes. And in the most unexpected places. Not just the police – even government officials. By the time Timmy was included in my increasing concerns, I was brushing aside – or appearing to brush aside – allegations personally hurtful and sometimes legally libellous. The day before I met Timmy, for example, a young woman who worked in an Ontario government office telephoned to ask if I were aware that rumours were spreading about my 'disgusting interest in young boys.' She was indignant because, she said, she'd met me and she'd become interested in the problems of these kids. The rumours had been spawned, she thought, by the original disagreement over permission to permit a photographer into the Ontario Reformatory for the magazine article on David. I remember telling her lightly that, as a Liberal, I wasn't impressed by the opinions of Progressive-Conservatives. It was a flip comment. When I hung up the receiver I didn't know if I might burst into tears of hurt rage, or slap a libel suit on someone.

But Timmy. Timmy who held significance because he was a writer.

We met anonymously one night while I drove home from a Saints' meeting. I had stopped for a red light and, reaching for a cigarette on the seat, my hand found sheets of paper. They were stories, each unsigned. I pulled over to the curb. I don't know how long I sat there, while the traffic swept past, but I remember my excitement. The writing was immature, but it was good. And it had to be one of the Saints. Someone had slipped them on the car seat, forgetting, in his excitement, to sign them.

That Saturday night a tiny, black-eyed, dark-haired boy stepped hesitantly up to me. 'Excuse me,' he said and stopped. A brief, mirthless laugh filled the beat of his embarrassment. 'I wondered if you had read my stories,' he said in a rush.

'You wrote them?' He was far too young. The whole world was too young, but this was ridiculous. Small-boned and thin, he looked almost frail. His face was narrow and pale, shadowed with a cynicism that hinted at experience with life's bruising powers. At his age? 'I'm sorry,' I said when he looked amused by my surprise. 'But you do look young.'

'Are they any good?' he persisted.

'Yes. Very good. I'd like to talk to you about them.'

He sagged against the door frame, his breath a long, slow release of relief. 'I haven't slept since I put them in your car,' he said.

'I'd have tried to get in touch but I didn't know your name.' When he told me, his voice still limp with relief, I said, 'Forgive me, Timmy, but how old are you?'

He looked around the hall. The minimum age for membership in the Saints was sixteen. 'Fifteen,' he said, 'but I'd appreciate it if you didn't tell on me.' When I said his secret was safe, he nodded. 'Thanks. When can we talk about my writing?'

We agreed it would be impractical to try to talk then. We also agreed he would come to my office on Monday. When I asked 'After school?' he gestured impatiently. 'I dropped out. What about three o'clock?'

And he was early. When he walked in he looked pointedly at the glass walls, the black-topped desk, the blue and white striped door. 'Nice place you have here,' he said with amused sophistication.

'It's humble, but it's home,' I agreed. And we got down to his writing. He agreed the themes were beyond him; he laughed indulgently over the shapelessness of his writing and he pinned me to a solid commitment of help. I was accustomed to a writer's determination, but I had never been nailed so skilfully or so quickly. He asked if one story might make a television play. When I said television writing was a craft in itself, he said he knew that, but how did one learn it. I choked back the suggestion that he age a little. 'Maybe,' I said idly, 'it might be an idea for you to talk to a television producer.'

It was a gamble to introduce a fifteen-year-old into the hypnotic, beguiling, cannabalistic arena of television. It might distort values or overwhelm him. And yet – I looked into the pleading young face. He saw the doubt. 'Please?' he said urgently. 'Right now?'

The producer I had in mind worked on the drama series. He was also a sensitive, compassionate and intelligent human being. Timmy would be safe with him. I called him and explained that I had a young man 'here' he might like to meet. 'Am I booked up?' he laughed, catching the code of 'here,' 'or is he for real?'

'For real,' I said, with Timmy's eyes on me. 'I've read some of his stories. He's good. He's also fifteen. We'd both be grateful,' I added to the 'fifteen?' gasp. When I said Timmy could come any time, no school problem, Timmy slid his stories back into the manila envelope. When I said, 'Three o'clock tomorrow. Thanks,' Timmy was on his feet.

'I'll let you know,' he said. 'I gotta get to work on these.'

When he left I realized I had asked no practical questions. This boy, with his fevered purpose, might have a police record.

Timmy kept his promise to report. He returned at five the next afternoon, looking grave and breathless. 'I have a lot to learn,' he said thoughtfully. 'Leo says one story does have possibilities. He says I might be able to pull it off. He'll work with me.' He grinned, 'Along with you, he says.'

I sat back, shaken. In one interview this child had established a first-name basis with the producer, picked up a little television jargon, and fastened his sights on the near impossibility of 'pulling off' a television play at the first try. 'Great,' I breathed. My reaction was split. I was delighted to find a Saint with ambition. How much other talent was being wasted in that subculture, I wondered. But I was deeply concerned that he might encounter a crippling disappointment. I had to know more about him. 'Do you live at home, Timmy?'

He waited, as if he were trying to see behind the question to the real reason for it. 'Yes,' he said warily. When I asked, 'Do you work?' he

twisted uncomfortably in the chair. 'I gave up the last job. I have to
have one that won't interfere with my writing.'

I coughed to hide a giggle. 'And how do you live?'

'Not by stealing,' he said sharply.

'I didn't mean that. But it takes time to make a living from writing,
you know.'

Another flickering laugh. I wondered when he had chosen that weapon as an instrument to fend off prying adults. 'My mother works. In
an ad agency.' Satisfaction shone in the black eyes. 'My father is a hospital orderly.'

'Why did you join the Saints?' That was the real question.

'Because they're interesting.'

'As material for your writing?'

'In a way. But I know something about their life, too.' He picked
up the manila envelope. The question period was over. He said he had
to get back to work; he thanked me, assured me he would report progress, and left.

We weren't to know Timmy's story for a long time, and when it came it
was in bits and pieces, through his stories and through fragmentary
references.

When he was a baby, his parents, who were battling serious financial
and emotional problems, asked a Negro family to take Timmy, their
only child. It was not an abandonment of him. They knew the daughter
of the family, who was a nurse, and they respected and liked the family.
Timmy would be safe with them. And Timmy was absorbed into his
home, finding values and kindnesses which sustained him.

But unintentionally and probably inevitably, the black family gave
him something else, the emotional identity of a Negro. He learned
what it was to be black in our society and he learned it at a time when
black was not beautiful. His parents, who visited him occasionally, became 'those white folks.'

When he was eleven, 'those white folks' decided they wanted their
son back. Timmy was uprooted again. This time he took that dual
emotional identity into the troubled world of his natural parents. His
father blurred problems with the bottle. 'One night he got me drunk,'
Timmy reminisced. 'Maybe he wanted me to lose interest – like it was
there and so what? But I just got sick.' His mother, fitfully and wearily
fought the spectre of total defeat. And both gave him the knowledge
that life could disappoint and demolish.

111

When he found the Saints, Timmy channelled his gropings, confusions, angers, and restless dreams into his writing. He worked furiously. Sessions with Leo and me became part of every week. An intense fifteen-year-old had discovered a new world, one not to be enjoyed but to be captured. The irritating necessity of finding a job was grudgingly considered. One day he telephoned, his voice heavy with regret. 'I got a job,' he said, 'nine to five and I lift heavy stuff. I don't know if I can do it.' A week later he called again. 'I quit,' he said happily.

'But you're hunting again?'

'Oh sure.' His voice brightened. 'Anyway, I got another draft of the play. You got time to see me today?'

During that session I suggested Timmy return to school. 'I can't!' He looked astonished. 'I have to work to help my parents. And there'd be too much to make up. Anyway,' he added defiantly, 'you can't be taught to write in school.'

'True. You learn to write by writing. Except for the finger exercises. The technique. But I'm talking education, which means developing as a person. Which you need to do if you're going to make it there,' I said pointing to the manila envelope. 'And if you can't go back regularly, there are correspondence courses. I know,' forestalling his objection, 'but you do have the time and you have a talent which mustn't be wasted.'

'Well,' he said lamely. 'Maybe. But in the meantime – ' and he opened the manila envelope to show me the latest draft.

Chapter Fifteen

Perhaps because the emphasis was on getting to know them in that stage, the night of John was a shattering personal shock. It was the first time I glimpsed what had begun to happen within myself.

He wasn't a club member. I had never seen him until Aaron headed anxiously toward me during a dance and whispered, 'He's here?' Startled, I looked around the hall. 'Who's here?' I asked.

'John.' At my look: 'You know, the guy Father Orr's helpin'. The one in hidin'. He's here and the detectives are due any minute.'

'Get Father Orr,' I said sharply.

Aaron shook his head. 'He's in a meeting upstairs.'

'The bouncers,' I suggested wildly.

'He's a friend,' Aaron chided.

I threaded through the crowd to a tall, dark-haired young man, standing in a corner. 'I'm sorry,' I said, 'but you must leave. If the detectives find you, the Saints are in deep trouble. So, I gather, are you. I'm sorry,' I repeated as he started to speak, 'I know nothing of all this, but whatever your problem is, it's going to treble any minute.'

Ron edged toward us, followed by several Saints. 'He can't just walk out,' he said practically. 'He might bump into them.' He looked thoughtfully at John. 'We might lose you in a crowd of us.'

'But if he's caught,' I interrupted, 'it implicates everyone.'

'Maybe he won't be caught. They don't look too hard at a crowd.'

The reasoning seemed weak. 'I could go with him, just the two of us,' I said impulsively and knew I must be stricken with a death wish. 'If we're caught at least I don't have a record.'

'You would by morning,' Ron grinned.

The Saints crowded around. 'If there was a bunch like Ron says,' Mike suggested, 'and we had a few girls and Jeann and we looked like we was goin' to the restaurant – you know, laughin' and talkin' it up and in a hurry.'

'Not too much of a hurry,' Bruce cut in swiftly, 'that makes them notice us.'

'Well, you know, goin' to the restaurant.'

'You game to try it?' Ron asked me. I looked at John.

'Are you?'

'I got a choice?' he muttered.

'Not really.' I took his arm and started for the door. The crowd was rounded up.

Outside John inserted himself in the middle of the group. We reached the sidewalk and a Saint murmured, 'Okay. Talk it up.' We talked it up. One of the girls slipped her hand into mine. Ron walked with his head down, his eyes swivelling toward Number Six. Bruce, as tall as Ron, changed positions. 'We make a good wall,' he whispered. David looked frightened. But he was there.

Halfway to the corner there was a bustle of activity from Number Six. 'Shift's changin',' someone whispered. 'We've had it,' Tony groaned. The police would spill out into the night. Our pace quickened. One officer strolled to the curb. His interest seemed to intensify. A Saint laughed noisily. The temptation to run was almost irresistible.

And in that moment I was appalled by my act. The repercussions could be staggering. I went cold at the image of the Inspector's face when I turned up behind bars. And Father Orr. His eyebrows would fly right off his face.

I could hear my heart pounding. What possible explanation was there for this action? Because Father Orr was helping him? Not good enough. Father Orr was not walking down this street with this wanted boy breathing heavily beside him.

I frowned into the darkness. Was this an act of defiance toward the police, a way of striking back at their hostility and insults? I had responded to Saving a Boy. But it was also Outwitting the Police. And I hadn't entered this subculture with this attitude. The Inspector; Detective x; the officers who asked, 'You his girlfriend?'; the whispers about my interest in young boys; the contempt – all of it had contributed to this moment. Now my back was beginning to arch toward all authority.

And this wasn't genuine help for these young people at all. I was joining a battle against authority – not a crusade to fight delinquency. It was all wrong. But if I stopped now to say I had been wrong, it would be an unexpected and unforgivable betrayal of the trust of these young people.

We were almost to the light. If that officer had a good memory for faces – my hand tightened around the small confident one. 'It's all

114

right,' she whispered. 'We'll save him.' Sure we would. And I'd self-destruct in five seconds.

John moved closer, his head turned from Number Six. 'You'll all get in trouble,' he whispered. And he vanished into the darkness. The next instant we were under the lights.

'Where's John?' someone hissed.

'Gone,' I whispered, bewildered by the suddenness of his disappearance. Conversation died. In silence we continued to the restaurant. No one broke away. No one looked back.

When we returned to the church hall, Father Orr was coming down the stairs. He looked inquiringly at me. 'We were smuggling out one of your caseload,' I said. 'John. He was here. We thought he'd be caught. We got him out.'

'That's . . . nice.' Father Orr said. 'Shall we talk in the study?'

'If I can make the stairs,' I said. 'My knees are going backwards. I make a rotten smuggler.'

'That's nice,' he repeated.

John's story reminded me of Paul's. He had been placed from babyhood in a series of foster homes. When he was no longer a child he put away childish things and took up crime. That led to confinement in a variety of training schools and reformatories.

But there was a major difference between John and Paul. His rebellion had not been solely against society. He also rebelled against being, technically, an orphan. Somehow he discovered his mother was alive. He decided to find her and the search became an obsession. He appealed to the Children's Aid for help. They refused him. They also underestimated the drive of his obsession.

He supported himself largely by stealing. Regularly he was caught and the search suspended while he served time in limbo. Eventually he narrowed that search to Toronto. Somewhere, in the million and a half people, his mother lived in ignorance of the relentless pursuit of her son. Through the grapevine he found the Saints and through them he found Father Orr. And Father Orr had taken up the cause with the Children's Aid.

'I wouldn't say they were bowled over by my persuasions,' Father Orr smiled, 'but we were making progress.'

John's money ran out. Either it didn't occur to him that Father Orr would be good for a loan, as he had been with several Saints, or he was so accustomed to stealing that he didn't consider any alternative.

He pulled a caper. He wasn't caught on the scene, but a warrant was out for him.

'And of course,' Father Orr said, 'he won't give himself up when he's this close to meeting his mother. I can't say I'm unsympathetic. It's been a long time for him.'

'When he finds her,' I asked, 'what happens if she's a . . .'

'Mess? Yes, I've thought of that. I think he must know the truth, whatever it is.'

'Suppose she doesn't want him?'

'Then he must know that, too.'

'Wouldn't it be marvelous,' I said, 'if she did want him.'

Father Orr smiled. 'Now you're romanticizing. Perhaps it wouldn't be marvelous at all.'

John did meet his mother. He walked up a flight of shabby steps one afternoon not long after that night and ended his search. They met alone. She was a dispirited woman who lived a disorderly existence. She didn't welcome this reunion, out of guilt, or perhaps because life already presented too many problems. John surrendered to the police the following day. He told Father Orr he would take care of his new-found mother, that he would 'make it up to her.'

Perhaps it was too late for both of them. Or perhaps his dreams couldn't stand up to the reality. When he was released, he tried to find work. Nothing lasted. He pulled another caper. And that time he made the big time, Kingston Penitentiary.

Chapter Sixteen

Early in May Ron mentioned that he had returned to his parents' home, and he asked, 'You want to come to dinner? To meet my folks?'

When I said I would like that, whenever it was convenient for them, he said, 'I asked them. They want to meet you.' And he set the date. 'I'd better draw a map for you,' he offered an indulgent grin, 'so's you won't get lost.'

'I can get lost going down a one-way street,' I confessed. 'I think it has something to do with my glands.'

'That's what I thought.' His laugh was triumphant. 'I'll make it simple.'

But I got lost anyway. Ron's family lived in a suburb of Toronto in a neat, pretty community of carefully tended homes. None of the houses was large, but they were attractive, set primly on manicured green lawns, with well-mannered bursts of colour from flowers and bushes, with tubs of evergreens and nylon clotheslines and bright blue, green, or pale pink shutters, and a blended scent of freshly mown grass and cleanly curving roses. And the streets looked identical.

Despite the map, I roamed the area for an hour. When, finally, I pulled into a gravel driveway, Ron ran down the front steps. 'Okay,' he yelled, 'what happened? Nobody, not even somebody with glands like yours, could get lost with that map.' Dolefully shaking his head, he opened the car door.

I was accustomed to his teasing, but I was warm and concerned about my lateness. 'Not a word,' I snapped and climbed out. He grinned uncertainly. And I saw his father behind him. A tall man, powerfully built like Ron, with Ron's cat-like co-ordination. Grey eyes, with the same closed-in, perceptive, appraising depth. Handsome. Fine laugh lines. Yet serious. You'd be serious, too, I told myself, if you had two sons who were penitentiary veterans. Gravely he shook my hand. They were pleased to have me, he said, and Ron followed us into the house while I apologized and explained my search.

Ron's face had relaxed, but a surprising wariness was still in his eyes. Perhaps his parents had not been so anxious to meet me. Or perhaps,

I thought, they are very anxious about this woman involved with their son and their judgement holds special significance for him.

Ron's mother walked into the hall. Short. Slender. Attractive. Dark hair, a thin pointed face, frown lines. Reserved. And appraising eyes. Her smile was polite. I said I was glad to meet her. She said Ron had talkèd about me. Ron was a great help in the club, I said, groping for an indication of their attitude toward the Saints. She smiled and gestured toward the living room.

I went to a deeply upholstered chair. Ron chose the chesterfield, one hand straying toward a magazine. While I tramped on verbally, he picked it up. Either I was on my own, or he was signaling against idle chatter. I reviewed my search, trying to make it amusing, and re-echoed my apologies.

'It's all right,' she said, 'I'm only sorry' – with a glance at Ron – 'that the map confused you.' Her tone held a rebuke.

'It wasn't the map,' I said quickly. 'It was my own stupidity.'

She smiled and left the room. Ron gave me a rueful glance. 'Sorry about that,' I murmured.

'It's okay.' He went back to the magazine and silence gathered. Ron's parents seemed attractive, sturdy, middle-class people. They did not look like the parents of criminals. But what had I expected? And I wondered what it was to experience the deep trouble of this family. You couldn't live constantly on the peaks of emotion, or in the valleys, either. And you would be sensitive, especially with strangers. That would explain the emotional moat around them. But Ron's withdrawal was curious. Did he shed an armour here that he wore at the club? Or was this the armour and if it were, why did he find it necessary within his family?

The front door opened and a slender, unsmiling girl glanced in at us. Ron tossed our names into the silence. This was one of two sisters. She was glad to meet me, she said. I was glad to meet her, I replied. She disappeared into the kitchen and we sank back into silence.

When Bill came in moments later, I greeted him enthusiastically. He muttered hello and ran up the stairs. He had barely disappeared when the front door swung open once more. A younger girl this time. And again the casual introduction, the exchange of greetings and Ron's younger sister vanished into the kitchen.

When Bob arrived he was a minor surprise. This was the brother who had spent five years in Kingston with Bill. He resembled Bill, with the same finely drawn features, the same haunted cast to his face, but he looked more relaxed. He told Ron his father wanted him. Without a word, Ron hurried from the room. Bob flipped a finger against his forehead at me and ran up the stairs.

I sighed into the emptiness, reacting to a critical tension in the air and wondering if I had introduced it or if it were a permanent resident in this home.

Beyond the window the street's shine began to dim. Lights flared in a house across the street; tree branches moved in the cooling wind and a little boy sauntered down the middle of the road, kicking a rock patiently in front of him. He looked a little lonely.

When Ron's mother called us to dinner, her voice had a quality, a blend of impatience and the expectation of opposition, that made me feel guilty without knowing why. We gathered around the table and the conversation rolled over me; questions were asked of each other, answers given with reluctance. Ron sat across from me, still slumped within himself, elusive and remote. I reminded myself that I was the intruder, and I took refuge in light comments which brought momentary, almost startled, silences as if everyone kept forgetting I was there.

Ron's father cleared his throat. 'Did you get the job?' he asked Bill. Bill didn't look up. 'Filled,' he said.

'They always are,' his father observed with an edge to his voice. His mother echoed the criticism. The girls ate in silence. Either I was regarded as a member of the family, or they had forgotten I was there again. When his father shot another sharp remark at Bill, tempers flared. Bill screeched back his chair and left the room. Anger filled the air. Ron's mother turned to Ron, and again the shafts flew. Ron stamped furiously from the room. Bob was next. His chair squeaked back. Now we were five.

When there was no longer a reason to stay at the table, Ron's father disappeared. I could hear Bob and Bill upstairs. The girls, refusing my offer of help, joined their mother in the kitchen. Ron was touring the house, restless and angry. I went into the living room and studied the rug. I wasn't sure if I had been forced on them or if they were generally uneasy. I didn't know either if I were expected to leave. But if the flaring tempers had been the outgrowth of uneasiness, I wouldn't help by withdrawing. And anyway I was curious. This inclusion of Ron in the overall criticism was strange. Or perhaps his association with the Saints was the problem. Perhaps they had hoped this son would cut all ties with the subculture that had provided so much heartache and destruction.

Ron passed my chair, his eyes down. 'I think we've met somewhere,' I said.

'Yeah.' He collapsed into a chair.

The women reappeared and we tried to talk to each other. 'Have you ever considered combing your hair?' Ron's mother asked suddenly. I grabbed my hair, but her eyes were on Ron. He grunted, one hand going to the thick, unruly hair that resisted ducktail discipline. 'You might try it some time,' she said. And I looked at her while she studied her son. Her scrutiny seemed a mixture of impatience and disappointment, with another indefinable quality. Anxiety, I wondered? Is she afraid that the mysterious something which went wrong with her two older sons will happen again with this one? Does she see the vitality of resistance in him toward authority? Or is there guilt, acknowledged or denied? Either way guilt contains that venom which, like revenge and hate, can be self-destructive but can also destroy others. It is painful to be the victim of another's guilt. Yet, as someone has said, behaviour is only the outer envelope of a personality. It was pointless to speculate, but as her eyes lingered on her son I found myself wishing that I could reassure her, could relieve some of the suffering she must have endured. She caught my scrutiny of her. 'This is pretty around here,' I said inanely, embarrassed in case my expression had revealed my thoughts. Everyone stared at me. 'Very pretty,' I insisted. 'And you have a lovely home.' She murmured 'thank you' and her eyes softened.

The arrival of Ron's younger brother gave our attention a focus. And Allen was a shock. Quiet, good-looking, gentle-mannered, he bore no resemblance to anyone. Ron had mentioned that he was an artist and he looked pleased when I asked about his paintings. Yes, he would be glad to show some to me. No, he didn't think he would become a professional artist. Yes, he did enjoy it. And he went upstairs. I didn't expect him to return. His exit had the mark of an escape.

While I hunted for a neutral conversational topic, Ron's older sister tossed a teasing comment at him. He responded with low rumbles, like a lion whose tail is being pulled. This might be part of the answer to Ron's fierce need to dominate any relationship with a woman. He tried to dominate Lillian. He tried, as well, to dominate me. Perhaps this atmosphere of oddly critical femininity had bred it. And unexpectedly I found myself stepping verbally beside him, as if I wanted to ally myself, in the eyes of his family, with him. Ron's mother looked at me with new interest. 'I've become very fond of Ron,' I said.

'Yes,' she said without expression.

'I don't know what we'd do without him in the club.'

'Yes,' she repeated.

My fervour seemed unnecessary in the face of their calmness and again I wondered what, in this atmosphere, made me so edgy. 'You haven't been to our dances,' I went on. 'You and your husband might find them interesting. Noisy,' I smiled, 'but interesting. We'd like you to visit us.'

'Perhaps sometime,' she said.

Allen reappeared, carrying a collection of paintings and as we bent over them I intercepted a look of pride from Ron. When his mother referred to Allen's hard work, Ron shifted his gaze to her, and there was a hint of something, a fleeting acknowledgement of an isolation. Our eyes met and he smiled. 'Mom's glad she's got one son who's worth something,' he said lightly.

'Hardly only one,' I said. But no one endorsed that comment.

As the evening crackled on, the darting words, the flashes of criticism, the exchanges with their tiny nips and bites became less disturbing. They reminded me of a lively Italian or Jewish or Irish family that indulges constantly in high-pitched emotional outbursts and probably is more closely knit because of it. And I wished I could have met them under different circumstances.

When I made a move to leave, Ron's father appeared as if on cue. He repeated his wife's invitation to visit them again and when I said to Ron, 'See you Wednesday, friend,' he glanced with a smile at his son.

I didn't subscribe to the theory that every problem of the young could be 'blamed' on parents. It had to be partially true, of course, but if you chose that answer, you had to carry the reasoning back to the problems inherited by the parents from their parents, and by those parents from their parents – back through the stretches of generations.

But standing there, my hand held in the strong firm grip of Ron's father, I looked into this father's steady grey eyes. In Shakespeare's *Henry IV*, when the King is voicing disappointment in his frivolous son, he says about himself, 'My blood hath been too cold and temperate.' This man's blood would not be cold, I suspected, or too temperate. I thought of the flaring temper, the criticism. Had he been too demanding, too uncompromising with the wilfulness of the mysterious rebellions of his sons, too bewildered, perhaps, when his sons didn't measure up to the standards he set for himself and for them? I turned to Ron's mother. Strong personalities, both of them. Good people. And hurt people. I went home carrying the question with me. Why, in such a family, would two sons choose spectacular criminal careers? What were they rebelling against?

A few days later, when I returned from lunch, there was another invitation from Ron on my desk. He wanted me to join a group of Saints and their girlfriends the following Sunday for an afternoon of horseback riding. He had signed the note, 'Your loving son.'

He telephoned later for my answer. 'I don't ride,' I confessed, 'and I think my bones are too brittle to learn now.'

'So you'll be in the sun,' he insisted. 'You need it. We'll go in Dad's car. Bill's driving. There'll be seven of us. I'll sit on your lap.

It was a lovely Sunday, warm and clear, and I was surprised how many of the Saints rode. Ron was an expert horseman and I was watching him, bemused by the gentle firmness of those hands holding the reins, hands which could crack a man's skull, when Mary joined me.

She was a tiny, childlike girl, under five feet tall, with a sweet gravity. Her hair was pale brown and curly; her eyes were large and grey and heavily lashed. Under the baby-fat roundness, she was finely boned. Mary was fifteen and she was the girlfriend of Ernie, one of the Saints. Like most of the Saints' girlfriends, she seemed immeasurably older than her boyfriend, with nest-building instincts that were so fervent they seemed more a need to escape personal rootlessness than a genuine commitment to a partner.

Over the months I had come to know some of the girls. We talked at the dances and sometimes one would telephone, to discuss a quarrel with a boyfriend or a home problem. Father Orr and I agreed there should be a girls' club to duplicate the Saints, but we agreed, too, that the practical limitations on time and energy made it impossible. At least until the Saints were – as we always called it – properly organized.

But I knew Mary lived with her mother, who was separated from Mary's father. I knew she had one married sister, that she worked as a waitress, as Ron's girlfriend did, and that she watched over Ernie. There was one word to describe Mary. Dignity. Even at fifteen she possessed that intangible capacity to be self-sustaining, with a quiet, inoffensive sense of personal worth.

Now she smiled at me and hesitated a moment. Then: 'Jeann, can I ride today?'

'Do you know how to ride?'

'Sure,' she smiled. 'I was born on a farm.'

'Then?'

'I'm four months' pregnant,' she said simply.

My heart stopped. 'I see.' I looked toward the ranch restaurant. 'Probably you shouldn't ride then. Let's have a coffee instead.'

The restaurant was empty and we carried our cups to a corner table. Mary settled expectantly. She was so composed I wondered, for a moment, if she wanted to discuss it. Yet, if she hadn't wanted any discussion, she wouldn't have asked her question. 'Are you sure?' I asked. 'Have you seen a doctor?'

'I'm sure.' She poured milk into her coffee.

'And the baby's father?'

'Ernie. Of course.' She looked up in surprise.

'Of course. Do you plan to marry?'

Her lashes lowered. 'No.' The single word held a note of obstinacy. 'He wants to marry me, but it isn't fair to either of us. We're too young to marry.'

'Do you have any plans?'

Her gaze was steady. 'I want the baby. I won't have it adopted.' Her voice faltered for the first time. 'Nobody can make me, can they?'

'Not unless you were judged by the courts to be an unfit mother, which I doubt would happen. But there are practicalities. For instance, how could you care financially for a baby?'

'I'll manage,' she said stubbornly. 'I live alone right now and I guess I'll have to give up my job soon but . . .'

'You live alone?'

'I moved out,' she said quietly. 'It's kind of mixed up. Mother lives with another man. Not my father. She was upset. So was he.' Her eyes dropped. 'Funny, isn't it. I mean, considering.'

'Is there anything I can do?'

'No, not really. I've been to the Children's Aid and I'm still working. But I have this kidney disease,' she paused to sip her coffee, 'they didn't think I'd live this long,' she said, her tone as casual as if she had referred to a hangnail. 'I fooled them.' She smiled again. 'The doctor says I got to take it easy, but he says we'll pull it off. He's nice. Big and redheaded.' When I murmured, 'A Parkdale man?' her looked reminded me of Timmy's patience with adults who didn't understand. 'He's at the clinic,' she said. 'I couldn't afford my own doctor. Most of them are nice except one woman.' She hesitated. 'Every time I go she starts in on me. She says I must have the baby adopted, that they'll take it away from me. And she always asks if I have' – another pause – 'some other income. She means I'm a . . . you know.'

'Probably she doesn't mean that. She may just be clumsy.'

'No,' brown eyes flashed, 'she acts like a frustrated old maid who hates young girls. You know the type. She makes me mad. But I'm fine really, another smile. 'You've helped already, just talking to me.' The afternoon sun streamed through the window, throwing a spray of pale gold over her face. 'It's good to have somebody to talk to,' she said. 'I guess that's all anybody ever needs, really.'

I thought of suggesting she move in with me until the baby was born, but as I began to phrase the invitation she said, 'I think I'll move in with my sister. We get along fine and I can practise on her kids.'

She gave me her telephone number and she tucked mine in her small handbag. And together we went back out into the sunshine.

The next morning I telephoned Father Orr about Mary. 'I see,' he said, 'am I supposed to know?'

'I think she wants you to know. I'll call her and tell her I've talked to you. May I suggest she call you?'

'Of course. And we are united in attitude?'

'I hope so. Unless you think she should marry to give the baby a name.'

'I don't.' He said it quietly. 'And neither do you.'

That afternoon Mary's young voice on the telephone sounded relieved. 'I didn't want to tell him myself,' she said. 'It's kind of woman's business. But thank you.'

It was woman's business when they talked, too. Mary controlled that conversation, sitting sedately on the couch while he asked pertinent questions. She was adamant on the subject of marriage and adoption. And no, she wouldn't go into any home for unwed mothers. 'I can manage,' she said calmly, 'especially if I have you and Jeann to talk to.'

At the door she looked back. 'I know I made a mistake, Father. And thanks for not – you know – bugging me about it. Don't worry,' she offered that serene, elderly smile. 'Everything will be all right.

It was that Saturday night at the dance that Ron sidled up to me. 'About Mary,' he said abruptly. 'Everything okay? Anything I can do – anything she needs?'

'You know?'

'Of course,' he lifted a surprised eyebrow. 'We're friends. I know she talked to you. I just wondered if I could help. I mean, sometimes you don't want to go pokin' in, you know.'

'I know. I don't think she needs anything right now, except' – remembering the grave, young face – 'somebody to talk to.'

'Yeah,' he said with a faint smile. 'Yeah.'

124

Chapter Seventeen

The middle of May a Saints' meeting was devoted to a mystifying proposal. Ron introduced it as a motion. He said it was time the Saints' club held a banquet. 'Every club has formal banquets,' he explained. 'The club is six months old, which is an anniversary and you gotta observe anniversaries. It would be good experience for us, too.'

'A banquet?' I whispered, astonished, to Father Orr.

Someone seconded the motion. The membership's agreement, without a single dissenting voice, was just as astonishing. Aaron got right down to business. A banquet, he told the meeting, had to be well organized. 'We got to have committees,' he said, 'and the committees can't horse around. But maybe we should choose a date first.'

Ron stood up again. 'I move we hold it on the twenty-first of May. That gives us time to organize and it's during the week, so it won't interfere with the dance, and it's also the anniversary of the night we got formally organized in the restaurant.'

My birthday, I realized with a start. It would be appropriate to spend my birthday with these new friends, even if they were unaware of the coincidence.

The meeting moved into organization of the banquet. Committees were appointed. Father Orr agreed they could use the main hall and, if they made proper arrangements, they were welcome to use the kitchen as well. But they had to remember that they were completely responsible. Any breakdown would not be mended by the adults.

The warning came from our growing uncertainty about the Saints' ability to follow through on any project. This banquet was the first venture, apart from the dances, with reasonably heavy responsibility, and we had been struck over the weeks by a disheartening characteristic of the members: they talked a lot, planned constantly, and stalled on concrete action. Their concentration on setting up the club's constitution, for instance, had been verbal and repetitive. But it was no further advanced than it had been in February. They spent hours discussing a variety of future plans, but the plans never moved beyond the discussion stage. Sometimes we wondered if they merely enjoyed fantasizing, or if they were fearful of the responsibilities inherent in action.

This time we waited – or I did – for the adults to be assigned specific tasks. But they moved forward with no reference to us. The catering committee, they decided, would get the food, arrange for its preparation and serving. Another committee would set up the tables, find clothes and decorations. A third would act as internal publicists, advising absent members of the event and establishing the attendance. 'Don't forget,' Aaron warned, 'we want the actual number. We don't want to be left with a load of stuff.' He made a last note in his book. 'All clear?' he asked the meeting. A murmur of agreement. He turned. 'Oh,' he smiled at us, 'Jeann and Father Orr, on behalf of the club, you're invited, of course.'

Father Orr glanced at me, received my silent nod and looked back at the Saints. 'Thank you,' he said, 'we'll be pleased to accept.'

The meeting adjourned. Father Orr and I went into his study. 'Now what is that in aid of?'

Father Orr tidied the couch, stacking the books on one end of the piano bench. 'Presumably,' he said, 'they understand what is expected of a club. I think it's a fine idea.'

'So do I. But I'm surprised. One minute they act like irresponsible children. The next minute, they're adults.'

Father Orr smiled broadly. 'Even,' he murmured, 'as me and thee. But I hope they follow through.'

And they did follow through. Their interest didn't vanish or even wane. Reports on committee progress were submitted at the next meeting. An incompleted task was criticized by the entire membership. And still they asked nothing of the adults.

The banquet was scheduled for six o'clock on the twenty-first. When I arrived at the church hall, shortly before six, Father Orr was standing on the steps. Several Saints were grouped about the door. I stopped to stare at them. They looked different, standing self-consciously in the pale sunlight. Of course. No shrieking crimson jackets. No jeans. They wore neatly pressed trousers and shirts. They had dressed for their banquet. Affection for them surged up. They looked so pleased with themselves and so proud of this achievement.

We walked together into the hall. The decorating committee had done its work well. Tables were set carefully and attractively, each place laid with shining silver and plates. Glasses of tomato juice were

126

already in place, red and gallant against the white cloth. And there were flowers. The piano had been moved from the stage into this room ready for later festivities.

From behind the kitchen doors came the sound of dinner preparations. The fragrance drifted pleasantly into the hall. The catering committee had not failed them. 'I was going to bring sandwiches, just in case,' I whispered to Father Orr.

'O ye of little faith,' he murmured.

Chattering and laughing, we took our places. They had even thought of place cards.

During the meal an envelope was passed down to me. Inside a birthday card announced that 'a friend' wished me a happy birthday. I looked down the rows of young faces in search of the Saint who knew my secret. No one responded to the silent inquiry. A few minutes later another card was slipped into my hand. Another wish from 'a friend.' Again the futile scrutiny. When the third card arrived, I concentrated on each face. David caught my eye and his pale face looked pleased – but with the banquet's success. Tony grinned, hoisting his empty tomato glass in a joyous salute – without acknowledging anything. Bruce spared me a fleeting smile. Father Orr lifted an eyebrow, seemingly as surprised as I by the banquet's professionalism. But the handwriting was young. It wasn't Father Orr. They had invited Bill and he was concentrating on his food. The rest of them returned my look proudly or shyly or with open pleasure.

Then I found Ron's face. He smiled back gleefully. I pointed to the cards and mouthed 'You?' His grin broadened. How had he discovered my secret? While we giggled across the rows of faces, I realized how deep this friendship had become. It held no shadow of the self-consciousness predictable in a friendship between a woman of my age and a nineteen-year-old. We met on mutually understood and mutually agreeable levels of communication. I felt as if I had known him all my life; confident of the dependable honesty and loyalty of a trusted friend; impatient sometimes with the dangerous mischief of a kid brother, and sometimes, too, I thought, concerned, proud, or worried over a son whose talents must not be wasted, whose life must not be scarred.

The kitchen staff cleared the tables. Either the Saints had employed a catering service, or the ladies of the church were participants. I turned to ask a neighbour when the kitchen door opened to the accompaniment of an outburst of clapping.

Four Saints, walking with nervous caution, were carrying the biggest birthday cake I had ever seen. And the Saints began to sing 'Happy Birthday to You.' For a moment I didn't understand. Then the laughter, the sheen of proud merriment got through to me. The Saints were giving me a surprise birthday party.

Aaron made the speech. When the clapping died down and a birthday card, signed by all the members, was pressed into my hand, I managed the strangled announcement that I might disgrace us all by weeping.

'Saints don't cry.' someone shouted and the clapping resumed.

Aaron handed me the knife and, blinking, I made the incision while the Saints called their interest in my wish. Ron yelled I wasn't to spoil it by putting it into words.

'I won't,' I gulped and thought that the wish was easy. I wished I would not fail these young men, these friends who had swarmed into my life, that I would have the common sense, the intelligence, the – whatever it took – to help rather than damage them.

When the excitement died down, Aaron stood once more. 'Well, Jeann,' he said seriously, 'you've had the singing and the card and the cake. Now,' with a flourish he held out his hand, 'here's the present.'

Again the thunderous applause, the laughter, the passing of a box from hand to hand. I fumbled with the ribbon, peeled off the tissue paper and opened the box. A wrist watch, gold and delicate, lay against the black velvet. I stared at it and could find no words.

'And Jeann,' one of the Saints hollered, 'it ain't even hot! We paid for it!'

Chapter Eighteen

The end of June I made two major moves. After eight years I resigned from the agency. The summer would be spent free-lancing, while I finished a book and made personal decisions.

The second move was a literal one. I left the apartment that had been the setting for my introduction to David to move into another only two blocks north, but six stories up.

The exit from the agency held both advantages and disadvantages for the Saints. On the debit side, they no longer had an office to visit, which was a pity. They had enjoyed the Land of Oz. But on the credit side, I would be more available without a fixed schedule. And that became useful almost immediately. We were pitching into the time of action.

The call from the police came one morning at four-thirty. Ron was in jail. He had asked that I be notified. 'He was in a fight, ma'am,' the voice said. 'He'll appear in the morning.' He didn't ask if I were Ron's girlfriend. He said the Crown would be Stanton Hogg. And I hung up with a sigh of exasperation.

The next morning I arrived at Stan's office at twenty minutes to ten. 'Morning, counsellor,' I saluted him, 'I have a client.'

'I know. I'm not impressed.'

I sidled into the office. He couldn't be irritated by a disturbance of the peace charge. 'Is it that serious?' I asked.

'It could be very serious,' he said sternly. 'The man could die. He's in a coma now.' I stared at him. 'Your client,' Stan swaddled the word in sarcasm, 'hit him with a brick. One inch closer to the temple and the man would have died instantly. As it is Ron may face a manslaughter charge. You see,' he went on carefully, 'the man was in the middle of the street when the brick hit him. It was not an accident. It was not self-defence.'

Alarm, confusion. 'What happens now?'

'We wait. While the man is alive, it is assault. If he dies . . .' Stan spread his hands. 'Meanwhile Ron stays in custody.'

'I'd better see him.'

I hurried out of the office and telephoned Father Orr.

When I arrived at the Don Jail a half hour later, Father Orr was there. 'We'll see him now,' he said. 'You know I have special privileges? No? Well, I fall roughly into the category of a lawyer. Private conversations with the prisoners. I'll see if I can get you through on my push.'

He explained to the guard about the club and about Ron. 'And Miss Beattie,' he gestured, 'is also associated with the club.'

The guard asked for my identification. 'No offence, Father,' he said, as he scrutinized my driver's licence and the Saints' membership card. 'I guess it's all right,' he said finally and shoved a big book toward me. 'You can sign here.'

We walked down a corridor to a large room, tiered with rows of barred cells. Involuntarily I shivered. The room was quiet, a watching, waiting quiet. I tried not to look up at the cells, not to speculate about hidden eyes that might be staring down. A series of narrow stalls stretched along one side of the room.

Ron sat in one of the cells.

'Good morning,' Father Orr pulled up two chairs.

Ron's smile was self-conscious.

'Okay,' I was quivering with nervousness, alarm and the infectious tension of the room, 'what happened?'

'The guy hit me,' Ron announced. The grey eyes were filmed with defiance.

'We assumed as much, but who hit who . . . whom first?'

'He hit me. Then this other guy picks up a rock and starts for me. I grab him. I give him the knee and he goes down. Real down, you know? So I look around and the other guy, the one who hit me first he's startin' to run away. So I pick up a brick. And I throw it.'

'Did you act impulsively?' Father Orr interjected.

'I threw it,' Ron repeated.

'Father Orr means did you stop to think before you threw it, or did you just throw it?'

A second's hesitation. He looked at me. 'I stopped to think.'

'Great,' Father Orr murmured.

'You know the man is in hospital,' I said.

'Lucky he ain't dead,' Ron muttered.

'His luck may run out,' Father Orr said quietly. Ron's eyes widened. 'He's in a coma. You know what it could mean if he dies.'

'He could die?' Ron's gaze turned abruptly inward. 'I didn't mean to kill him.' Silence. Then, 'Oh. That's why you asked if I stopped to

130

think. Voluntary manslaughter.' His normal refusal to accept disaster faltered. 'How long? I mean until we know?'

'There's no way to know that,' Father Orr said. 'They say if the brick had been an inch closer to his temple, we wouldn't be wondering. He would be dead now.'

'I didn't mean to kill him.' Ron sounded as if he were talking to himself. 'I didn't even know him. He hit first. I was mad.'

'He hit you without any provocation?' I asked. 'He just hurled up out of nowhere and smashed you one?'

'No,' he sighed. 'We had a disagreement. I got mad.'

Father Orr looked at his watch. 'Well,' he said, 'there's nothin' to do now except wait. We'll be down again. No bail, I'm afraid.'

Ron nodded. 'Mom and Dad know?' he asked and I was struck by the curious change in him. The leap of fear, when he knew his impulse could end a man's life, that was one change in the normally confident manner. Now there was another quality. Anxiety? Apprehension? Concern? I couldn't tell.

'They know,' Father Orr said. 'I called them.' He pushed back his chair. 'Do you need cigarettes?' When Ron nodded silently, Father Orr replaced his chair. 'I'll leave money at the desk.'

We went slowly out of the Don. 'There's no point in speculating,' Father Orr said as I climbed into my car. 'But if it's manslaughter, we should certainly consider defence counsel.'

'Yes,' I said, caught up in my own apprehensions. As I drove away the look on Ron's face returned in memory. It is true that if you are attempting to understand anyone you must try to understand the needs that motivate him and rouse him to action. And to get at the truth you must be able to distinguish between the mask we all wear and the basic substance that is the true person.

Ron would wear a mask. It had slipped at the news of the victim's condition. Fear for self? Natural and normal. Shock and fear, too, that he might be responsible for another's death. But the question about his parents, that had produced a different reaction. He cared whether they knew, but was it out of concern for them, or out of apprehension about their reaction?

Abruptly I wondered how Ron saw himself. It was one thing to try to see him as he was without his mask, even to compare that personality with the masked one. It was another to try to see him as he saw himself. And maybe that was the only way you could understand people – from their point of view.

The man remained in a coma for eight days. They were the longest eight days I had known since the club was organized. On the ninth day Father Orr telephoned. The man had regained consciousness. 'He'll live,' Father Orr said. 'The charge will be assault.'

'Thank God.'

'Yes. Thank God.'

Ron would be released on bail. No one knew when his trial would come up. The court calendar was full. It might take weeks.

'Maybe,' I said, 'there is some good in it after all. Ron's had a bad scare.'

'Maybe,' Father Orr's tone was sardonic, 'although humans are woefully slow to learn from experience.'

Later that afternoon it began to rain and the rain came in a rush of heavy, grey sheets, slashing through the city. As the wet twilight deepened, I pulled the drapes against the deluge. And, standing alone in the middle of my living room, I was invaded by a strange uneasiness, unreasonable and elusive. I told myself I was tired, that rain always depressed me, that I needed food. But none of these could be the real reason for this perplexing sense of something wrong, something just beyond my comprehension.

I had dinner and after I washed the dishes and cleaned up the kitchen, I creamed my face, filed a broken fingernail and slid out of a black sheath dress into a loose blue housecoat. And still I couldn't shake the uneasiness.

It was almost as if some crack had appeared, as if I were trying to intercept warning signals. Impatiently I shook my head. Ron's act of violence had come from temper. A fanged, savage temper. I turned away from the nebulous feeling that glowed softly like a distant light.

We began what seemed to be an endless series of court appearances. The day of the third remand, I realized that Bill had not attended any of those appearances. That was surprising. They were brothers of togetherness. When I mentioned it to Ron, he scowled. 'I thought you knew,' he said, 'he's gone back.'

'Gone back where?'

'To the reformatory. Where else?'

Where else. There was no shock this time, only the mournful surprise of incomprehension. He had spent five years in Kingston. He had been on the street only weeks. He was intelligent and he had been the prison route. Yet he had gone back. There was no sensible explanation.

'No, I didn't know.' I touched his arm. 'I'm sorry. What . . . what did he do?'

'Sold hot stuff,' Ron snorted. 'Big deal. They'd pick up stuff in a delivery van, like they came from a wholesalers or manufacturer, or something. Then they'd sell it to a fence.' The shoulders shrugged. 'So they got caught.'

'How long is he in for?'

'Four.'

'Years?' I gasped.

'Months. But it's gonna seem like years. He's in Millbrook.'

Millbrook Reformatory was designed originally as a research centre to study the causes of crime. But the plan had broken down. Presumably the breakdown was caused by financial problems. Someone needed a new highway, or perhaps a million-dollar school building. Both would be considered more important than the study of crime. Millbrook had been changed to a top-security reformatory, dealing with the more difficult prisoners. 'The incorrigibles,' I thought. 'I'm terribly sorry, Ron,' I said again. 'Your parents must be upset.'

'They're used to it,' he muttered.

'I'd like to visit him,' I said, 'I like Bill. Or would that use up a visit your parents might make, or Bill's girl?'

'It would be okay,' Ron looked pleased, 'Bill would like it. I could go with you, as long as you didn't go on a Friday.' He grinned self-consciously, 'I couldn't go in, but I could keep you company. And you shouldn't be drivin' alone in the sewing machine.' My newly acquired mini-car, which, as one Saint pointed out, I could wear rather than drive, had become another point of relentless teasing.

It was lucky that Ron was busy the day I made the trip. He might have torn the place apart, top-security brick by top-security brick.

Millbrook is located near Lindsay, Ontario, almost a hundred miles from Toronto. I telephoned before I left to confirm visiting hours. The gentleman, who announced his rank as lieutenant, assured me I could see Bill.

It was a lovely afternoon, hot and clear and bright. Beyond the city, the highway curved through land slumbering in the heat. I drove slowly, relaxing in the stretches of green, the tall, motionless trees, the clusters of cows and horses that grazed sleepily on the land.

Millbrook had a tidy look, reminiscent of Guelph. Like Guelph it was surrounded by gentle farm land. The waiting room was empty. Facing the door was an enclosed office, presided over by a uniformed guard. I gave him the required information: my name, the prisoner's name and our relationship. He wrote it down, studied me with the look that is intended to be a moral and physical x-ray, and walked heavily to the back of the office to confer with a ledger. He returned, shaking his head. 'You can't see him,' he said.

'Why not?'

'He's in solitary.'

'In solitary?' I echoed. 'There must be a mistake. I telephoned before I left Toronto. I was told I could see him. What has he done in the last' –I looked at the round-faced clock, ticking solemnly on the wall behind him – 'two and a half hours?'

He checked the ledger again. 'He's been in solitary eleven days,' he reported. 'The lieutenant made a mistake. You can't see him.'

Perhaps, despite the luxurious countryside, I was tired or cranky. Or maybe, unknowingly, I had reached a point of no return. When balked my natural reaction is to go to the top. 'Is the governor in?'

The guard's surprise was swift and swiftly retrieved. 'The Colonel' – the title came out like a rebuke – 'is in Lindsay.'

'When will he return?'

'Not until six. And you can't see the prisoner.'

'I'll wait.' I turned to a chair. At his look I paused. 'Or would you prefer I wait in my car?'

He pressed his lips together. 'As you wish.'

The Colonel returned shortly after six. It had been a long, uncomfortable wait and I was squirming on the hard seat when I saw him approach the waiting room door. The guard hurried out, presumably to alert him. The Colonel paused to listen, glanced over the guard's shoulder and walked in beaming. It was my old friend, the former governor of the Don Jail. He apologized for the error. He was dismayed at the inconvenience it had caused. He would let me know personally when Bill was out of solitary so I could arrange another visit.

I explained I hadn't waited for an official apology. I wanted to know first why Bill was in solitary. He led the way into his office. It was bigger than the Don Jail office, more affluent, more intimate. More in keeping with the original intention of Millbrook.

We sat down. The Colonel settled back. Bill had refused to co-operate, he said. Bill had been unmanageable. Among other things, Bill

134

had tackled a guard. He had shown a spectacular lack of inclination to obey the rules. 'That would be no surprise,' I said and the Colonel smiled.

'We know this type,' he said. 'A stretch in solitary is very persuasive.' He added it would 'break this man's spirit.'

I thought of Bill's history: five years and it hadn't been the first time; two years in solitary; six months in the psychiatric ward. Society through confinement was saying 'surrender or we break you.' Since he suffered more by refusal than he would by yielding, his opposition had to be more important to him than anything else.

'We'll get him,' the Colonel said. And what would happen, I wondered, if they did 'get him,' if they broke that dreadful strength? What incredible need produced it, and if it were cracked, what revenge would it take?

I asked about the psychiatric facilities at Millbrook. The Colonel wasn't sympathetic to the idea. I agreed psychiatry wasn't the only solution. 'But it's a start,' I said.

'It's coddling,' he said.

Coddling. There had to be countless people like Bill, who, acting out of hidden trouble, committed crimes, were convicted, served time and returned to society with the same problems that triggered the first offence. They would repeat the cycle and we called them 'incorrigible.' An attempt to help was termed 'coddling.' If we were honest, we had to admit our system was designed for revenge, the law of retribution. If we were honest, we had to admit we demanded punishment for its own sake.

And melancholy anger stirred. This talk of 'breaking a man's spirit,' of 'getting him,' of 'the persuasive effects of solitary,' this relentless echo of a primitive time in man's history, of a primitive thirst in man; this barbaric talk in this building, this barbaric monument to past failures in the fight against the social disease of crime, this monstrous testimony to man's disastrous refusal to relinquish traditional methods – however inadequate, however savage, however doomed to failure, and however dooming to man himself – this, I looked furiously at the barred windows, this damned and damning rigid authoritarianism which is interested in facilitating without searching for the truth. . . .

'You don't agree,' the Colonel's voice punctured my rage and the memory of that first evening in my kitchen, the conversation with those two relaxed detectives, crashed back.

'No,' I said, too angry to put words coherently together.

He smiled, the practical, efficient man, doing his job. He had wound up his case, for the prosecution, I thought. He expects me to leave, preferably graciously. And my angry stubbornness held. 'I was told I could see Bill,' I said, 'Thank you for the apology and for explaining your views. It's been most interesting. Now, I'd like to see Bill. Please.'

He was silent. I had no idea what I would do if he called my bluff. I considered what would happen if he merely left the room which, I admitted, he had a perfect right to do. A sit-in would be interesting, but a little foolish. Yet I was angry clean through, with the kind of anger that isn't on speaking terms with common sense. I had had enough of unyielding, self-righteous authority.

The Colonel's look combined bewilderment at my attitude and an urgent need to guess right about any alternatives I had in mind. He must be a government appointee too, I thought with sudden bitterness. His shoulders lifted a fraction. He reached in silence for the telephone. 'Bring the prisoner from solitary,' he said. 'Miss Beattie may see him.' I thanked him.

The visitors' room was a sterile, white-walled, narrow room, divided down its length by a sweep of glass. The individual cubicles gave an impression of privacy. Conversations between visitor and prisoner were conducted by telephone, placed on counters between them. And, of course, conversations would be monitored. This was a top-security institution.

Bill was brought in by a guard. He looked thin and white and astounded. He hurried to the telephone, picked up the receiver and muttered, 'How did you get me out?'

The guard had left the room. We appeared to be alone. At my questioning look Bill nodded and tilted his head. The monitoring was taking place around the corner, over my right shoulder. 'Through the generosity of the Colonel,' I said into the telephone and Bill grinned.

We talked only a few minutes, conscious of the listening, hidden guard. Before I left Bill said, 'I've been thinking. Remember you asked once if I'd like to talk things over with a head shrinker? Well, I guess I would. You choose him. I can't go on like this. When I get out, I'll see him.'

The guard reappeared. Our time was up.

Chapter Nineteen

A week later I came under official suspicion as the head of a teenage crime ring. Father Orr gave me the news by telephone. He began briskly: 'You were in Parkdale today. Could you give a verbatim report of your conversation with six Saints, while you sat with them in a booth, and with two girlfriends of the Saints, while you stood with them at the cashier's desk?'

'Possibly, if I try hard enough. Do I win dancing lessons if I'm right?'

'Not exactly. I've received a call from the Markham police. They believe you're the head of a teenage crime ring.'

'Oh really?' I tried to match his gravity. 'I think I like that better than the girlfriend image. It's more sophisticated. Today the Saints. Tomorrow the Mafia.'

'They are serious,' he said.

'You're joking.' I listened to silence. 'You're not joking.'

'I'm not. Neither are they.' And he told me the story. The previous evening a service station had been broken into. A farmer had seen the thief and shot at his fleeing car. The Markham police believed the bandit was hiding out in Parkdale.

That afternoon a detective had seen me come into the restaurant, had watched me join the Saints and talk with them. He recognized the Saints. He took down the licence number of my newly acquired car, and he learned, presumably from the restaurant manager, that I was frequently in Parkdale and in the company of these questionable young men. He checked out my identity through the car ownership, followed the link, with Father Orr and the Saints' club and arrived at the only conclusion that seemed reasonable to his official mind.

'I tried to clear you,' Father Orr's gravity was cracking, 'but I don't know if I succeeded. I'm not sure if they think I'm being hoodwinked by the lot of you, or if . . .'

'You're our real leader,' I noted. 'Mr. Big!'

'Anyway,' Father Orr's voice choked, 'he said he believes you know the whereabouts of the fugitive and he wants that information. I don't suppose you actually do know.' His voice took on slight alarm.

'Actually I have him stashed in the frig. He's cooling off.'

Father Orr waited. 'Please,' he urged, 'this detective will call you soon and I would strenuously advise a serious approach with him.'

'How can I be serious, for crying out loud,' I sputtered.

'Well,' he laughed, 'I'll get Stan if they close in.'

The detective called a half hour later. He started in smartly. 'You were in Parkdale today in the company of teenagers who call themselves the Saints,' he said. When I said, 'Right,' he stepped on the admission. 'We know of your association with them.'

'It's no secret.'

'You know there was a holdup last night.'

'Father Orr told me of your call to him,' I interrupted, 'I'm afraid I can't help you. I don't know where your fugitive is.'

'Would you tell us if you did know?'

'Depends on the source of information. If it came from a Saint, which is your inference, no, I wouldn't.'

'You realize this makes you an accessory.'

'We're talking in the "if" department. Since I don't have the information, it's also irrelevant.' The cold interrogation was beginning to irritate.

'But you do know the Saints are involved.'

'I don't. Neither do you.'

'Will you find out where the fugitive is hiding?'

I tried to explain about the club. 'Since trust is the only thing we have going for us in our efforts to help these young people,' I said, 'I don't intend to turn into an informer for the police. Surely you understand that reasoning.'

He didn't. I had a social responsibility, he said, and if the Saints really were innocent, they would want to co-operate with the authorities. 'Now that is sheer nonsense,' I retorted, 'and you know it. They may have changed their life-style, but they haven't changed certain attitudes. They aren't about to become informers, either.'

'We have good reason to believe the man is wounded,' the detective broke in. 'He may need medical attention urgently. You could help him.'

That was good psychology. The mental picture of a wounded man in hiding rose up. 'I doubt if he'd give himself up anyway.' The image became more vivid. 'I admit the Saints do have a remarkable grapevine. It's possible they might be able to spread the word and it would reach him.'

'You could tell him it will go much easier on him if he gives himself up,' the detective pressed on.

'I couldn't tell him a thing, because I don't know where, or who, he is. But. . .' A wounded man? 'I could try to get the message through.'

Would I report back to him? 'There'd be no point in that,' I sighed. 'The report would be only that I kept my word. Look, I'm not head of any crime ring. I'm not lying. But if you think this man is wounded, I'll try to get the word on the grapevine.'

'That's all?' When I was silent he said 'all right' in a suspicious and unsatisfied voice.

Ron would be the one to contact, I decided, and I telephoned the restaurant to leave a message for him to call me. Ten minutes later the telephone rang. 'Now hear this,' I said, 'I've just completed a marvelous conversation with a Markham detective who has me tagged as the head of a teenage crime ring.' His laugh blasted my ear. 'I'm serious. I'm acting at their request because he thinks a wounded fugitive is hiding out in Parkdale.' And I gave Ron the details. 'If you know anything about this, I don't want to hear it. If you don't, tell anyone you can collar that the police say it will go easier on him if he gives himself up, and if he's wounded – well, anyway, the news may reach him. And, judging from the detective's suspicions, I wouldn't be surprised if this line is bugged, so if you get news of him through whatever grapevine we crime-ringers use, don't tell me.' The echo of the joking comment swung back. But I did believe it was possible. In our society? I could believe my telephone might be bugged?

'Okay,' Ron said and hung up.

I was annoyed, frustrated and impatient. I trudged back to Father Orr's insistence that we must always try to see it 'from their side.' All right, fairly, what justification could this detective have for this suspicion. He found if difficult, impossible apparently, to believe that anyone – with the possible exception of professionals – would become involved with 'young offenders' without a questionable, even criminal motive. Unless he had a psychic kink, which was unlikely since his view was demonstrated with astounding frequency, that had to mean that people without questionable motives were so rare in the offenders' world as to be suspect by their very presence.

Most citizens were so apathetic, so self-absorbed, so indifferent, or so confident in the rightness of our system, that the machinery of authority was a separate world never to be questioned or challenged by the average citizen? But the average citizen who did become involved, judging from our experience, was received with more than initial suspicion or curiosity. That was the knife-thrust, the shock.

As a society we had moved out of an era when social structures were easily understood, solidly and clearly defined, and supported by a set of values and code of ethics generally acceptable. We were moving into an era of turmoil, in which all structures had to be questioned in a thousand ways to accommodate new social needs – and newly recognized ones – to incorporate new scientific findings, to make our shrinking planet capable of maintaining, let alone improving, human existence.

Yet so vital, so powerful, so complicated a machinery as Authority would resist questioning, or participation, or examination by the citizens whom it was designed and intended to serve? It would respond with scorn ('Since you are so successful in this work, perhaps you should go into it professionally,' 'What kind of friend?'); with threats ('You realize this makes you an accessory?'); with insinuations, humiliating analyses of involvement that could discourage further questioning?

Old faiths, like old loves, die painfully and leave a residue of regret – that sad ash of the heart's dead longings. I was losing something that would change me forever. It was the slow extinguishing of a cherished, bred-in-the-bone faith that our system of authority was usually right.

But now the suspicion was spreading like a brightening, unwelcome dawn that something was going wrong, if not with the structure of authority, then with the attitudes toward and within it. I thought of my speech to the Saints, the night of the newspaper headlines. 'Society has flaws and injustices, but they have to be fought from within.'

There were flaws. There were injustices. We had assembly-line justice too frequently. We had magistrates who, for the most part, were political appointees and whose justice, too often, was a blend of self-conscious 'honour' to their responsibility and contempt for the victims of that justice, or the result of personal prejudices. We had an authority – I thought of Millbrook – with rules that facilitated, and were not concerned with the search for truth. We spewed young offenders back on the street without even the mark for Cain on them – a mark which, after all, was not an advertisement of guilt, but a sign of protection. We permitted, even encouraged, authority to meet the growing violence with the threat of violence. We called eight-year-olds, or ten-year-olds, or thirteen-year-olds failures. We slapped labels on young people, 'punks,' 'hoodlums,' 'incorrigibles,' forgetting – or not caring? – that people usually behave as they are expected to behave.

140

The ultimate irony, I decided, the real leap to conscience's jugular, was the fact that this slow death of my innocence had been caused by association with reformed young bandits, some of whom probably weren't reformed at all. I hadn't lost my unquestioning faith that our system was usually right in any civil-rights battle.

Or was even that true? In a way this was a civil-rights battle, a battle to ensure that the rights of certain human beings be recognized and respected, not only in the legal aspects, in the 'innocent until proven guilty' categories, but in the infinitely more important and infinitely larger sense that their human-ness be recognized and respected. I was in a battle demanding that these young people be regarded not as a breed apart, to be hung up on sociological meat-hooks for mass tabulations and analyses, or tucked away where they wouldn't be social nuisances and where that primitive hunger for revenge would be satisfied, but that each one be considered first and individually a human being, with human problems and conflicts and needs to be taken into account and perhaps even some day solved.

And what did you do in a civil-rights battle? I looked at the telephone and pictured Ron spreading the word. You stayed involved. You yelled when there was injustice. You fought. And you said to hell with the humiliations and the threats – if only because in the final analysis you were also protecting and fighting for yourself.

The telephone rang. 'Message on the way,' Ron reported.

'Thank you,' I said gravely. 'Over and out.' And, with a laugh, he hung up.

I wasn't to know the end of that incident for seven years, but it delights me to this day because of the delicious irony.

The Saints had not been involved in the holdup, but some did know the fugitive and where he was hiding. In Parkdale. After my call, one sped by cab to the hide-out. The message was delivered. As a warning. The fugitive, who was not wounded, had been unaware that the police suspected he was in the area. He slipped out and, because a detective insisted I get the message to him, he got away.

Today he is in business in Toronto. Legitimate business. And he is still grateful to that Markham detective.

Chapter Twenty

Throughout July and August we seemed to leap from incident to incident, each one foreshadowing the ultimate question yet to come, yet to be recognized and, in some ways, never really to be understood.

It began with the rumble threat. Ron called one Saturday afternoon to say there was 'big trouble.' A north Toronto gang's application for membership had been turned down because they would have 'tried to take over the club.' The problem stemmed from their lack of grace about the rejection. Friday night two members of the gang had beaten up a Saint. The gang promised a 'return match' which, under the rules, could involve the entire Saints' club. Ron wanted me to come to Parkdale. I assumed I was to try to prevent trouble.

When I arrived at the restaurant the Saints were crowded around their wounded comrade, who sipped a coke while he muttered angrily about the damage he would inflict 'next time,' and winced when anyone admiringly touched the splashy stains on his face. 'And if they don't come tonight,' a Saint declared as I slid into a booth, 'we go to them.'

'There's a hell of a lot of 'em,' one Saint said and shivered.

I opened my mouth to deliver the reasoning speech. Ron's voice cut in. 'Don't worry,' he said, 'I can pull in reinforcements. I can have a thousand guys here in two days. From the States.'

The first vision to cross my mind was that of a stony-faced horde of teenagers swarming across that great, undefended border like locusts – or would it be lemmings – and occupying Toronto. All because of our little club. Then Ron's words bounced back. A thousand reinforcements? I stared at him. What possible connection could he have with – and 'gangs' had to be the word – in the States. His brothers again? But why would he even think of it? Suddenly he looked an experienced young man who lived in a threatened and threatening world.

'I could,' he said to me quietly.

'I see,' I began. 'Well, actually, I don't see,' I amended, 'but aren't we being a trifle dramatic? This was a fight. Turning it into a riot . . .'

'Rumble,' someone corrected automatically.

'Rumble,' I repeated obediently and tried to clear my mind of the images that word invoked, 'is absurd. No, listen,' as they glanced at each other with thinning lips, 'I know I'm a square, but I'm not choked up with admiration for people who try to solve something or prove something with violence. It doesn't accomplish a thing, except to increase the violence. And you might remember we have an interested neighbour. Number Six.' Grins broke over their faces. 'It will . . .'

'It will scare the . . .' Ron glanced at me, 'breath out of them. They'll drive around with the windows rolled up.'

I left them, owl-eyed with excitement, and hurried to the church. Father Orr took the news calmly. He said probably the less attention we paid to it the better. His eyebrows raced up his forehead when I mentioned Ron's promise of a thousand reinforcements. 'Oh?' he grimaced. 'Let's take that as a not-very-interesting statement. Otherwise he might think he has to prove it.'

'You think he could? Or would try?' Astonishment jumped.

'I think there's a good deal we don't know about Ron,' he said, 'and probably about the rest of them. Let's,' he smiled, 'keep cool.'

The day passed slowly. At the dance the detectives patrolled more deliberately and the teenagers beamed excitement. By eleven-thirty they had scattered. Father Orr and I agreed not to make it a death watch, and I went home, to sleep fitfully, dreaming of Parkdale exploding in a full-scale rumble, with the Stars and Stripes fluttering everywhere.

The next afternoon the atmosphere in the restaurant was electric. 'They came,' a Saint yelled as I walked through the door. 'It was a hell of a fight. We won,' he added needlessly.

'Great,' I sighed. 'Now what?'

Ron was standing by the booth, his thumbs hooked into the pockets of his jeans, his fingers fanning slightly in an alert, expectant way. It was a characteristic pose, head up, tilting back enough to invite and give inspection, legs apart as if he were braced against something. 'Up to them,' he said. 'They want another go at it, we're ready.'

The cruiser from Number Six drove slowly past. The windows were rolled up to within an inch of the top. Despite the reluctant laughter, I thought how sad and wrong it was that Father Orr and I couldn't talk over this problem, or any problem, with these experienced men. 'Well,' I said lamely, while the Saints doubled up in laughter, 'I'll see you later.' And I headed for the church.

Father Orr had heard of the victory. 'And?' he prompted.

'I don't think he's called for the Americans. Yet.'

'It still bothers you?'

'Yes. I don't know why. Something in the way he looked. It wasn't teenage boasting.'

'Why not ask him about it?'

'Because I don't want to go mucking around. I want him to talk voluntarily, not because I'm asking the right questions and he's honouring a promise.'

Father Orr looked through the window toward Number Six. 'Yes,' he said, 'providing he understands that your lack of questions means acceptance of the truth, whatever it is, and not merely a desire not to know it.' He looked back at me. 'You two have become good friends. I think the friendship has a special significance for Ron. Some day he'll want you to know all there is to know. How you receive it may make a big, a vital difference. To him.'

Sunday drifted past. On Monday Ron telephoned. 'All clear,' he said.

'Good. I'm glad we didn't need to provide international complications.' At his silence I added, 'The reinforcements.'

'Oh. Sure.' His voice dismissed it. 'Well, see you Wednesday.'

The next week David came to the apartment to ask me to keep another weapon for him. This time it was a bicycle chain, securely wrapped in Christmas tape, which made it a provocative blend of glinting cruel grey and warm merry scarlet. He sauntered through the door when I opened it. 'See?' He gestured. 'I remembered. Through the door.'

'I'm glad to see you,' I said and hoped it was true. Despite all the months of association, there was still this reflex of coiled apprehension.

'How are you?' he asked, as if he hadn't asked that three nights earlier. When I said I was fine and asked if he wanted a coffee, he shook his blond head. 'Meetin' the guys. I just wanted to ask a favour.' He didn't stage it this time. He reached into a pocket and pulled out the chain. 'Will you keep this for me?' he asked and handed it to me. He saw the innocence of my look and grinned. 'Rap it against your palm,' he instructed. Automatically I obeyed and winced. 'See?' he said. 'You could use it like a weapon. To protect yourself.'

'I could use it?' I looked from the weapon to him. 'You're giving it to me for protection?' I was exasperated with his air of knowing and with this reaction to him. 'Okay, what's up? Do you have "that feeling" again? Do I prepare for another court appearance? Or is this a joke?' He was silent, as if I had deflated him. 'I'm sorry, David,' contritely, 'I didn't mean to sound sarcastic. I guess I'm tired. What's wrong?'

'Nothing,' he said, the hazel eyes empty of expression. 'I've been carrying that thing around with me. I decided it would be better to ask you to keep it for me. Just in case. But,' – and the engaging grin pushed his mouth – 'you could use it, if you ever needed to.'

I wanted to make up for the impatience and for the weeks of not being openly, actively concerned about him. 'Thanks. And I'll be glad to keep it. Sit down. We haven't talked in a long time.'

He turned to the door. 'I'd like to, but I got to meet the guys. Don't worry. And thanks.' He left me standing in the middle of my living room, with the bicycle chain in my hand. And I didn't know if my manner had turned off another intention, if he were issuing another warning, or if, indeed, he had displayed another symptom – of something.

A couple of days later I dropped in to see Father Orr. He was behind his desk, staring down thoughtfully. When I asked if I could help to find it, he looked up. 'You've heard?'

'Haven't heard a thing. You looked as if you were hunting for something.'

'The study was broken into today. Only an electric razor was taken, but I've been robbed.' He sat down. 'And I'd like to know why. I assume it was one the Saints. Aaron was here a while ago. I've asked him to . . . look into it.'

'It wouldn't be a Saint,' I objected. 'They know you trust them.'

Aaron's voice came from the doorway. 'It's possible Jeann. The guys are checking now.' He turned worried eyes to Father Orr. 'And we've decided to do something to protect you in future. The guys think a reinforcement down the door is best. We'll get a new lock, too. And if it turns out to be a Saint,' he said formally, 'he will be expelled. Immediately.' Solemnly he left us.

'Actually I'm fascinated,' Father Orr admitted. 'The stolen item was personal.' He smiled quizzically. 'If we're up on our psychology, we know that could have significance. As the child who steals from mommy's handbag is really stealing love.' He waved a hand. 'Simplified version, but you know what I mean. The idea intrigues me.'

'The stolen item is also the only thing easily pawnable here,' I reminded him.

'True.' He paused. 'But I'd still like to know who did it and why. Perhaps I could be a witness for the defence.'

The Saints put the reinforcement on the door and despite Father

Orr's interest in possible psychological significances, it challenged an attitude I had proclaimed, months earlier, at a meeting.

Habitually I left my handbag with my coat on a chair. That night a Saint brought it to me. 'I wouldn't leave this just hangin' around,' he chastised, 'not in this crowd.'

'Look friend,' I retorted, 'when I'm concerned about that bag, I won't be back.' Trust, I believed, like the Biblical bread, does return to you. A little soggy, sometimes, but it does return. That time I was right. Ron told me about it. An unnamed Saint had visited my office one afternoon while I was momentarily absent. He saw my bag open on my desk. He saw my wallet, with a five-dollar bill in it. He took the money. Halfway down in the elevator he changed his mind, returned, and replaced the money. 'I couldn't do it to her,' he had said to Ron. 'She trusts us.'

The day the Saints reported they were 'reasonably sure' about the thief's identity and that he wasn't a Saint, I was only half-relieved. By that time I had a premonition of my own.

And then Paul returned. I hadn't seen or heard from him since the day he walked from the courtroom. Then he came back, one July night, while a friend was helping me refinish an old table in my apartment.

When the soft rapping came on the door, I opened it, unprepared and unguarded. 'Hello,' he said without a smile. 'Hello, Paul,' I said politely. And we stared at each other. Until this moment I hadn't realized how deeply I wanted that second chance with this boy. 'Come in.' I stepped back. Paul edged inside and saw my friend. I introduced them. 'How are you?' I asked.

'Okay.' He waited. I hadn't asked him to sit down. I had done nothing but stand there, resisting a flurried response to his re-entry into my life. 'I didn't know you were busy,' he said. 'Maybe I should come back.'

I wavered. This would be more than a casual reunion. 'Perhaps it would be better,' I said. 'I'm sorry.'

He reached for the doorknob. 'See you,' he said and the door closed behind him.

When I stepped out of the elevator the following morning, Paul was coming into the lobby. It was almost nine o'clock and I had a business appointment. This wasn't the time for a heart-to-heart talk. But maybe – I looked at the set expression on his face – he didn't want a heart-to-heart talk. 'Hello, Paul. You're out early. Something wrong?'

He took three steps toward me. 'I need money,' he said.

The words dropped into silence. His eyes didn't waver. We weren't to mince around with apologies or explanations or even lies. We were to get to the heart of the matter.

'You're asking me for money? Just like that?'

'Yes.' he said.

I looked at the pale face and felt a stab-thrust of hot, disappointed anger. 'I'm sorry.' I took a breath. 'I know I made mistakes with you. I'm sorry about them. I intended to try to undo the damage. If there was any. But now – no.' His eyes were expressionless. 'Not just because of your lies at the trial, or because you stole from the department store and betrayed both me and my friend,' I could hear my voice recounting his sins and I knew, even as I tried to halt it, that I would go back to that original wound, the secret wound. 'Not even because this demand, under the circumstances, is something less than tactfully phrased. You see,' I took another breath, 'I know about your analysis of my interest in you. I've known about it for a long time.' I tried to sound sarcastically amused. 'You talked a lot about it.'

He looked as if he were about to deny it. Then his eyes slid from mine. And astonished shame washed over me. It had been there, festering, all the time. 'I guess,' I reached for the front door, 'I can be hurt by that kind of. . . .' I stopped. Of what? Ridicule? 'Maybe I'm that petty,' I finished. 'But now I can't see any point in becoming your resident target again. It can't do either of us any good. So, I'm sorry. And good luck.' I turned from the silent face and walked away, telling myself not to think about it.

I didn't think about it until evening. I decided to work on the old table. I put newspapers on the broadloom and sat down – and the morning swept back, carrying the white, guarded face of one of the waifs of the world, a waif filled with yearning and rage and need and contempt. 'Do they all have to look so alone.' The echo of that first impression of Paul. And the alone can deny safety even as they reach for it. They can defile tenderness even as they seek it.

While my hand moved back and forth over the table and the fine dust drifted in little puffs to the floor, I felt my face wet and knew, with surprise, that I was crying. I didn't know why I wept. Mourning the loss of tenderness for a young stranger? Or was it the rediscovery of some hurt, an earlier, long-buried, long-denied sense of loss? I didn't know, either, why I had denied this boy so swiftly, so ruthlessly, why I had renounced a commitment so totally. And it was a commitment, not an impulsive, reacting-to-a-moment gesture as it had been with David; not a curiosity-spawned, sympathy-endowed alliance as it had been, originally, with the Saints. It was the commitment of caring for reasons that lingered hidden and unsuspected. And I had withdrawn, not out of fear as, even yet, I feared David. Or out of impatience, or frustration, or even wounded pride. I had withdrawn because I had been hurt.

You couldn't do that. You couldn't reach out to a troubled boy, still childlike in his gropings and denials, and say, 'You are safe with me as long as I am safe with you.' But I had done that. And I had said that. Out of a buried, painful need of my own. I had penalized a boy.

The apartment was full of that thundering silence that follows a moment of distressing self-recognition. I thought of the Saints. And an inexplicable thrust of emotion, like a forecast of calamity, shot through me.

When the Saints decided, at the next meeting, to suspend club operations for a two-week summer vacation, it was like a period of grace. I had gone to the meeting invaded by guilt, shaken by that inward glance, and disturbed by the influence this new-found capacity within myself to be so pained might have on these vulnerable Saints.

The motion to suspend came unexpectedly, as they groaned over the smothering heat. Some, including Ron, opposed the idea of suspension. 'You know what it's like to try to get things goin' again,' he said darkly. But for once he was overruled.

'Then we gotta find another meetin' place,' someone moaned, 'or there won't be nobody left. We'll all be dead from the heat.'

'I'm afraid I can't solve the heat problem,' Father Orr remarked. 'Our budget doesn't run to air conditioners.'

'And the club's doesn't either,' Aaron said.

'Maybe we could pick one up . . . somewheres,' a Saint called. A moment's silence. Side looks at the adults. And a burst of laughter.

'And there ain't no other place we can get, not for free, not easy, like,' a Saint pointed out.

'So,' Father Orr summed up, 'a vacation would be best. I'll be away two weeks anyway and,' he looked at me, 'you, too?' When I nodded, he said, 'And presumably some of the members will be out of town, too.'

'Not unless the fuzz catches up,' someone grunted and the Saints laughed again. We've come together nicely, I thought; now they can joke about themselves in front of the adults. The motion to suspend carried.

148

Chapter Twenty-One

I left the city the first week in August for a camping trip in Algonquin Park. Stan said Ron's trial wasn't apt to come up until September. Mary was padding placidly through the final weeks of her pregnancy. David revealed no other trouble symptoms. And Timmy said the television play had 'gone a little stale'; he thought he'd recharge by trying a new story. He'd have it ready for me when I got back.

In the whispering silence of the Ontario northland, I tried to sort out the questions. The clean, pine-scented air, the glimmering waters, the winged glimpses of deer, all jolted the world of the Saints into clearer perspective. I decided to concentrate on the important question: where were we now, as a club, six months later?

The meetings had a set format: the guest speakers, the arguments about the still-incompleted constitution, the passing problems of the dances, the new members, the occasional resignation or disappearance of a member without formal notification, the vague complaints about the lack of other activities, and the insubstantial discussions of the future.

But they resisted all efforts to inaugurate other activities. They weren't interested in study groups. When we spoke of learning projects, they groaned and asked if we meant making licence plates, like at the reformatory. Even sports activities collapsed when they discovered they would not be instant champions. The success of the club still rested on David's claim of being together and having some place to go. And that claim, so far, was unchallenged by any outbreak of criminal activity.

The Saints were attracting community interest, too. Toronto's Crest Theatre had invited them to attend what, for most, was a first experience in live theatre. They had been guests of Alex Barris at the telecasting of one of his shows, an event which had been highlighted also by meeting Shirley Harmer. And Shirley had visited a Saints' dance. Father Orr also arranged a weekend at a church summer resort, which had not been a total success. The city-bred Saints couldn't see the attraction in doing 'nothin' but listen to yellin' birds.' The parishioners of St.

149

Mark's still grumbled about their occupation of church property, but a few had offered to help and one women's club had invited me to speak to them about the Saints.

But what about that insight they should be receiving into their past – and present – problems? 'To get at the why is the first step in prevention,' I had insisted to Stanton Hogg. I believed that, but I appreciated, more than ever, the complexity of the how. A form of group therapy? That meant shuttling the club into a radically new structure, with a measure of take-over by the adults, which wouldn't be welcome. It also meant finding a psychiatrist to work on a no-fee basis. Which wouldn't be easy.

Probably the only sensible answer lay in our personal relationships. Father Orr had his special interests among the members. I had mine. But there were too few of them. I remembered G. K. Chesterton's 'In everything that matters, the inside is much larger than the outside.' We didn't know enough about the inside of the Saints. So, I decided, we had to push harder, even if, sometimes, we intruded.

When the meetings resumed, the warnings about suspension seemed valid. Some Saints didn't show up at all. 'That's normal in any club,' Father Orr said, 'but I think it's time we got into the act more forcefully, but of course' – his laugh ruefully recognized the challenge – 'as unobtrusively as possible.'

We got into the act more forcefully that Saturday night. There was nothing unobtrusive about it. It was the first time I saw Father Orr lose his temper.

During the dance it was evident that some dancers were drunk. They weren't Saints, but they were there and the detectives were due and that made it a crisis. The bouncers went into action. Five minutes later the crisis ballooned. Outside the drunk teenagers challenged the bouncers and everyone in sight. Within seconds the original exchange was lost in mass upheaval. The parking lot threatened to become a riot scene.

Father Orr rushed into the core of the fighting. They ignored him and he exploded, his face white. 'If you are not inside in one minute,' he shouted, 'I'll call the police.' No one paid any attention. He waited one minute. Then he strode down the lane toward Number Six while I stood paralyzed on the steps. He had to stop it, but to ally himself with the enemy? One by one the teenagers fell silent. Father Orr looked back. 'I will not have this property turned into a setting for violence,' he announced. You' – to the troublemakers – 'have thirty seconds to go. The rest of you have thirty seconds to get inside.'

One by one they left. One by one they went inside. The riot had been averted, but there was the problem of the drinking.

Both drinking and drugs had been a major concern from the beginning. Of the two, drugs were my special worry. Young people had not found it fashionable yet to turn on, and society had not become aware, yet, of the potential attraction in drugs for the young. But it seemed logical that the Saints with their emotional knots, their thrill-seeking, their excitement in experimentation – especially with the forbidden – would try drugs. The question of the source of money to support a habit was only another threat. I mentioned my concern once to Ron and he laughed. 'Don't worry,' he said, 'we got enough trouble. That we don't need. Matter of fact we've had offers. One guy got awful friendly, offerin' rides in his convertible, gettin' interested in the club. Real friendly type. Finally he asked did we want to make real money, easy like. We asked how.'

'He was a pusher?'

'Somethin' like that. We told him to get lost.'

Drinking was something else. Most Saints were eighteen and older. They were veterans of reformatories and prisons. They were not the high school crowd and no one could term their lives sheltered. It was unrealistic to think they didn't drink. There were also occasional references to 'big weekends,' offered with the same satisfaction in the 'wickedness' displayed by many adult men. We greeted them with controlled disinterest. All we asked was that they abstain while on church property. Apparently the rule had not been transmitted effectively to their guests.

The Saints held an emergency meeting. The bouncers insisted that the dancers hadn't been 'that drunk' when they arrived, or 'we'd never have let 'em in.' That meant a hidden supply. Flasks weren't carried in by the young men either, the bouncers claimed with professional certainty, but they might be in cars. A crew of parking lot spies went to work. The cars were clean. The Saints came up with another possibility. The girls. They could be hiding flasks in handbags or, as one Saint put it, 'Under their dresses, wherever there's room.' The bouncers couldn't 'frisk' on so intimate a level. Father Orr was similarly restricted. But there was someone else. They looked at me. I could search any suspects in the ladies' room.

The prospect didn't delight me, but something had to be done. And for the first half hour next Saturday night I conducted my inquiries with the tact usually reserved for church socials. But one girl tried too hard to push past. 'Excuse me,' I put a restraining hand on her arm, 'we have this problem. There's been some drinking during the dances and of course that's against rules and – ' I stopped. Her skirt was caught back by the stair post. A bulge was visible on her thigh. Either that girl had a serious physical problem, or a flask. She followed my look. 'Do you have a flask on you?' I asked.

'You nuts?' She tossed her head.

'That isn't the issue right now,' My voice firmed. 'Will you come into the ladies' room please.'

She spun on her heel and shoved open the ladies' room door. It closed noiselessly behind us. She put a hand on her hip. 'You want me to strip?' She tilted an eyebrow. 'You want a thrill?'

'Those are two unrelated questions.' Adult irony was automatic. 'Will you take off your dress, please? Or even,' I eyed the bulge, 'lift it a little higher?'

She yanked it over her head. Taped to one leg was the flask. We both looked at it. Silently, almost triumphantly, I held out my hand. When she slapped the flask on it, I watched her wordlessly. This was the wrong way to do it. In the moment of confrontation with young insolence, I had relied on the superior and supercilious manner of the outraged adult. 'I'm sorry, but – ' I began. She stopped me with a look of scorn. 'Have a ball,' she said coldly and, pulling the dress back on, she swept from the room. When I went into the hall she had vanished. The threat of search worked, but I thought, 'here we go again.' Rules are rules, because we say so. We – adult authority.

The third week in August, Bill was released from Millbrook. He arrived in Toronto at eight-thirty in the morning, called me from Union Station, and arrived at the apartment fifteen minutes later. He stayed ten hours.

We talked about the day I 'got him out of solitary' and he laughed when I admitted that my insistence on seeing him had less to do with rescuing him, however briefly, from solitary than with an extraordinarily fierce and unexpected rebellion against the rule-book authoritarianism of Millbrook. 'I think I was trying to prove I wouldn't buckle down,' I confessed.

'So was I,' he said wryly.

He said he couldn't talk about his time there, that it had been too terrible to put into words. He said, 'I could never go through that again.' And he shuddered. The Colonel had said solitary was persuasive. 'You mean you don't intend to get into trouble in case you'd go back there?'

'Oh I'd go back,' he said quickly. 'The Colonel said he wanted me back. He said he'd asked that I be sent back there if I get into trouble again. I think he'd like it.'

'I doubt he's a sadist,' I objected, 'but at least you can beat that rap. Don't get into trouble again.'

'Sure, but it doesn't work that way,' he muttered and the 'why?' trembled on my lips. But it was pointless to ask why, as pointless as it had been to put that question to David the day at the Don Jail.

Bill began to talk as if the words had been accumulating inside him for years. And I listened, watching him lean back in the pale grey chair, the thin hard body tense, the soft slow voice talking steadily in a monotone; memories and fears, questions he didn't expect to be answered, fragments of bitterness and confusion spilling out, unrestrained and unrestrainable. I listened, still disbelieving that this quiet man had wasted long years in the walled-in world; that this gentle-looking man, with the sardonic smile, the good intelligence, the self-dismissing shrug, had huddled in solitary for two years; that this man, who paused to make coffee for us, to ask if he were imposing on me, to apologize for the moving, winding river of words that flowed from the depths of him; that this victim of himself and of each of us was capable of armed robbery. Over a hundred armed robberies.

The words kept coming, lighting up dark swamps of desolation and loneliness within him and, hours later, emptied of words, he paced the apartment, pausing to lift a book from a shelf, to leaf through it, to ask about the writer or read aloud a sentence which pleased or puzzled. And I had the eerie sensation of watching him prowl a prison cell, stalking the unidentified prey within himself. With no one to help him.

'Did you know I learned to read on a training farm?' he asked.

'Did you know I wanted to be a social worker?' he asked.

'Did you know the last time I was in there' – pointing to Mount Pleasant Cemetery, spreading beyond the apartment building – 'the cops were shooting at me?'

'Did you know?' 'Did you know?' 'Did you know?' This man, labelled the most incorrigible man in Canada, was digging out the ironies, the shames, the pieces of a life he wanted both of us to look at, to evaluate, perhaps to find, somewhere in the desolate depths, the identity of the man he should have been or might have been or, I wondered, could be.

'What will you do now?' I asked. And he halted, to stare wearily, hopelessly.

'Do?' he echoed. 'Do? I don't know.'

'Get a job?'

'A job?' The sighing, defeated smile. 'Sure, they're clamouring for guys like me.' He balled a fist, pounding it absently, rhythmically, into his palm. 'I can't think,' he said. 'That's crazy. I've done nothing but think, but it wasn't really thinking. I mean,' he said, more to himself now, 'it's like waking up from a nightmare and finding the nightmare isn't over. You're still in it. I couldn't figure out which was real. Or maybe . . .' and his voice trailed. Or maybe the two were the same? The reality had become the nightmare and the nightmare reality? 'There's something wrong with me,' he said and swung to face me. 'Isn't there.' Not a question. Not a challenge. Not a plea for denial. An acknowledgement. An admission that was another assault. And I shook my head, a spontaneous response to helplessness.

'There's something wrong with each of us,' I said. 'Maybe the miracle is that we survive at all.'

'It's worse with me,' he said. 'Why do I do these things?'

'I don't know. Maybe that's the first step – to ask yourself why.'

'So who's gonna give the answer? Who's gonna spell it out so's I can understand. A head shrinker?'

'Not spell it out. Help you do it, maybe. I called one. He's good. He said he'd be glad to talk to you any time. There's a sliding fee scale,' I added. 'No worry about the money angle.'

'I got to do something,' He sank into the chair. 'I can't go on like this. But you want to know something? Now I'm even scared of going to a head shrinker.'

'There's no need to be scared, but of course,' I smiled at him, 'saying that doesn't help a bit, does it?'

When the telephone rang and he lifted a questioning eyebrow and I said, 'You answer it. Tell them I'm dead,' he picked up the receiver. A smile spread over his face. 'Ron,' he said to me. 'He wants to know if he can come over. He says he'll make lunch for us. I told him I was coming to see you first.'

Ron arrived with two Saints and Bill's pretty, redhaired girlfriend. Ron went into the kitchen, while Anne and Bill settled to talk pri-

154

vately. The Saints needed no hostessing. They roamed the apartment, glancing through books and magazines, rebuking me for the smallness of my television set and hanging over the balcony to watch the traffic flow along Mount Pleasant Avenue. They also made telephone calls. To save dimes.

And it was after Ron had washed the lunch dishes that the little incident happened that stuck to memory like a burr. He had sauntered to the balcony and he bent to examine the door lock. 'You should do somethin' about that,' he said. 'A guy could get in easy.' When I protested that I was six stories up, he shook his head. 'Doesn't matter. A guy could swing up easy. Even I could do it and I'm too heavy for much monkey work. And that front door,' he gestured, 'three seconds would get it open. There's that milk box, too. A thinner guy could squeeze through like butter.'

'Stop this,' I waved a hand. 'You're wrecking my sense of security.'

'In this place,' he said, 'security is what you ain't got. I'll get them fixed for you.' And he went back into the kitchen.

I glanced from his disappearing back to Bill. Bill was watching me. There was a question in his eyes I couldn't decode. There was a question in me I couldn't decode either.

Shortly after five o'clock Ron left with the other Saints. I went out on the balcony to watch dusk settle over the city. A few minutes later Bill joined me. 'Sure hate to eat and run,' he smiled the slow smile. 'And thanks for listening.' His face sobered. 'Do you think people would ever believe the truth about guys like me?' he asked in a flat voice.

'If you told them the truth.'

'You think I lie about it?'

'No. I mean everyone interprets in the light of personal belief and prejudice. That's the name of the game of truth. Interpretation. To phrase it more profoundly, as a wise man by the name of Paul Tillich did, "We transform reality according to the way we see it and we see reality according to the way we transform it." '

'So I'm prejudiced?' he smiled.

'A little. So am I. Then, too, people don't always know what to do with the truth. Like me. It's fine to holler that locking people up isn't the answer, that punishment doesn't kindle urges to reform, that our system is wrong, but what is the answer? You can't have people stealing and generally running amuck.' I looked at him. 'What would help – or cure – you?'

Bill looked toward the cemetery, as if he were watching the ghost of himself running through it while gunfire echoed. 'Damned if I know,' he said softly, 'and that's the truth.'

Book Three

Chapter Twenty-Two

One afternoon the end of August, I arrived home hot and exhausted. It had been a blistering, hard, long day. I was soaking in the bath when the telephone rang. It was Father Orr.

'We have a breaking and entering,' he said. 'They were caught this morning. I've been trying all day to reach you.'

Here it is, I thought. One of the 'unconverted' finally has exploded. 'Who?' I asked, half curious and half exasperated.

There was a tiny pause. 'Bruce. Ron. And Ron's brother, Bob. The one who was with Bill in the Kingston Penitentiary.'

I thought I had misunderstood. 'Who?' I said, my voice skidding up. And, disbelieving, I listened to the repetition of the names. 'I don't believe it,' I said flatly.

'According to the story they told the police,' Father Orr said, 'they are all innocent. Ron and Bruce admit that they talked of . . . pulling this caper,' he said the phrase carefully. 'Bob is supposed to have heard about it and rushed to stop them. But in the meantime, and at the site of the planned caper, they changed their minds. A remarkable coincidence is supposed to have occurred. The police arrived at the moment of their mind-change. They ran. But they were caught. So was Bob. Right at the scene.'

'I knew it.' Relief lifted my voice this time. 'They're innocent.'

'Oh really?' Silence. Then: 'Jeann, the factory was robbed. A cash box is missing. They ran at the approach of the cruiser. They refused to stop when they were ordered to stop.'

'And the inference is that only the guilty run?' I burst in indignantly. 'You know perfectly well that the Saints would run if they spotted a cruiser – or were ordered to stop – on their way to church.'

'You accept this astounding coincidence then?' Father Orr paused again. 'Well,' he said when I didn't speak, 'they'll appear in court tomorrow. Are you available?'

'Yes.' Steady now, I told myself. 'I have a nine o'clock meeting, but I'll get there as soon as possible. We'll get the truth.'

'I'll see you there,' Father Orr said. 'In the meantime, be realistic.'

I hung up the receiver. The pink telephone looked smug. I crawled back into the tub. Bruce? The club's vice-president? The critical cynic, lips curling over the antics of these – what had he called them – these hoods. Bob? After five years in Kingston? Of course he would go to stop them if he thought they really were going to commit a robbery. And Ron? My bodyguard and mentor? My friend? The one who had seen the destruction in his brothers' lives? The one who was fighting to keep others from that same destruction? He would rob? It was beyond belief. They had been boasting. Or perhaps a joke had gone too far, had become a challenge, at least to the point of pretending, of actually going to the site of the alleged crime. Except it wasn't an alleged crime. A crime had been committed. The factory had been robbed. It had to be a coincidence, an outrageous prank of fate. And I clung to that thought throughout the night.

Recess had been called the next morning when I arrived at the courtroom. Father Orr waved from the corridor. 'I talked with them,' he said, 'before court convened. I have the impression of pure fright. I also have the impression,' his eyes held mine, 'that they are guilty and afraid to admit it. I asked three blank faces and three blank faces said they were innocent.'

'You think they're lying.' It wasn't a question. 'Ron won't lie to me.' At Father Orr's lifted brow, I frowned. 'Remember our pact. He will never lie if I ask the right question.'

'And I didn't ask the right question? Or is the pact an exclusive one between the two of you?'

'I don't know. I don't know anything right now.'

Father Orr gestured toward the empty courtroom. 'The Crown isn't Stan, but perhaps he'll permit us to speak with them. You could put your right question to Ron. I think we should get the truth as quickly as possible.'

The Crown listened doubtfully when we made our request. 'It may save the Court some time later,' Father Orr said as an extra inducement. The Crown hesitated. Then he nodded. The prisoners, he said, could be brought to the box for five minutes.

They were ushered in by police officers. Ron's chin was tilted up. Bruce's mouth was rigid. Bob looked anxious. As we neared, Ron looked away. 'Okay,' I said abruptly, 'I know what you've told Father Orr. Tell me. Did you rob that factory?' Silence. A dismaying silence. Ron's eyes were fastened on the middle distance. 'Ron?' His head

159

snapped back, grey eyes looking into mine. 'Did you rob the factory?'

'Yes,' he said promptly, his gaze drifting to Father Orr, to skim over his face and return to me.

And coldness filled me. I still carried remorse over Paul, or perhaps it was more than remorse, perhaps it was a morbid uneasiness, even a fear of wounding and being wounded again. I stared at Ron, this young man into whom I had poured belief, trust, acceptance, loyalty, affection, all the indefinable ingredients of friendship. He had been a human being of known and unknown dimensions. The known ones – the intelligence, the loyalty, the honesty, the vitality, the humour, even the gusty rebellion – had pleased. Now, sharply, another dimension was jaggedly revealed, one that was both unbelievable and dismaying.

In his flickering gaze there was no hint of apology, or defiance, or embarrassment. He was waiting quietly for a verdict. And the crisis – because it was a crisis for both of us – passed almost without conscious recognition. The tumbling emotions of my response, the mixture of frustration, confusion, anger, disappointment, bewilderment, even a residue of disbelief, couldn't be translated into one emotion. But when I said, 'Thank you,' his head dipped slightly and his eyes darkened with satisfaction.

The other two were silent. 'You'll be remanded, of course,' I glanced at the Crown. He was signalling the end of the interview. 'We'll get the details later at the Don.'

Silently they followed the officer from the prisoners' box. As they walked away I realized I hadn't asked if the story of Bob's intended intervention were true. It mattered if Stanton Hogg was the Crown at their eventual trial. Our friendship was based on the mutually understood premise that I would tell him the truth always as I knew it. This charge would have to include a defence lawyer. And if Bob's story were a lie, designed as an escape route from prison, I couldn't tell Stan Hogg. Yet I couldn't lie to him, either. The only solution, I decided wearily, lay in not asking Ron for the truth about his brother. It made no moral sense, but it was the best I could do.

As Father Orr and I walked from the courtroom, he said, 'We'll need the best lawyer we can get. What about David Humphrey?'

David Humphrey was considered by many to be the dean of Canadian criminal lawyers. And he was enormously expensive. 'You think it's that serious?' I asked.

'I think,' Father Orr said, 'it's very serious.'

160

Later that afternoon we swept past the guard at the Don barely pausing to scribble our names in the official visitor's book.

The three sat in a cubicle. Bruce focused on a spot slightly past my right ear and to the left of Father Orr's face. Ron scrubbed at a spot on his sleeve. Bob twisted his fingers and examined the side walls of the cubicle. There was no swagger and no bravado. They seemed to have shrunk, as if the jail had peeled off a protective covering.

'Greetings,' I said grimly. No one spoke. 'First,' I blurted, 'I don't get this.' Their eyes swivelled to Father Orr. 'I mean it,' I insisted. 'I don't understand at all.'

'You're mad at us,' Ron observed, sober-faced.

'You're damned right I'm mad,' I snapped and glared at the sudden small smile on his face.

'I think I can understand,' Father Orr interrupted quietly. 'If you were sitting in a restaurant with nothing to do . . .'

'With another trial hanging over your head?' I glared at Ron.

'Especially then,' Father Orr said calmly. 'I can understand how it might happen.'

Anger gave way to surprise. This was the first time we had shown a disunited front to the Saints. Perhaps he was signalling against splutter. Or perhaps he was giving honest support, I thought, when they need it. 'Well,' I sighed, 'let's have the details.'

Ron looked steadily at me. Bruce and he had been sitting in the restaurant and they decided to rob this factory. They went there, broke in, and found the cash box.

He isn't saying it was a new experience, or a challenge, or a joke that went too far; they had 'decided to rob this factory.' And memory threw up the moment in the restaurant the day of the rumble threat, when he had promised a thousand reinforcements and suddenly, inexplicably, he had looked like an experienced young man in a threatening and threatened world.

'How much was in the cash box?' I asked and marvelled at the calmness of my voice.

'We don't know.' Exasperation flooded his eyes. 'We didn't get a chance to find out. We got outside and there they were, runnin' and yellin'. So we ran. I stopped long enough to bury the box. But one of the cops was shootin' at me, so I didn't wait to open it.'

'Shooting at you?' I repeated, startled.

'Coulda killed me, the damned fool,' he confirmed with disgust.

'He ordered you to stop?'

A grin spread over his face, 'He yelled, "Stop or I'll shoot every mother's son of you," and I yelled, "Shoot your mother, I ain't stoppin'." '

I was speechless. Weren't there rules governing the circumstances under which the police could legally shoot at someone? 'Did any of you have a gun?' I asked sharply.

'Gun?' Ron looked honestly bewildered. 'Course not. What did we want with a gun?'

'And they shot at you?'

'If I'd ducked my head to the left instead of to the right,' he grinned again, 'I'd be dead now.' He turned to the other two. 'Right?' They nodded silently. 'The cop told me later,' Ron said casually, 'that he didn't know how he coulda missed. He said he had a dead aim.'

'You discussed this with him?' This was pure madness. I was not here listening to the ludicrous recital of events which made no sense. Father Orr's hand touched my shoulder, its slight pressure a signal. Or a reminder, I thought, of a conversation we had once about the position of the Saints in any situation involving the authorities. In a charge against the police by known offenders, we debated, whose word would be more acceptable to a board of inquiry?

'So you were caught,' Father Orr deflected the conversation.

'They got us,' Ron agreed.

I looked at Bob. 'And you went to stop them.' I didn't make it a question. There was a little silence. Ron's eyes went to the table top. I had no pact with Bob. There was no reason for him to tell the truth if it differed from the official story. But he might and this time I pleaded silently 'please don't.' Mutely he dipped his head.

'Has bail been set?' Father Orr asked.

'Dad will put it up,' Ron volunteered. 'It'll be property bail.'

Their parents. In the excitement I had forgotten their parents. Once again. Once again, I thought, and this time it's Ron.

'In the meantime,' Father Orr said, 'do you need anything?'

'A good lawyer?' Ron grimaced with a glint of the old mockery.

'We've discussed David Humphrey,' Father Orr said, 'but I meant things like cigarettes.'

They glanced at each other. 'Thanks,' Ron said. 'We're out of cigarettes. But,' he frowned, 'Humphrey is awfully expensive.'

'Yes. Well, we'll see.'

And we trailed out into the sunlight. 'Do you really understand any of this?' I demanded of Father Orr.

He stopped on the jail steps. 'If we expect them to act according to normal standards,' he said with a half smile, 'we're done for. And yes, I think, with them, I can understand.'

'Ron?'

He looked at me. 'Maybe the time has come,' he said softly, 'for you to know at least part of what there is to know. It's up to you now, isn't it.'

'Yes.' I turned to go to my car. Then I stopped. 'About this police shooting at them.'

'Before we hit the front pages,' Father Orr's smile brightened, 'we should be certain of facts. The police did give the warning.'

Anger again, this time at the whole absurd mess. 'Even when the dangerous criminals to be apprehended are two teenagers who aren't firing back?'

'The police might not have been aware of their ages,' Father Orr pointed out, 'and remember there were three. They might have recognized Bob. And his previous charges were armed robberies, right?'

'The police weren't being shot at and don't you think it was a somewhat reckless use of police guns?'

'I know. I know. But right now, first things first.'

We drew lots to see who would approach David Humphrey. I lost. In the oppressive heat, his office was cool and orderly and by that orderliness rebuked human foolishness. Mr. Humphrey, behind a wide desk, was calm and speculative, but his professional manner didn't quite conceal his ability to find the outrageous humour in the human condition.

I had heard about this colourful 'dean' of criminal lawyers. The reports were true. He did have a vibrancy of personality, a swiftness of smile, and a vitality in his voice. He was an attractive man with a manner which indicated his awareness, coloured with resigned amusement, of the human habit of getting into trouble. He also had penetrating eyes and they fastened me to the chair as I tried to meet the organized efficiency of his questions.

But I had the jitters. My mind refused to concentrate on facts. My report began to bog down. Mr. Humphrey leaned back in his chair. 'What happens with these kids? That's your real question?' He smiled. 'I think I can tell you. Irresponsibility. It's that simple. Once they get into trouble it's all over. They've lost the only thing that matters, in the final analysis, to anyone – a good name. From the point of that loss, nothing matters.'

I thought of Congreve's line: 'To be honest is nothing; the reputation of it is all.' And Othello's cry, 'I have lost my reputation. I have lost that immortal part of myself.' But that didn't answer the question of the original act which cost them their good name. And if it were a matter of 'we have the name, let's have the game,' why choose a game that provided only more trouble?

Yet I was looking at the Saints, and especially at Ron, with split vision, tallying up their acts on a scoreboard of common sense. Maybe I was reducing it all to a personal struggle, to prove that there were answers to the unanswerable. Or maybe it was a matter of not knowing enough about anything.

Mr. Humphrey leaned forward. 'All right,' he said, 'I'll take the case.'

Relief. Gratitude. And caution. 'About your fee,' I began, 'I do thank you, but maybe we should discuss fee before making anything definite.' I had heard he charged five hundred dollars a day.

A quick smile. 'Tell you what,' he said, 'I'll make a bet with you. I'll bet my fee that they're back in the courts on a similar charge within a year – providing they don't go to jail for this one. If they aren't back, no fee. If they are, we talk money.'

'You believe they'll consider an acquittal or probation as merely beating the rap?'

'I believe it will have no obligatory significance,' he picked up a letter opener and tapped it absently, 'that it won't cure them, change them, rehabilitate them. And that's what you have in mind. I believe they have made their decision. They don't want to kick the crime habit.'

I thought of Ron. I didn't want to discuss Ron. 'But the club,' I said.

'The club didn't prevent this,' he pointed out.

'Maybe it's too soon.'

'Or too late.'

'They want to do something about delinquency,' I said stubbornly.

'They're doing it,' he laughed.

'The bet is unfair to you. You'll lose.'

'You'll take it then? Good,' he smiled. 'I thought you would.'

Stanton Hogg was next on my visiting list. He might not be the Crown at that eventual trial, but he was involved.

He was alone in his office and he looked up, unsmiling, when I knocked on the door frame. 'Learned colleague,' I went toward his desk,

'I bring tidings. David Humphrey has agreed to take our case. You know about our case.'

'I know.' He smiled. 'Bringing in the big guns? Wise decision.' His face lost the smile. 'And they're guilty, Jeann. All of them.' He wasn't previewing the courtroom scene. He was stating a conviction. 'You don't seriously believe that "going-to-stop-them" story of Bob's?'

'You don't buy it?' I hedged. This man was experienced in spotting lies. His derision alarmed me a little.

'Of course not,' he said shortly. 'Neither do you.' He shoved a pencil aside. 'What do you expect for the others?'

'Is the word leniency, clemency, or mercy?'

A short, exasperated laugh. 'On what grounds?'

'The grounds' – I thought of the night of the Markham detective's call – 'that they are human beings. I don't know what happened, especially with Ron. I have no case, except two human beings. Sending them to the reformatory won't accomplish a thing except turn them into more successful criminals.'

'And Bob?' Stan shot the question in quickly. Like a good lawyer should, I thought.

'Under the circumstances, I don't have to defend him.'

'But if he's guilty,' Stan waved impatiently, 'if the story is a lie?'

'Same reasoning. If he's lying and he did intend to rob that factory, surely that's an indication that Kingston made no difference.'

Stan leaned forward. 'You seriously believe that if these young men get off it won't seem to them to be getting away with something? They committed a crime. This country has laws for the good of society. Even you concede that' – he held up a hand – 'no, listen to me. Maybe our system isn't perfect, but you don't correct the imperfections by wrecking the system. That's what you do when you work to protect people from the law's punishment.'

'Even if the punishment is unjust?' Now I was back in Millbrook, listening to the Colonel's voice. 'Putting them behind bars won't change anything, except to increase their problems and inflict more expense on the public. How much does it cost – three thousand a year? – to keep someone in a reformatory?'

Stan rapped the desk angrily. 'I'm talking principle and you know it. You're giving these teenagers a dangerous impression and you know that, too. They could believe that with you and Father Orr fronting for them they can get away with anything. You aren't teaching them respect for society and for law. You're teaching them to outwit both.'

'Wait a minute,' I jumped at his condemning tone. 'If anyone is teaching people to outwit the law, friend, it's the legal profession. It won't be Father Orr or me who "gets them off." It will be one of your professional brothers. And if there's something to be learned from that, it's obvious. You want a chance in court? Get yourself the best lawyer you can afford. Okay,' as he started to protest, 'so that's an old argument. But nobody comes before the Bar of Justice in the old tribal sense of being judged by his peers these days and you know it. Not every lawyer is inflamed by a passion for truth and justice and you know it. There are the earthbound ones who want to make a buck, and to make a buck you must make a reputation, and to make a reputation you must be good. Very, very good. When you prosecute a case, when David Humphrey defends a case, it isn't only the accused who's up for judgement. You and Humphrey are up there, too.'

'We've sold our integrity for thirty pieces of silver?' He was watching me with impatient amusement.

'Not every lawyer,' I conceded. 'I don't think you would and I don't think Humphrey has, but that isn't the point. There's a materialistic sheen to the legal profession that makes for competition. It turns court trials into contests and don't think kids like the Saints don't know that. So when we're giving them airy philosophy about truth and justice, they can jettison us with facts.' I yielded to his look. 'All right, so that's another debate. You said we were giving them the wrong impression, or confirming an idea they have. Maybe so. But if I have to choose between the law and justice, there's no problem. I take justice.'

'But you must be certain which is justice and which mere sentimentality,' he said softly.

'Point for you. Okay, so they can't go around stealing and conking people on the head. But the answer is not revenge. We're wrong; as a society we're wrong and stupid and indifferent and maybe just plain savage in our approach to the whole problem.'

He sighed. 'Well, Dave will have a few points, too.'

And I smiled at him. 'Sorry. Didn't mean to blow off at you. I'm a little . . . unnerved. Anyway, they'll be released on bail?'

'You're putting it up?'

'Ron's parents. Property bail?'

'Fair enough. And we'll see what happens.'

The three were released the following morning. Ron telephoned at noon. 'We can't afford Humphrey,' he said urgently, 'and you and Father Orr can't either.'

'It's been taken care of,' I shunted off the subject. The bet was a private affair.

We didn't discuss the robbery, or his motives. I was operating on two levels. He knew I believed his act to be wrong, morally and practically, and that I would struggle to understand it. He knew me that well. But as his friend I was honouring the rules of our friendship. You didn't demand an accounting from a friend. Any explanation had to come voluntarily from him. All that concerned me – and I realized it only half-consciously – was the battle for him, and for his future.

At the next club meeting Ron was there when I arrived, sitting in a corner with Bruce. The emotional climate of the club seemed different. A cluster of Saints wandered near Ron and Bruce, exchanging grins or whispered comments, but another group had gathered across the room and their faces betrayed an agitation. They cast glances at the offenders that weren't admiring.

David sidled up, his face solemn. 'I'm sorry, Jeann,' he said.

Sorry? Of course. About Ron. He knew the extent of our friendship. 'Thank you, David,' I said and wondered if I imagined the glint of laughter in those porcelain blue eyes. Aaron was sombre, too. When he called the meeting to order he maintained a funereal seriousness.

After the meeting I stopped to talk with him. 'I'm sorry,' he said, 'about . . .' and delicately waved a hand. He had heard rumours, he said, that we had engaged David Humphrey. 'Are you and Father Orr paying for it?' he asked.

That tricky question again. 'He's being generous. We talk money later.'

Aaron hesitated. He was a businessman; he knew successful criminal lawyers were seldom vague about money. 'Oh?' he said and let his voice lift invitingly.

'Aaron, how do the members feel about this?' The question was suddenly important.

He considered it. 'Some think it's, you know, a lark. Some are kinda mad. I mean it gives the club a bad name.'

'And they do care about the club's name?'

'Sure.' He glanced at Ron. 'I hope it goes okay with them,' he said.

Perhaps, if we had talked longer that night, I might have learned something. But we didn't talk longer and I didn't learn anything. Not that night.

Chapter Twenty-three

The trial of the three was remanded again the next Friday, and the next, and the next. Ron's trial on the assault charge was also set ahead on the crowded court calendar. We were on the wheel of suspense that is part of our system of justice.

Each Friday morning Father Orr and I took our places, with Ron and Bruce and Bob, in the courtroom. Each Friday a group of Saints, in their scarlet jackets, distributed themselves throughout the room. And each Friday Ron's parents were there, sitting white-faced and quiet, waiting.

The meetings and dances seemed unaffected by the question mark that hung over the future of their vice-president and the Saint who was a major strength in the club. But beneath the surface a beat of strange new dissension could be heard. The Saints listened when Ron offered his commands, but the faces of some looked less eager and they were less obedient. Even Bruce's brooding glance, which once held power over them, seemed less potent.

For me, the ring of the telephone after midnight, which once had signalled only a Saint's need to talk, became a curious disaster alert. I answered in hushed expectancy.

A month later its ring at one-thirty one morning carried a distinct premonition. When I picked up the receiver and a man's voice asked if I were me, I said only, 'Which one is it?'

'Ma'am?'

'I'm sorry. I assume you're a police officer and that you're calling about one of our Saints.'

'It's the police station,' he confirmed, 'but I don't think we have any Saints here.' I explained and he laughed. 'Saints, eh? Odd sense of humour they have.' And he got down to business. Did I know Ron? Again I thought I had misunderstood. He repeated it. 'He asked us to call you,' the officer said. 'He's here. He was in a fight. Disturbance of the peace. He said to tell you – '

'You've told me,' I cut in angrily, 'and you can tell him he can go straight to – '

'Yes, ma'am,' he interrupted. 'A pleasure, ma'am.'

The connection broke softly in my ear. Furiously I banged down the receiver. I wasn't interested in explanations. I wanted to break every bone, misunderstood or not, in his body. I looked at my watch. Father Orr might be awake. I was too angry to keep this to myself.

When Father Orr said Hello, I jumped in: 'You won't believe it!'

'We're having a scene?' he asked calmly. 'Which one is it and what won't I believe? Try me.'

'Ron.' I could barely say the name. 'He's . . . he's . . .'

'In jail. I see. Why?'

'Disturbance of the peace. Disturbance of the peace!' I repeated incredulously.

'Well, at least he didn't kill anyone. Why is it unbelievable?'

'Why!' I almost screeched.

'Steady now,' he said. 'What happened?'

I told him of the call. 'Ron asked them to call me. I told the officer to tell him he could go straight . . .' and I stopped.

'Yes, of course. But you'll do more. You'll go down in the morning. In the meantime, try a cold shower. It's too hot for temper tantrums.'

I tried the cold shower and I tried, as well, to imagine what might have happened. He could have become accidentally involved in a street fight. But this was the third collison with the police. Three charges. It was unbelievable.

The next morning at the station Ron greeted me with a cautious half grin. 'The cop said you told him I could go to hell.'

'That was the general idea.'

'I told him you might say that but you wouldn't really let me go.' And the grey eyes met mine.

'That may be. But it was close. Just what do you think you're doing?' I demanded.

'It was a fight. A bunch of guys. Somebody hit me. I hit back. A cop broke it up.'

'And everybody's locked up?'

'No,' he said slowly, 'but you shoulda seen the guys who got away.'

'So now we pencil in another court appearance?'

He shook his head. 'Simple disturbance. A fine.'

He was right. But as we walked out into the glowing day, I stopped on the steps. 'Look, I know I'm supposed to be up to the eyeballs in understanding and patience and all that stuff. But I'm getting very confused. No, wait,' I said when he started to protest, 'so it was a fight. I know. Could have happened to anyone. But it didn't. It happened to you. Again. And even to my numbed mind that suggests something. Ron, what is it? What's happened?'

He turned his head slightly from me, and I thought of the early days with the Saints when Ron had been a complex, absorbing teenager with a mysterious interest in helping to organize an anti-delinquency club. The mystery of that interest was solved when I met his brothers. The assault charge warned of a savage temper. In the restaurant, the day of the rumble threat, the note of experienced authority in his voice had puzzled. The trivial bits and pieces had piled up, had changed my concept of him slightly, had altered my mental picture of his personality. The shift had affected none of the emotions of affection and loyalty and respect I felt for him, but it had introduced another emotion. Now I worried about him for a simple, even crude reason. I wasn't tangled up in motivations or self-questioning. I wanted to keep him out of jail. He had erupted in this baffling way for baffling reasons. Finding them was second on the list, if that meant a prolonged search through some inner darkness. Right now he was on a collision course. He had to be stopped – or diverted.

'Nothin' is bothering me.' He looked back at me. 'You can't figure me out, can you?'

'No,' I said. His head went back in a familiar gesture of exultant, triumphant laughter. 'Is it so important to you not to be figured out?' I asked gently. And his laughter dwindled. His expression changed. For a second, only a second, I caught a glimpse of Ron's anger at being vulnerable, as all humans are vulnerable, of his resistance to the danger of trusting, of a destructive, flaming satisfaction in remaining isolated and yet a streak of resentment at the lack of a genuine, deep communion with someone. He has taught himself to be cautious, I thought with astonishment. This volatile young man has taught himself to risk, even invite, rejection. This wary boy-man has conditioned himself to be satisfied with superficial relationships, to deny needs as urgent as the hungers of the flesh. Why? His brothers again? The scars of that time, the scars of social reaction, of family response?

'Yes,' he said simply. 'It's important to me not to be figured out.'

'Why?' And the question was gentle. Who called us all 'frightened strangers on a frightened planet?' And why are we so frightened, I wondered desperately.

'I don't know. Although,' he glanced at me quickly and as quickly glanced away, 'I've told you things I wouldn't tell another soul.'

170

Chronologically he was twenty now, yet the expression, the edge of bitterness, the curt defiance and the defence of inner privacy was ageless and never young. 'What is it, Ron?' I asked, daring, despite the threat of intrusion to penetrate – or try to penetrate – this barrier. 'This series of explosions makes no sense. If something is wrong that is none of my business, then, okay, say so, but – '

'There's nothin',' he repeated stubbornly. 'But I've been thinkin' maybe I should get out of Toronto. I mean later, if I'm free to go,' and the bitterness touched the qualification.

'I don't understand,' I said helplessly.

'I just think it's time I got movin'. I always move around. I'm a movin' target.'

'Who's shooting at you?' He gave me a sealed look. 'You don't want to talk about it?' Silence. 'Whatever it is, we can work it out.' Silence. 'I'm with you, you know.' His head dipped. 'But you haven't decided definitely to leave Toronto?'

'No.'

This was new, too, this doubt, this indecision. Something had happened. Since the robbery? The thought led to swift, savage rage. He could not be put behind bars. To cage this man like an animal, to confine this restless, clamouring rebellion, to try to 'break his spirit' – this must not happen.

'The trial will go all right,' I said and he was silent. That was wrong, too. He was seldom suppressed and never had he seemed submerged. 'It will,' I repeated fiercely as if saying it emphatically would make it so.

He gave me an absent smile. 'You know why we're such good friends?' he asked. When I shook my head he stared at me. 'Because you're always honest with me. You never lie to me, not even the kind of lies people tell when they think the truth will hurt, or make them seem, you know, something worse than they want to be. Like at the jail and like last night. You were real mad and you let me know it. That's how I knew you wouldn't . . . you know.'

'We have a good friendship,' I said. 'We can both trust it.'

'And I told you I would always give you an honest answer to any question,' he said slowly.

'I know.' I chanted the rule: 'That means I must know the right questions.' My voice was light, but the questions, right or wrong, begged to be asked. Yet if they were asked, if the answers were given because he was honouring that pledge and not because he wanted me to know,

171

I could lose my friend. And maybe, I thought, he would lose something, too. 'I don't have any questions,' I said. And silently he nodded his head.

Chapter Twenty-four

Autumn did not come proudly to Parkdale. The houses, which had gasped for air all summer, began to lose their green camouflage of bushes and trees, and the emerging skeletons weren't pleasing. The night wind, rolling in from the highway and the lake beyond, took on a dusky, damp chill. The people moved less wearily but more slowly, as if they wanted to savour the last thready warmth before winter put icy claws into them.

And one morning it was time for Ron's trial on the assault charge. When his name was called, we all started in surprise. There had been so many remands it seemed the trial would never be held.

The magistrate listened to the evidence, while a subdued Ron stood, as Paul had stood, as David had stood, with hands clasped behind his back. Finally the magistrate reached his decision. It was his opinion, he said, that Ron's hands constituted a lethal weapon. He would put Ron on probation this time, but if Ron ever appeared before him again on a similar charge, he would be judged in possession of a lethal weapon.

I didn't know if he could make such a decision stick, but it sounded firm and that, judging from Ron's expression, was good.

When court adjourned I caught up with Stanton Hogg. 'Thank you. You could have been tougher in your recommendations. Is round two coming up soon?'

'I don't know,' he said slowly, 'and you're welcome.' Then he paused and gave me one of those appraising looks, half-searching and half-puzzled. 'You're still convinced the older one went to their rescue?' When I said yes he shook his head. 'You're wrong,' he said. 'Dead wrong.'

Round two came up one morning a couple of weeks later. And Stanton Hogg was the Crown Attorney after all.

I was bending down to pick up a fallen handkerchief when I heard the court clerk call out the names of Ron and Bruce. My head snapped up. The two rose to face the Court. Stanton Hogg looked sombre as the charge was read. David Humphrey looked imperturbable. Our threats to society stood in silent expectation.

I hoped someone would remember Gibbon: 'When the offence inspires less horror than the punishment, the rigour of penal law is obligated to give way to the common feelings of mankind.'

The magistrate was a solemn figure in black. People shuffled their feet and whispered among themselves. He frowned and the courtroom fell silent. This was the Bar of Justice. You did not whisper or shuffle your feet when men approached the Bar and asked for that Justice.

I suppose it was during that trial that, for the first time, I tripped over the 'justice' in the awe-inspiring privileged responsibility of magistrates and judges. This stranger in black, who sat with dignity looking down, severely interested, from his raised seat of judgement, this magistrate who was, after all, a man and subject to man's moods and prejudices, contempts and compassions, would decide not only the guilt or innocence of the accused, but, in the case of guilt, whether the convicted would spend months or years behind bars. I found myself hoping he felt well this morning, that no pain twisted a joint to irritate and distract him, that his marriage was a good one, that his breakfast had been serene and that the last person to whom he had talked before he climbed to that judgement seat had not displeased him. For, however honourable a man he might be, however carefully he might listen and meditate and decide, the thousand incidental influences would be within him to contribute or to distract from his objective judgement. And that is wrong, too, I thought wearily. A human being should not have this much power over other human beings.

The facts were presented. Police officers testified. I looked at the one I knew had shot at the fleeing Saints. We had met outside the courtroom one morning. Ron, with a grin, had introduced us, and we had sat together on a bench while he exchanged subtle shafts with Ron. Shooting at the trio had been legal he had said, when, slightly stunned by this air of competitive friendliness, I had asked the question. He had given the required warning.

Now, on the stand, he matter-of-factly restated his acts of that night. Questions were asked and answered. The young men had raced from the scene of the crime. They had not obeyed the police order to halt. The net appeared to hold no escape for them.

When court recessed Father Orr and I went into the corridor to greet Ron's parents, to wave to Stanton Hogg, to talk with the sombre three. David Humphrey said it was going well. 'It would have been better,' he said, 'as I told you earlier, if you'd surrendered that damned cash box.'

'But we buried it,' Ron reminded him.

'It would help?' I asked David Humphrey and when he said, 'of course,' I looked back at Ron. 'Could you find it again?' He hesitated, exchanged a glance with Bruce. 'Ron. Could you find it again?' The cash box might represent buried treasure for them. That would be childish, but it was possible. Anything seemed possible now. 'The truth,' I said to resigned eyes.

'I think so,' Ron muttered.

'And if we brought it back?' I looked at David Humphrey. He smiled. I didn't ask if he would defend me if we were caught in the car with a stolen cash box. 'Come on,' I said to Ron. He signalled Bruce and we took off.

The factory looked too small to be so great a factor in their lives. I parked the car, pleaded with them to be careful and watched them run across a field and disappear. Ten minutes later they were back. Ron carried the cash box. 'Got it,' he said and climbed into the back seat of the car. 'Now,' settling comfortably, 'let's see how much we got.'

'No!' I twisted to glare at them. 'Leave that box alone!' Their disappointment was acute, but, with a sighing shrug at Bruce, Ron put it on the floor. Stiffly I started the car. There was time for a quick lunch. Ron's mother had invited us to stop at their home.

While she made sandwiches and we talked with the new ease born of the weeks of waiting together, the trio disappeared into the basement. When they reappeared, their half-gleeful, half-defensive look said it all. They had forced the cash box lock.

'All right,' I sighed, 'what would have been your reward for this brilliance?' They looked at each other. 'How much was in that box, Ron?'

He held it out. 'Sixteen dollars and seventy-nine cents.'

I have never driven as carefully as I drove during the trip back to the court. We delivered the box, with the money, to David Humphrey. Court reconvened. The ritual began again. The prisoners faced the court; the magistrate glowered down on them; Stanton Hogg prosecuted; David Humphrey defended; the two Saints had reached the critical moment of judgement.

The magistrate grunted his displeasure. Ron and Bruce were pale, inward clamourings hidden behind impassive faces. Absurdly I hoped the magistrate's lunch had been one of the most delightful of his life. And Aristotle's line endorsed my concern: 'It is best,' he had said, 'that the laws be so constructed as to leave as little as possible to the decision of those who judge.' Factually there had been as little as possible left to the decision of the magistrate. The two were undeniably guilty. All that remained was his opinion of justice.

He launched into a lecture. While he gave his views of youthful offenders, I hunted for the traces of prejudice that lie buried in the emotions of even the most responsible of older men toward young people, especially young people in trouble with the law. Now I was praying he liked and respected David Humphrey. He paused. I held my breath. At the word 'however,' I let the breath out slowly. 'However' I had learned was a key to intention. 'And therefore' was another, more ominous key. However, this time, he said, he would give them another chance. He would put them on two years' probation. The shoulders of Ron and Bruce went down a trifle. And my eyes went to Bob, sitting white-faced in the prisoners' box, waiting his turn at the Bar of Justice.

His trial began. Stanton Hogg confined himself to facts. David Humphrey confined himself to interpretation. The spectators watched and listened and murmured. A few looked with curiosity at this man who had gone to save his brother – or so he said. Some thinned their lips. Bob's anxious voice answered the questions and his fingers curled over the edge of the witness stand. He knew, he said, what it meant to be in prison. He had wanted to spare his brother that experience. He sounded honest and even a little defiant, as if he were embarrassed by this admission of brotherly concern.

It did make sense, far more sense than the alternative, that a grown man, who spent years in prison, would risk his future with two teenagers in a foolish, petty theft. Stanton Hogg hunted the gaps in the story, the slips which would prove it a lie. David Humphrey suggested by his manner that Bob should be congratulated by the court. The magistrate rustled his papers.

One of the Saints leaned over to whisper, 'It's okay.' I didn't know the grounds for his decision, but it was encouraging. The magistrate agreed with him. The charge against Bob was dismissed.

Relief was paralyzing. Ron's parents smiled at each other and at us. Ron and Bruce inclined their heads in grave appreciation of the Court's wisdom. Bob's face melted into a smile and behind us, to the right, I could see Bill, sitting very still, disbelief on his face.

When court adjourned we went into the corridor. Ron's parents hurried toward Father Orr and me. 'Thank you,' they said and we hugged each other. Bill came up slowly. 'This is the first time this family ever got a break,' he said to me. 'You won't have to worry about us, ever again.'

Stanton Hogg beckoned from his office door. When I went in he closed the door and sat down on the edge of his desk. 'It's over now,' he said. 'You can tell me. You never believed that story of Bob's, did you?'

'Yes,' I said emphatically. 'Yes. I really do believe it. It makes more sense.'

He sighed. 'You're the one who's incorrigible,' he said.

I told him of Bill's promise and he sighed again. 'Probably right now he means it,' he said, 'but . . .'

'But you don't think it will stick.'

'I hope so. I doubt it.'

In the corridor, when I caught up with David Humphrey to thank him, the quizzical eyes narrowed. 'Now for the bet,' he smiled, 'now we'll see.'

For the next couple of weeks I had the feeling we were marking time. Ron appeared to bounce back from the visible alarm and depression of the pre-trial days, yet his manner had a peculiar quality, one of relaxing domination without yielding the right to challenge. He was more thoughtful, too, considering questions without the previous grand sweep of emotion. Neither of us referred to his speculations about leaving Toronto. Instead he announced one day that he was job hunting. He seemed sincere about it and he took a deliberately offhand suggestion without resistance. Instead of hunting just any job, I asked, why not be scientific about it? Why not find where his talents lay, so that he could build a future which wouldn't waste them?

'How do I go about that?' he asked.

'Aptitude tests, probably,' I said. 'They offer guidelines at least. And the experience would be interesting for you.'

Who gave them, he asked and how much would it cost? I told him I would investigate and the following week he took the tests. The results were interesting to both of us. As I had suspected, he ranked high in a number of fields, but the highest rating was in mechanical ability, especially automotive. 'I take after my Dad,' he laughed. 'But that means taking courses and serving apprenticeships. I'll need money. So I'd better make some.' He threw me a sly look. 'Legally,' he said.

The next week he invited me to use the services of a floor and window cleaning business he had established with another Saint. 'We'll give you special rates,' he assured me. And later I had another fragment of evidence that he intended to make his money – legally. He telephoned late one night to say he needed advice. 'You know I got a place of my own now,' he said. 'Well, I got an offer from some guys. They want to rent my apartment. For floating crap games. I can get a couple of hundred. Maybe more. I don't get involved. Just collect the money.'

'You mean a gambling outfit wants to rent your apartment?'

'That's it,' he said. 'What do you think?'

'I think I'm too tired to make trips to Kingston Penitentiary or even Guelph Reformatory to visit you. The answer is no. Just no. I don't even want to discuss it.'

I could hear his laughter. 'The money sure would come in handy.'

'No,' I repeated. 'Tell the men it's darling of them to think of you and the answer is no.'

He dropped the subject.

And Bill had called the week after the trial to ask that I make the psychiatric appointment for him. He broke the appointment. When he broke a second one, it seemed likely that he was trying to keep an unspoken promise – to himself, if not to me – without seriously wanting to undergo therapy. That would cancel out any benefits. Apparently the suspicion was right because his voice sounded relieved the day I suggested he meet a friend of mine, who happened to be a probation officer, and talk to him instead of to a psychiatrist. 'This man is practically a contemporary of yours,' I explained. 'He's had plenty of experience helping people with problems. He has a sense of humour; he listens and you couldn't shock him. I think you'd like him.'

Bill's sessions with the probation officer began immediately.

Bruce was less receptive to any overture. He returned to his private world. The no-trespassing signs were hoisted and when I mentioned it to Ron he said, 'I'd leave him alone. He's got problems, but I don't think he wants to talk to anybody about them.' He added that day that his brother Bob was job hunting, too.

And David, always the question mark, David. He wasn't changing. He still drifted through the meetings, voicing infrequent opinions and showing no surprise over anything. But he was working; he was cheerful; and he wasn't in jail.

Timmy was still writing, but a new quality of resolve had been born in him, too. Earlier Timmy's father had died with shocking unexpected-

178

ness. Timmy no longer talked of jobs which didn't interfere with his writing. He took a permanent job and he announced one afternoon that he had decided to finish his high-school education through correspondence courses. 'I don't know how I can manage it,' he said, biting his lip, 'but it must be done. I was wondering too if maybe, later, I could . . .' he took a deep breath as if the idea were too big to be encompassed by words, 'go to university.' I stared at this boy who, overnight it seemed, had changed from a wistful child into a resolute young man. Without my noticing he had shot up in the startling manner of adolescents, and now he seemed taller and bigger and abundantly mature. 'I think that's a fine idea,' I said, and let go of the child, 'Tim,' I added deliberately and he gave me a wide smile.

Then, one lovely October evening, Mary's baby was born, a healthy, vigorous boy. Two weeks later she telephoned to ask if I would be the baby's godmother and the next Sunday we met at St. Mark's. The christening was private and the dim, quiet church was empty. Mary was waiting for me at the back of the church. 'I want to tell you something, she whispered, 'but I don't want Father Orr to know just yet. I'm going to be married. To Ernie.'

My eyes went to the baby. 'That's wonderful, of course, if it's what you want, but I don't understand. Why have the baby christened today? Why not wait until – '

She stopped me with a smile and touched the baby's face. 'This is between us,' she said gently, 'the baby and me. I want to marry Ernie. I wanted to marry him all the time, but I didn't want anybody to think I had to marry him. I mean,' she glanced up at me, 'I didn't want Ernie to think it and I didn't want to think it myself. And when he grows up,' she smiled down at her son, 'I didn't want him to think that, either. But this christening is between us.' And lightly she touched the baby's cheek.

'That baby is a lucky boy,' I whispered, and I slipped an arm around the shoulders of this remarkable child.

Chapter Twenty-five

The Saints' club court had functioned spasmodically during the year, trying, as I recall, only two cases. The first had been a surprise. I expected raw young emotions, 'nature red of tooth and claw,' a combination of *West Side Story* and *The Blackboard Jungle*. But the Saints were polite and orderly and sensible. They also knew a great deal about court procedure, which wasn't surprising. But it did occur to me that the legal fraternity had lost potentially good lawyers when some of the Saints had chosen another line of work. At any rate, my imagination was so thwarted that I don't even remember the results of the trials.

The serious escapades of Ron and Bruce demanded a trial, yet no one pressed openly for it. It crossed the adults' minds that the Saints might fear retaliation, but that was overly dramatic, too, a throwback to imagination's concept of gang conduct. Neither Ron nor Bruce would be squeamish about settling grievances by force, but they did insist vehemently that the club's rules be enforced, and pride alone might prevent any attempt to reconcile violence and principle.

As the trial continued to be delayed, a peculiar revolt swelled in the club, like a spot on the skin that, almost imperceptibly, becomes a boil. The character of the membership was changing. Either we had been infiltrated by teenagers who had no personal interest in defiance of authority, or something was happening to almost everybody.

I don't remember what triggered the outright demand for the trial, or even if it were an articulated demand. I remember only that one night a Saint moved that the offenders be brought before the club's court and that the motion passed.

The court convened downstairs in the big hall and that was a mistake. The echoes of the dances cast an air of frivolity over the proceedings. The room was too big and the membership couldn't dominate it, which set up the wrong psychological climate.

'Who needs this?' one Saint muttered as he slid onto a chair. 'Why not hang 'em both and get the hell out of here.'

The Crown Attorney and the defence attorney shared a table. The magistrate, who looked as if he regretted the whole idea, drummed his fingers on the top of another table. The accused sat together and their determined jokes sounded hollow. The magistrate wrapped a handkerchief around a newly discovered cut in his finger. He took a long time. Then he rapped for order. The court was in session.

The Crown stood slowly, fingering papers. He had right on his side. The magistrate's court of society had recognized the guilt of the accused, even if, according to club rules, that was inadmissible evidence. The Crown confined himself to facts which, he said, would prove 'beyond reasonable doubt' that the accused were guilty.

The defence attorney waived his right to opening remarks. Everyone became appropriately solemn. Ron was sworn in first. Earlier he had faced society's Bar of Justice. Now he asked justice from his peers.

While Ron answered the questions and the magistrate caressed his wounded finger and the Saints watched, I wondered what kind of justice Ron expected from his peers. Would he be right to expect influences on their judgement which would not press in on the adult courts? And I hoped, with sudden serious fervour, that these young people, products of his culture, would find a justice that had significance for him and for us, whatever its consequences.

Ron left the stand, winking at Bruce in real or pretended amusement. And Bruce, when he took Ron's place in the stand, duplicated Ron's attitude.

The Crown summed up without looking at either of them, an approach that seemed more a gesture of self-preservation than courtroom technique. We waited expectantly for the defence counsel's reasoning. When it came I grimaced. He praised the contributions made by both Ron and Bruce to the club. I remembered my own plea to Stanton Hogg, 'Was the word leniency, clemency, or mercy.' Yet St. Augustine said 'charity is no substitute for justice withheld.'

The magistrate cleared his throat. He glanced at the spectators. 'It is the judgement of this court,' he said, 'that both accused are guilty as charged.' Ron and Bruce looked at each other. 'It is the further judgement of this court,' the magistrate stopped to clear his throat again, 'that they be put on probation.' His thin young hand reached thankfully for the gavel. 'It is so ordered,' he intoned and rapped the gavel.

The Crown leaped to his feet. 'May it please the Court,' he said, 'will His Honour tell us how long the probationary period is to be?'

His Honour stared uncomprehendingly. His Honour had lost the thread of the whole business. 'Oh,' he said. 'Oh,' he repeated and looked at everybody, 'for a period of . . . six months.' Firmly he rapped the gavel again. 'This court stands adjourned.'

A rumble went through the spectators. Some criticized the decision. Others rebuked the grumblers. Ron and Bruce smiled at each other. But there was neither pleasure nor relief in the smile. The judgement of their peers had been no surprise to either of them.

At the next Saints' meeting, an emotional bomb went off. It began like an average meeting. They gathered to push and shout as they had over the months. Aaron demanded 'order' and 'silence' and 'quiet' and they ignored him, as they usually did. The only strangeness was a shortening of Aaron's patience. He shouted, 'Simmer down! This is a church hall!' and when someone called out, 'But we ain't here to repent,' his anger unaccountably shrivelled into indifference. He sat down.

It was Bruce who got them under control. His shoulders hunched, he stood up. 'Everybody shut up,' he growled. 'Now.' And everybody shut up.

The grumbling, which should have been soothed by the club trial, seemed more prevalent. I tried not to be dismayed, even when the secretary announced four resignations. Clubs were always receiving resignations, as well as new members.

Father Orr left early to attend a parish meeting. He whispered to knock on the study door if there were any bulletins. When, finally, a Saint moved for adjournment, the members stampeded for the door. Aaron touched my arm. 'Could I speak to you for a minute?' He led me to a corner. 'I think some of the guys are stealing,' he said in an anxious whisper.

'What makes you think that?'

He looked around to confirm privacy. 'Something I overheard. But I think they're stashing the loot in the church locker.'

Father Orr had given the club permission to use a locker in the downstair hall as storage space for the dances' music equipment. The Saints had a key. Father Orr had a key. It was mutually understood that he would not use it without permission – as a sign of trust. On both sides. 'That's interesting,' I said and wondered why I didn't faint.

'I thought you and Father Orr would want to check it out.'

'It should be the executive's responsibility,' I said.

'I know.' A helpless shrug. 'I didn't know what to do.'

182

'I'll tell Father Orr,' I said and knew that the admission that the club might not deal adequately with the problem was as unsettling as Aaron's suspicions. 'And thank you, Aaron.'

Father Orr called, 'Come in,' to my knock. I opened the study door and leaned against the frame. 'Trouble?' He decoded my look. I told him. 'You believe it?' he asked.

'I find I don't disbelieve it,' I said and went unhappily to a chair.

'I see. We have lost our innocence.'

'Aaron may be wrong.'

Father Orr shook his head. 'Probably not.'

'We've grown so cynical?'

'Not cynical. Realistic.' He stood up and started for the door. 'Which one of us opens the locker?' he asked.

'Wait a minute,' I put out my hand. 'If Aaron is wrong, the breach of faith is ours.'

'Yes. But my first responsibility is to the church. Which one?'

We were staring uncertainly at each other when there was a soft knocking on the door. When Father Orr opened it, one of the parish men grinned. 'What did I interrupt?' His eyes travelled between us. 'You two look so . . . is guilty the word? Or is stricken a better one?'

'Relieved,' Father Orr said and drew him aside. 'You told me once you'd be glad to help out any time. This is your big night.' And he explained.

'You want me to open that locker? You want it on my conscience?' The man held up his hand when Father Orr protested. 'Only joking. Trying to relieve tension. Sure, anything I can do to help the cause.' He took the key from Father Orr. 'But if it turns out to be the crown jewels or a million dollars in cash, don't forget I'll need a passport, quick. Those Saints of yours aren't babies.' The door closed behind him.

'We're going to feel very mean if there's nothing in there but dance equipment,' I said accusingly.

'I'll try to cope with that feeling,' Father Orr murmured. 'I'll even welcome it.' We looked at each other.

'If there is stolen property in there,' I put a suspicion into words, 'it might only involve a couple of them. Or even just one. I mean it won't indicate that the whole club knew about it.'

'True,' he agreed.

Memory clicked. 'The arsenal!' I gasped and fell into a chair.

'Please.' Father Orr said and closed his eyes.

Footsteps. Approaching slowly. That was bad. If the locker held nothing illegal the man would have rushed to reassure us. The study door opened. I stiffened, staring at the man's expressionless face. He leaned against the door frame and studied the ceiling.

'Anybody want thirteen teakettles?' he asked. Relief flooded through us like a gale. Father Orr rolled on the couch. The room rocked with our laughter. The parishioner, wiping tears from his eyes, nodded furiously. 'Thirteen teakettles, that's what's in that locker. Thirteen of the newest, shiniest teakettles you ever saw!'

'Thirteen teakettles!' I howled.

'Thirteen teakettles,' Father Orr repeated breathlessly.

The man blew his nose. 'What on earth are you going to do?'

That sobered us. However absurd, however impossible, the nature of the stolen goods was not, after all, the point. The point was their presence in that locker. Father Orr took off his glasses, peered through them and carefully, thoughtfully, he cleaned them. 'Yes,' he said. 'And that's my problem, isn't it. I'll have to think about it. We'll tell the club how and why we investigated. Or I will tell them.' He put the glasses back on. 'We'll have to know who is involved, of course. But until I make my decision, say nothing to the Saints.' He shot a look at me. 'Not even to Ron.'

When I left that evening I stopped in the front hall to look into the locker room, my gaze going compulsively to the locker containing thirteen teakettles – the stolen goods. And horror grabbed. Stolen goods! In that locker. In this church. And any minute someone. . . .

'You thought of it, too,' Father Orr's voice came from behind me.

'We must get them out of there,' my voice dropped instinctively to a whisper. 'We can't leave stolen goods in a church locker!'

'No.' he said.

'How?' And we exchanged a look.

And so it came to pass, one cloudy night, that thirteen teakettles were carefully piled at the rear entrance to Number Six Police Station. There was no card left with them.

Chapter Twenty-six

The Saints' dance that Saturday night was laced with uneasiness. We didn't know if word had travelled about our discovery. The Saints who removed the equipment would notice the absence of the teakettles unless, as we hoped, they had been put there during the week and none of the executive was aware of their existence. But a group of dancers whispering in a corner made me edgy and Ron's glances brought a flush of guilt.

During the evening Father Orr beckoned me to the study. 'I've made my decision,' he said. 'You may not agree with it, but my first responsibility is to the church. So,' he took a breath, 'I have decided to issue an ultimatum to the Saints; they must be told the circumstances of our discovery, of course, although we needn't involve Aaron if you think it might be troublesome for him. But the Saints will be told, too, that the guilty teenagers are no longer welcome on this property. If they decide not to expel the offenders then the club must find a new headquarters. Do you understand and agree?'

'I suppose you have no choice,' I replied, without answering his question. And silently I wondered. Justice again? The guilty were to be told that this betrayal barred them from a church? A church's property, I amended, but if they followed that reasoning, might they conclude that a church was for those who were without guilt? No sinners need apply? 'You think they'll understand the finer points of the moral issue?' I asked.

'Perhaps not. But my first responsibility – '

'I know,' I looked at his serious face. My own responsibility was just as clear. I hadn't said to the Saints, 'I'll support you as long as you obey my ground rules.' I had made no ground rules. If they decided to leave instead of expelling the offenders, I would have to leave with them. And I would have to make it clear, too, that my decision was not a protest against Father Orr.

The following Wednesday evening the Saints seemed subdued as they mounted the stair and filed into the meeting room. Before the meeting convened, Aaron knocked on the study door. 'I'm sorry to intrude,' he said, 'but there's more news. The guys know about the discovery. And they know who hid the stuff in the lockers.' A beat of silence. 'I'm sorry, Jeann,' he said.

'David,' I said and didn't know how I knew.

'Yes.' He hesitated. 'And,' he hesitated again. 'And Bruce,' he said finally.

David Humphrey's voice. 'I think they have made their decision.'

Stanton Hogg: 'You're giving these teenagers a dangerous impression.'

Bruce? 'Bruce?' I repeated. Aaron nodded. 'One more,' he said and Father Orr turned quickly toward me.

'No,' I said.

'No,' Aaron said hastily. 'It's Lennie. One of the new guys.' He waited a moment. 'I thought you should know now.' he said.

'Yes. Thank you, Aaron,' Father Orr said, 'Perhaps we should see the three of them before the meeting.'

Aaron left the study. I looked at the deepening darkness beyond the study window. 'Isn't that strange,' I murmured. 'Bruce is more of a surprise than David.'

The three walked in slowly, scenting the climate. David was stripped of his easy manner. The other two, and especially Bruce, were tight in their defiance. 'You know why you're here,' Father Orr said.

'I didn't do it,' David blurted.

Frustration. Anger. Guilt. 'Come off it, David,' I cut in. His face crumpled. He was guilty, he said brokenly and he was sorry. He didn't know why he'd done it; he looked beseechingly at me. Bruce sat on the edge of the chair and listened with open scorn to David's appeal. Father Orr interrupted the monologue. He explained the ultimatum to be given the club. David's eyes became a frightened, hungry blue. 'No,' he cried frantically, 'no, please. I gotta belong. I gotta be president. I won't do nothin' no more. I promise. Please.' And tears slid down the white face.

I tried to see behind the tears and the voice and the eyes. This might be the moment, the breakthrough. Father Orr shook his head. 'I'm sorry,' he said, 'that is my decision. Perhaps the club will choose to move rather than to expel you. But you three are no longer welcome on this property.'

'Not even for the dances?' Lennie inquired, more inquisitive, it seemed, than concerned.

186

'Not even for the dances.'

David resumed his pleading. Father Orr was silent. David looked at me. 'I'm sorry, David,' I said.

'Put me on probation then,' David swung back to Father Orr.

'You've been on probation.'

I caught Bruce's eye, watched his shoulders lift and fall, watched the square hands smooth a jacket sleeve. 'I'm sorry,' I repeated to him and a smile etched his mouth and was gone.

We went silently into the meeting. The Saints eyed one another. Ernie, the new father, looked as if he wanted a lead. Tony squirmed on the chair. Peter shuffled his feet. Timmy took his mental notes, standing against the wall. And Ron, hunched in the chair, his eyes moving narrowly, watched us all.

Father Orr sat down. I slipped into a chair beside him. Aaron uneasy and embarrassed began the formal explanation of the problem. His voice dribbled off and he looked at Father Orr. 'Maybe,' he said, 'you want to tell us yourself, Father?'

Father Orr issued his ultimatum. Aaron seemed excited by it, as if there were more at stake here than the continued use of the hall. Some Saints looked genuinely distressed, even surprised. Others lounged in exaggerated nonchalance. 'If you prefer,' Father Orr finished, 'Jeann and I will leave to give you a chance to talk privately.'

'You're both honorary members,' Ron called out. 'You got a right to stay. Okay, guys?' A mutter of agreement, rippled on the surface by excitement. Aaron invited the guilty Saints to offer a defence. No one mentioned the club court. This was to be an immediate confrontation with justice.

David wet his lips. He had done it, he said, and he was sorry. He would never do anything wrong again. I was afraid he would conclude with the familiar, 'and I'll do or say anything you want.' Perhaps that was his intention. He started to speak, caught my eye, and fell silent.

Bruce confirmed his guilt with a snap of his head. Lennie said nothing. He didn't need to, his brown eyes whipped over the members, his mouth lifted in a grin which had a mark of self-contempt and self-amusement.

'I move the accused be expelled,' Ron said and even Aaron looked surprised by the speed of decision. I was stunned. Ron had given an impression of friendship with Bruce. There would be no second thoughts with David, but Bruce? The club was that important? Or was this disavowal of association with Bruce linked with the results of their

187

caper together in the summer. Another Saint jumped to his feet. 'I second the motion.'

'Excuse me, Mr. Chairman,' Father Orr said, 'I think in fairness you should examine the decision more carefully.'

'There's no need,' Ron said stubbornly.

'You understand,' Father Orr protested, 'this means that none of the guilty may come on this property for any reason.'

'We understand,' Ron said and gave David a look that denied the open appeal on David's face. He didn't look at Bruce or Lennie.

'Will you vote on the motion, please?' Aaron instructed.

A forest of red waving arms. 'Motion carried,' Aaron looked at David and back to me. Ron stood up. 'And I move we adjourn,' he said. They didn't wait for a seconder. The Saints scrambled up and hurried from the room. David seemed dazed. At the door he looked back, waited and then walked out. Bruce caught my arm. 'Why don't you give up?' he asked flatly.

'Why?'

'Because nothin' you do will make any difference at all.'

For almost a week I debated the talk I had to have with David. He didn't telephone, which was predictable, and I didn't know where to reach him. He didn't show up at the restaurant while I was there and I didn't want to call his mother. Ron said cryptically he was 'around.' 'He'll be back,' he said and I thought of the detective's remark, 'He wasn't hanged, you know.'

We met eventually on a street near the church, as I walked to my car after a visit to Father Orr. David was loping through the darkness and he had passed before I recognized the thin figure. 'David,' I called, 'wait a minute.'

He halted, turned and came back. 'Sorry,' he said with an easy smile. 'Didn't see you. These shadows.' We looked at each other. 'How are you?' he asked.

'David . . .' I began.

'I been meanin' to call you,' he said with no trace of embarrassment. 'I wanted to ask you somethin'.' He's excited, I thought, the 'g's' are falling off. 'You know the stuff in the lockers,' he went on conversationally, 'well, I was gonna tell you, I got other stuff from that same caper,' he smiled, the you-know-me smile, 'and some of it was, you know, women's under stuff.'

'Lingerie?' I supplied wonderingly.

188

'Yeah. Well, what I was gonna ask you, maybe you'd like some of it? I mean,' he added deprecating the generosity with a shrug, 'after all, I owe you a lot. There's just one thing.' In the dim light I could see a thoughtful frown. 'They're all size forty-four. I found out that's kinda big. It would be too big for you, wouldn't it.'

This could not be happening. I wasn't understanding properly. 'David. Let me get this straight. You're asking if I will accept, as a gift from you, this . . . this hot lingerie?'

'That's what I was gonna give you, but I didn't know about the size. I'm awful sorry about that.'

'That is what you wanted to talk to me about?'

He looked bewildered at my sharp tone. 'Yeah. Would you like it anyway? Maybe you could have them made smaller, or maybe' – his face lit up and then sobered – 'no, I guess not. I mean I was gonna say you could exchange them for the right size, but I guess,' he grinned, 'under the circumstances, you couldn't do that. Not safely, like.'

I swallowed. 'David I must talk to you. I really must talk to you. You can't be serious.'

He darted another look down the quiet street. 'Gee, I'd like to stand and talk,' he said, 'and I hate to sound rude and stuff, but I got this appointment and I'm kinda late already.'

'David!' The word was a command.

'I'll call you,' he promised as he turned from me. 'And I'm awful sorry about the wrong size.' And his slim figure, still in the Saints' jackets and jeans, disappeared into the darkness.

I told no one about the gift offer except Ron and Father Orr. I told Ron over the telephone. Now I wish I could have seen his face. At first there was silence. Then a laugh, scornful and dismissive.

Father Orr mirrored my own stunned disbelief. If he searched for the psychological cause, he gave no inclination. I was too shaken to search.

But we attended the next Saints' meeting with private anxieties. The expulsion of David and Bruce and Lennie had been too swift. The Saints might have reconsidered during the week.

When Aaron called for order, they seemed unnatural, unnaturally obedient and unnaturally quiet. A new painful grimness had taken hold. The locker incident might have shocked even the most insensitive. They liked the new image of themselves. Maybe David Humphrey had been right. They had lost their good name, but the club had been giving it back to them. They didn't need to be told that the locker incident, if it became public knowledge, could change that.

And beneath the grimness there was a wider split in the membership. The undercurrent of discord and discontent was more apparent. Some members took action that night. They resigned. And the resignations all reflected identical reasoning. As one Saint phrased it in a note I kept: 'I do hereby rezin from the Saints' Young Men's Club becuz it has not cept up to its name.'

Chapter Twenty-seven

Ironically, while the Saints as a group was disintegrating, the outside world took a new interest in the club's existence. Both *Maclean's* and CBC-TV decided they wanted 'to do' the club. The magazine article fortunately, was not to be a follow-up on David. The emphasis would be on the club, with only its origin linking it with David. The CBC-TV show was scheduled to be a documentary, for inclusion in a Sunday afternoon series. It would be taped in Parkdale, and the producer wanted the Saints to appear as themselves. The members agreed to turn up, 'if it's convenient.' I had the impression that nothing short of mass confinement would keep them away. But I told the membership that I needed help in research. They agreed to a series of taped, in-depth discussions.

It wasn't precisely true, of course. I had little need for intensive questioning after months of association, but the chance to ask questions without appearing to pry was too welcome to throw away. And I had the growing suspicion that if we didn't get some answers now, there might not be another opportunity.

The taped interviews had no planned structure. They were to talk among themselves, while a microphone eavesdropped, answering questions that were designed to spark discussion.

The night of the first session they gathered, shuffling and giggling, around the table. But as the lights shone down on faces too old and too young, they sobered and told the microphone and each other how it was with them. We began on a practical note. 'Gentlemen,' I asked, 'could any of you explain why the majority opposes the idea of working for a living?'

A wave of laughter. 'We're lazy,' one announced. 'No,' another broke in, 'we ain't got no education and you can't get no job with no education. And we got records, too, which don't help none.'

'So you don't even try?'

'Sure we do,' a Saint retorted defensively.

'Oh come on,' another objected, 'we make excuses. Sure we do,' he flashed a challenging look around the table. 'We say we're huntin' but

191

we just go and sit in the employment office. We see other guys and we know we don't have no chance, so we sneak out. Then we say we couldn't get a job. Sure we do.'

'So why not go back and get your education?'

'Who wants to get into that crap?' one mumbled. 'Sittin' all day while somebody who don't care nothin' about you yells at you and tells you you're dumb? Who needs that?'

'And anyway,' another piped up, 'school's for lawyers and doctors and stuff. They don't want guys like us – I mean if you ain't gonna be somethin' special, like go to college and stuff like that, they don't want you. They just try to cram stuff into your head and hope you don't pull down the ratin' of the class.'

'Any other reason?' I asked.

'We're too old.' 'We're dumb.' 'It's too much work.' The answers tumbled, reluctantly or excitedly.

'So you plan to go on like this, just drifting?' My glance slid to Tony.

'I did try,' he squirmed in his chair while the others hooted.

'We can make money in other ways,' a Saint called out and they giggled.

'Is that all you want? To make money?'

'What else is there?' a Saint asked in honest bewilderment.

'I could list a few things, but this is your session. However, if you believe that, aren't you being impractical? I mean if you think you need an education to get a job, and you're right up to a point, and you need a job to get money, and money is so all-fired important, then aren't you defeating yourselves by not trying?'

The microphone recorded no opinion.

'All right,' I switched topics. 'You mentioned police records.' They grinned at each other. 'Would anyone care to explain the fascination of stealing? Why would anyone want to steal.'

While they looked at each other, I was struck by a realization. During the months I couldn't recall hearing any of them reflect on the moral considerations of criminal activities. David had nodded in apparent agreement during our first dinner when I had said, 'I think it's wrong to steal and I think you agree,' but he would have nodded just as seriously if I had said that in Swahili. He would 'do or say anything I wanted.' And I remembered something I had read about the marked and unconscious failure of some parents to include genuinely moral teachings in their 'obedience training' of a child. Too frequently children were taught to obey out of fear of punishment, rather than from any understanding of the moral issue involved. 'You will do this because I tell you to do it.' 'You will obey me because I say so.' 'This is wrong because I say so.' Those were common approaches. And the child grew up responding and reacting, in one way or another, to the threat of punishment, rather than to any moral sense. It could be that these teenagers regarded stealing as an outgrowth of defying parental threats and demands.

'You steal for kicks,' one Saint said. 'You get bored, sittin' around with everybody tellin' you what to do and what not to do and you say to hell with this. So you steal.'

'Sure,' a blond nodded his head, 'and you're takin' somethin' somebody don't want you to have.'

'But isn't that childish?'

'No,' he shook his head, 'when you're stealin' you're smarter than the one who don't want you to have whatever you steal. You beat 'em and you're ahead. It's a good feelin', man. Sometimes you think it serves 'em right.'

'Revenge?'

'I guess,' he looked pleased.

'So you steal for kicks, out of resentment of anyone who has anything?' I took a breath, 'Okay, I don't want to get personal, but let's take my case. Would David have decided it served me right when he tried to steal from me?'

'We steal from people who can afford to lose it,' one said.

'But I couldn't. Which suggests, Robin Hood, that your judgement isn't all that good.'

'But you looked as if you could,' someone put in. 'You lived at a good address.'

'And there's somethin' else . . .' a dark-haired young man sat back in his chair. 'Adults got a funny split in their rules. Like, my father was an accountant. He did books for a lot of important guys. Not here in Toronto. Someplace else. And I used to hear him talk. And you know somethin' funny? These high-up guys, very important guys, goin' to church on Sunday, real' – he grinned – 'real pillars of society, my Dad used to call them, they'd ask him to cut every corner. Some of them asked for things that were crooked. Now that's stealin', right?' His eyebrows went up slowly. 'But they didn't call it that. They called it bein' smart. How come,' he challenged me, 'they were smart and we are thieves? How come?'

'They weren't caught,' someone shouted, 'that's the difference.'

'If they had been, the penalty would have been the same,' I said.

'But,' the teenager leaned forward, 'you know somethin' else? Those very pillars of the community were the guys who really hacked me and my folks when I got into trouble. Those guys were the ones who said I was no good. Now that's pretty funny. Right?'

'People who feel guilty are frequently the most vicious,' I admitted. 'But of course you're right. Stealing is stealing. Let's go back to the moral angle. And don't look so blank. You do believe it is morally wrong to steal whether you're fifteen or,' I looked at the accountant's son, 'fifty.'

'Who says?' someone chirped.

'Society?' I suggested. 'Which means all of you.'

They laughed and I thought of my conversation with Stanton Hogg. 'Do you believe in God?' I asked.

'Sure,' a boy piped up, 'but that's different from the church.'

'In what way?'

'Like, you can believe in God, but you don't have to go to church to prove it.'

'True. Were you taken to Sunday school as children?'

'Man!' One slapped his forehead, 'Was I taken! I was dragged.' And he laughed. 'Once they got me there my folks went back home. I think they wanted to get rid of me for a while. Or maybe do what they thought the neighbours said they should.'

'I think,' a Saint said thoughtfully, 'if there was only one God it would be a whole lot better. This way everybody's fightin' with everybody else. Everybody says his God is best. That's stupid.'

'A different God for each religion, you mean? Or a different approach to God in each religion?'

He threw up his hands. 'I never figured it out. It sure doesn't sound like they're talkin' about the same God.'

'And when do you believe you're old enough to decide such things – about the conflicts in beliefs and about God?'

'When you're old enough to steal,' Ron's voice rang out. He had been sitting quietly, studying the ceiling. Now he hunched forward. The membership laughed and he looked around. 'I mean it. When you get to be five or six and you're stealin', that's when you're makin' decisions.'

I focused on him. 'At five or six?'

The level eyes came back to me. 'Sure.'

'You mean stealing from your mother's purse?'

A smile flickered. 'No,' he said quietly, 'I mean real stealin'.' His brothers again, I wondered.

'But decisions wouldn't be very logical at that age, would they?'

'Maybe not,' he conceded, 'but you're makin' decisions. You grow old fast.' And he smiled at me. 'Anyway,' his eyes went around the table, 'you steal because you're selfish. That's the real reason. Even at five or six.'

'But isn't selfishness a natural condition when you're that young?'

'Then you don't outgrow it.'

'Is that why some don't steal? They've outgrown the selfishness?'

Tony crowded in. 'Maybe they're not smart enough,' he said, 'or they're too scared, or they think different. They're squares.' He offered an impudent grin. 'Like, no offence, but like you.'

'But something has to make a difference,' I insisted. 'So there's a difference between the squares and the . . . thieves. But the thieves didn't rush from the womb to pull their first job. So what made the difference. Do you think there are influences on kids – I mean within the home, or in society, the immediate society – which everybody calls the environment, that makes a difference? Or do you think thieves are just born different?'

The Saints considered it. They rejected the possibility that they had been products of crippling home conditions. No one opted for the theory that it was all mom's fault, or all dad's fault, or even a combined responsibility. There was such swift rejection I wished a psychologist had been guiding their discussion. They were talking with new interest and new freedom. The interview was turning into an amateur group-therapy session. But it was an amateur one.

'Maybe,' one Saint said, 'my folks shouldn't have put me on a training farm when I was only eleven, but I guess they didn't know what else to do with me.'

'You were an old man when you went,' another laughed. 'I was only nine.'

'Did the training farms and schools and reformatories teach you anything?'

'To be better bandits,' one said. 'To smarten up,' another called. 'To use a loid,' one volunteered and at my look, 'you know, a celluloid strip, like for breakin' through locks.'

'Did you learn anything that made your life better?' The answer was unanimous. 'No!' 'Did you learn anything that discouraged you from,' I thought of David, 'a life of crime.' Another unanimous 'no!'

195

'It taught me,' one muttered, 'that I had to be smarter than other people.'

'It taught me,' the blond boy said, 'that nobody cared what the hell happened to me as long as I was locked up.'

'It taught me you need a good lawyer,' one laughed.

'I found out,' a black-haired boy spoke softly, 'that I was alone.'

'Did anyone receive help from a reformatory or prison psychiatrist?'

The laughter, loud and derisive, swept the table. 'So this guy sits behind a desk,' one explained, 'and he talks to you because it's his job and he's got all the others to talk to and he wants to get it over with. So how's that help?'

'One helped me get a stretch in solitary,' another said. 'He asked his first question – when was the last time I slept with my mother. I hit him. I got solitary.'

He grinned at my look. 'I see,' I managed. 'Well, what about this club?' I looked around the table. 'What does it mean to you?'

The black-haired boy, the one who had discovered behind bars that he was alone, spoke up, 'It means that you're not alone any more.'

'It means,' a new member added, 'you got people you can count on.'

'It means,' a third said, 'when you walk along the street, you ain't by yourself, if you get into trouble, like.'

I looked at Ron. He was leaning back in the chair, lost in thought.

When the tape ran out, the Saints seemed disappointed. They were basking in this new contemplation of themselves. 'Hey, Jeann,' one yelled, 'you gonna quote us? I mean, like, give our names and stuff?'

'No,' I was busy with the recording machine, 'you'll be protected. No real names.'

'I don't want protection,' he said. 'I'd kinda like to see my name in that magazine. I mean, people would know I had ideas of my own then.'

The CBC-TV documentary was taped one cold afternoon. I was locked into the responsibilities of a new job, as editor of a magazine suffering birth pangs. But the producer agreed that one of the Saints should be employed, officially, as an assistant to the director and to the writer during the taping. Ron was appointed. The producer commented later on his efficiency.

The taping was completely satisfactory. There was only one incident. During the busy afternoon, the writer's car was stolen.

196

Chapter Twenty-Eight

The Saints' meetings limped through the last two weeks in November with dissent and dissatisfaction growling like a thunderstorm which threatens in the distance. And the first week in December I walked into the familiar meeting room with an alien reluctance.

The lights glared in the room and the night's cold blackness pressed against the windows. The wind howled and knocked around the church. It was noisy outside, but inside the Saints were quiet. Only about twenty-five gathered around the long table. Aaron said, 'We will come to order,' in a formal voice. And they began immediately to argue and contradict. But we had heard it all before, the complaints and the explanations; tonight it sounded flat, without confidence or enthusiasm.

Aaron looked worried. 'We got to get this club off the ground,' he said. 'Anybody got any real ideas?'

'I think,' Father Orr looked around the table, 'the most important question to be decided is whether you intend to continue this club?' He sounded like a judge summing up for the jury.

'I want it to continue,' one said, scattering accusing looks around the membership. Another pounded the table, 'It's got to continue,' he said. 'Sure,' Tony hopped up from his chair, 'I move the Saints' Young Men's Club continue.'

'I second that,' another yelled, too loudly. 'I second that,' he repeated in a lower tone.

'Wait a minute,' Ron lunged to his feet, 'Look at us.' The Saints studied themselves and each other. 'Look how few are here.'

'You're out of order,' Aaron rapped. 'There's a motion before the meeting.'

'So I can speak to the motion,' Ron said defiantly.

'Let's have the vote,' Ernie sounded tired. 'Let's not fight.'

'I forget the motion,' someone muttered.

'That this club continue,' Aaron glowered.

'I mean I forget why we gotta vote on it,' the voice sounded perplexed. 'Why are we talkin' like this?'

It was a good question. While a neighbour whispered to the confused Saint, I looked around the table. Why, indeed, had the club's existence become an issue. When had we started to fall apart? Summer? The suspension? The Downtown Trial, as the Saints called it, of Ron and Bruce. The expulsion of the president and the vice-president? Was there some point we had passed without recognizing it as the critical one?

'Okay,' the Saint shouted, 'I got it. Go ahead.'

They went ahead. The motion passed. 'Now,' Aaron looked at Ron, 'you want to say something?'

'I want to ask somethin',' Ron stood again, hands spread on the table top. 'What did that prove? We got to do somethin' except talk. We got to make the guys want to come back.'

A Saint jumped to his feet. 'I think we need a new executive,' he said and looked belligerently at Aaron.

'Is that a motion?' Aaron asked politely. With David and Bruce gone, Aaron virtually was the executive.

'Yes,' the Saint said firmly.

'Is there a seconder?' Aaron looked inquiringly around the table and murmured, 'thank you,' when another Saint held up his hand.

'Mr. Chairman,' Father Orr signalled for recognition, 'is the motion intended to elect a new president and vice-president or are we making,' he gestured elaborately, 'a clean sweep?'

The meeting lapsed into silence. I looked at Ron. He was studying his fingernails. Ron as president? He had seemed uninterested in any executive role which, when I thought about it, seemed strange. But the membership, small as it was now, was so split that even his candidature might widen that division.

'I meant a clean sweep,' the Saint said suddenly.

'The vote, then, please,' Aaron said, and meticulously counted the 'yes' and 'no' votes. 'The motion,' he announced, 'is defeated.'

'But Mr. Chairman,' I broke in, 'there is still the question of filling the posts of president and vice-president. Unless,' I looked at the Saints, 'they were always inconsequential.' Silence.

'Would the members like a week to consider nominations for president and vice-president?' Aaron asked as if he were hunting a lifeline out of trouble. All hands shot into the air. 'Okay,' he glanced apologetically at the adults. 'We take a week to consider it.'

Ron sighed audibly. 'But we still gotta have a goal,' he muttered.

Father Orr's expression was laconic. 'I thought we had one. To fight delinquency.'

'I mean a kind of project,' Ron muttered.

'Like a clubhouse,' someone yelled. 'That's it! We'll build a clubhouse, where the guys can have a real meetin' place, even some place we can stay when we got no other place, you know . . .'

'Mr. Chairman,' I plunged into the excitement which abruptly filled the room, 'it would take a great deal of money to build a clubhouse. There aren't enough of us to organize a fund-raising campaign, and I seriously doubt if we could get any major investors right now. Wouldn't it be more practical to take on a smaller project until we've rebuilt the club?'

They looked at each other again. As Father Orr said, the Saints might be frustrating, but they were never boring. 'Okay,' someone agreed gravely, 'let's hold a Christmas Rock.'

'With all proceeds,' Ron seemed to come alive, 'to be donated to needy families in Parkdale. I mean' – with a knowing look at Father Orr – 'other needy families.'

The members snatched up the idea. Committees were appointed. I was assigned the task of helping with the publicity, which involved the writing and distribution of news releases for newspapers, radio stations and CBC-TV. When I questioned such ambitious coverage, Tony was ready with the answer. They wanted to draw young people from all over the city. But they also wanted a 'big name' as master of ceremonies. 'We can't pay him much, so he'll want publicity to make up for it,' he pointed out. 'You know how celebrities are.' And he looked pleased with himself.

The day we delivered the releases is one of the times I remember more clearly than yesterday.

Six of us crowded into my mini-car; Aaron, who was businesslike; Tim, who hung over my shoulder from the back seat, arguing politics; Tony, who bounced happily and sobered only when he had to slide through the snow on his turn to deliver; and two other Saints who tried to duplicate Aaron's professionalism. Ron was working that day. His floor and window cleaning business had two customers that afternoon.

A gusty cold wind was blowing up a prelude to a snowstorm, the first flakes already spinning around the buildings and the sky lowering in a grey threat. It would be dark early. But for the first time in weeks I was buoyantly happy, there in the car with my young friends. Perhaps it had to do with Christmas, but the crawl through the city was an escape from the questions, an illusory time, like moments we all experience when we know, briefly, what it is to be free of the confines and to feel the liquid quality of hope.

We talked and laughed like people who belong everywhere and nowhere. We giggled as each candidate for the delivery grumbled out of the car and cheered when he returned to tell us it had been easy. These Saints might be blasé men of the world when they were in their own environment, but once 'in the city' as they termed downtown Toronto, they became shy, uncertain, and easily-intimidated teenagers.

The assignment took longer than we expected because of the snowstorm. By four o'clock it had turned from a threat into a reality. At six o'clock there was one more station to be visited and it was located outside the city. Darkness had dropped like a curtain. The Saints were tired and hungry. The temptation to call it off was almost irresistible.

'We might get stuck in the snow,' Tim pointed out sensibly.

'Of course,' Tony observed, 'we could always carry this car back.'

'And we'd feel better if we carried through on this assignment,' I said and a little silence fell. The question of the empty president and vice-president posts remained unanswered. At the last meeting the Saints had managed, again, to duck it.

'Okay,' one grinned, 'gotcha.' We headed for the station. An hour later we stopped to study the map. We were lost. Aaron laughed. 'Ron told us about your glands,' he said. Tony chanted, 'But we'll feel better . . .' and we nosed through the snow again.

It was seven-thirty when we arrived back at the restaurant. As the Saints tumbled from the car, Aaron looked back. 'Thanks for transporting the bodies,' he said. 'And if this Rock isn't a success, I'll kill myself.'

No one had to kill himself. The night of the Rock the hall was jammed with young people. A Christmas tree glowed in one corner and multi-coloured lights winked on the long windows. There was the 'big name' master of ceremonies. There was also the grey march of the detectives. Even that night they couldn't smile.

During the dance Ron whispered that a few Saints had decided to attend the Christmas Eve Mass at St. Mark's. 'We figure it's the least we can do for Father Orr,' he said, 'I mean, show up so's his parishioners can see us in church.' Then he snapped his fingers. 'Almost forgot to tell you,' he said, 'our president has a new job. He's learnin' to be a chef.' He mentioned the name of one of Toronto's better dining rooms. 'He's workin' there now,' he said. 'Next time you eat there, send your compliments to the chef.'

Unthinkingly I snapped, 'I'd rather help them count the silverware.'

'Hey!' Ron shouted with laughter. 'You're smartenin' up.'

On Christmas Eve the Saints came to midnight mass. They added colour, as well as numbers. Most of them wore their Saints' jackets. 'So's they'll know it's us,' one explained. I didn't point out that there was no way the Saints would not be recognized, unless they wore bags over their heads. And 'they' knew, all right. Some parishioners smiled, but most faces remained stony. St. Mark's had not lost its apprehensions. Later, while Father Orr and I talked in his study, Ron appeared at the door. 'I'll only bust in for a minute,' he said and dropped a parcel on my lap. 'Wanted to give you this.' He waited while I opened it. A crimson angora beret and a pair of crimson angora gloves lay on the white tissue. 'Mom made them for you,' he said. 'We figured they'd keep you warm when that car of yours conked out.'

When I got home that night there was another package at the door. A pair of carved African bookends. The card said, 'Merry Christmas from Tim.'

It was Christmas Night before I realized I had not heard from David. I didn't even think of him until I put Tim's bookends on the end table. The gift would not have been deliberate irony, but it did seem exquisitely appropriate.

Three days later Ron telephoned. David was in jail, charged with possession of stolen goods. 'I thought you'd want to know,' he said.

'Yes,' I agreed slowly, with calm acceptance, 'I'd want to know.'

I didn't go to the jail to see him. But I did help Ron persuade a lawyer to act for him, and I did go to the trial. When the clerk read his name and the charge, David looked over his shoulder and our eyes met. Time spun back to another courtroom and another look of expectancy. That other time seemed a lifetime ago.

David insisted the stolen goods had been put in his room by 'some friends' to whom he had given shelter. His lawyer did his best, but the magistrate chose not to believe David. I didn't believe him, either. David was sentenced to eight months in the reformatory. As he left the courtroom he looked back again. This time he smiled and I thought of his recurring comment, 'You know me.' I don't know you, I thought, and I don't know the answer to you. As our system stands now, I don't even know what can be done for you. There's something, but I don't know what it is.

David's return to the reformatory carried no backlash of remorse or self-condemnation. I experienced only the bewildered defeat. No miracle had been wrought. I wondered vaguely if this had any connection with his expulsion from the club. But under the questions – about him, and about our system of authority – I experienced, as well, a sense of relief as if something inevitable had happened and it was not as bad as I had feared.

Chapter Twenty-nine

I missed most of the meetings and the dances in January and the early part of February because I compounded the problems of the new job by tearing a ligament in my leg. Father Orr relayed the news and it wasn't good. We had new resignations. And everyone continued to resist the challenge – if it was that – of electing a new president and vice-president. There was no open discussion of David.

Ron telephoned or called regularly at the office, and his reports were less concerned with the club than with his own life. His business was doing well. He had a new girlfriend. Bill liked his new job. 'Even Bob's workin',' he laughed. 'It almost gives you the creeps.' I thought of Bill's 'you'll never have to worry about us again.'

The first Saints' dance in February was a shock. Attendance had dwindled; the age level seemed lower – some of the dancers looked about twelve. And the Saints seemed bored. But there were two news items and one forecast. Aaron and Veda were to be married in the spring. And Bill was getting married, too.

The forecast was a pretty, dark-haired girl in a white dress. Ron introduced her with studied nonchalance. 'Jeann, this is Marna. She's a friend of mine.' We smiled at each other. Marna had to be the new girlfriend. Ron gestured toward Veda's engagement ring. 'That kind of thing is catchin',' he observed. 'I've been thinkin' of settlin' down, too.'

The Saints did everything together. They had stolen together. They had formed the club together. They had launched job hunts together – because job hunting had become fashionable. And now, presumably, they would marry, as if they were responding to a mass infection. 'That's nice,' I said mildly and everyone laughed. The laughter was relaxed. Old friends together, I thought, and marvelled at the affection I felt for all of them. I no longer thought of the 'converted' and the 'unconverted.' It no longer mattered. I was a partner in their concerns and I couldn't imagine a time that wouldn't include them.

I thought of something I had read by the priest-scholar-scientist Pierre Tielhard de Chardin: 'Seeing; we might say that the whole of life lies in that verb, if not ultimately, at least essentially. To try to see more and better is not a matter of whim, or curiosity, or self-indulgence. To see or to perish is the very condition laid upon everything that makes up the universe by reason of the mysterious gift of existence.'

I had been pushed into seeing. Or trying to see. Some of the sights – about myself, about the troubled and troubling young and about our society – had not been welcome. Some had been deeply wounding. And all of them had combined to change my life.

The final blow to the club was Father Orr's unbelievable decision to leave St. Mark's. Of course it wasn't unbelievable at all. Father Orr, like me, did have a life that didn't include the Saints. And he had warned me of the impending decision one October evening over dinner in my apartment.

We were lingering over coffee when I asked if he had ever considered psychiatry as a profession. Casually he said, 'As a matter of fact, I'm considering it now.' And he laughed at my open astonishment. 'I can be both a priest and a psychiatrist, you know,' he said. 'It isn't definite yet. I want to do advanced academic work first.' Then he dropped the bomb right on my Irish linen cloth. He intended to leave St. Mark's. He couldn't study and meet parish responsibilities. 'To say nothing of the Saints.'

While he talked my mind tasted the possibility that all of this could end. And I didn't want it to end. But even as I tried to put it out of my mind, to shore up against the inevitable, to daydream – which is what it was – about a miraculous revitalization of the club, the continuance of Father Orr's participation and, most of all, the stopping of life at this stage, time moved heedlessly on.

The parishioners gave him a farewell tea. I attended it in a mood of disbelieving acceptance. He was leaving. The club was dying. The experiment was almost over – even as the civil-rights battle raged – and we had no way of knowing if that experiment had been a partial success or a total failure. Life had moved to another level of existence.

I think he shared the disbelief. He wandered through the room, looking a little dispossessed himself. When I asked if he would take a holiday before he assumed his new duties as curate at another church, he said, 'I can't spare the time. That's what all this is about.' And he turned to greet someone. Neither of us mentioned the Saints. With Father Orr's departure, the members faced the demand for a firm decision which, for them, seemed close to an impossibility.

At the final meeting the Saints were true to their habit of avoiding any head-on collision with reality. I wish the end of the club had been tidier. I wish there had been another banquet to mark the finish, or even two minutes' silence as a sign of respect for what, that night, I considered to be our dead dreams.

There were only fourteen at the final meeting. We grouped mournfully around the table. Aaron called us to order and this time we obeyed him.

'Now that Father Orr's leavin',' Aaron said, and the next words sounded like a worn recording, 'we gotta decide what to do.'

Ron groaned and looked up at the ceiling. The others frowned and looked accusingly at each other. Father Orr and I waited, half hopeful, half resigned. 'So what choice have we got?' Mike sputtered, as if Aaron's statement constituted a shocking new announcement. It didn't, of course. Father Orr had issued his warning to them weeks earlier.

'We can get the club going again,' Aaron began and Ron groaned again, 'or we can disband.' Suddenly his face lit up. 'Or we can suspend for a while.'

'And what will that accomplish?' Father Orr asked.

'I mean maybe we could transfer to your new church when you're settled.'

'I'm sorry, that's impossible. I'll contribute whatever I can, but I cannot assume the responsibility of the club at the new parish, even if the rector were willing.'

'So where does that leave us,' Tony asked, round-eyed.

'Right where we've been for weeks, Father Orr said.

'We gotta decide,' Ron glared around the table. 'You want this club, or you don't. If you do, we gotta find a new headquarters and a new place for the dances. If you don't let's get the hell out of here.'

They murmured among themselves. 'Maybe,' someone said, 'we could suspend, like Aaron says, for the summer. If the guys want to start up again in the fall, we can do it then. In the meantime, we'll be together in the restaurant and we can talk about it.'

'Is that a motion?' Aaron demanded.

It was over. We all knew it. We didn't know when, or why, or even if, the club had failed. But it was over. A Saint stood up. 'I move we suspend the Saints' club until fall,' he said.

'I second that,' another waved his hand.

Father Orr's shoulders lifted in a shrug of surrender and silently I yielded. 'And I move we adjourn,' someone shouted. 'I second that,' a young voice chanted. Chairs squeaked back, scratchy sounds now with none of the lost thunder. They stood up, some solemn-faced, others reverting to cheerful acceptance. And, elbowing each other, they left the room.

'Well?' Father Orr said, in an unconscious echo of his first word to me such a long time ago. I couldn't do it. I couldn't resurrect the fascinated, 'Whee!'

'Yes,' I said. And we walked out of the room.

That, as far as I was concerned, was the story of the Saints' club. Until I decided to write it.

The club never did reconvene. While Father Orr and I were gathered up by concerns in our private lives, the Saints spilled into adult life. Most of them assumed the average responsibilities and privileges of society, with families and jobs, worries and satisfactions. A few achieved the status of successful businessmen. Only a handful maintained the dreary, deadening, futile cycle of street-to-prison-to-street-to-prison.

David was one of those. He returned from the reformatory. He married, became a father, and inexplicably went back to the reformatory. I wasn't in touch with him. I knew he would greet me with the old, cheerful friendliness, the old 'you know me' and slip past questioning.

Several Saints stayed in our lives. For me the one to remain most fiercely and most deeply was Ron. He married Marna, fathered three children, and settled into that category of a successful businessman. He lost none of the reckless, joyful rebellion, but now that boundless emotional energy was channelled into the more socially-acceptable competition of business. And through the years he remained my bodyguard, that rare breed of friend who stays a partner, however dark or bright the climate and conditions of life.

But the club remained an unanswered question. Had it made any difference to anyone – except to Father Orr and to me? Through the years I thought of trying to write the story. Yet I could draw no conclusions and there was always the possibility that the Saints, even as adults, might interpret it as exploitation. I don't know what changed my mind. The passage of time itself, perhaps, would make the individuals less recognizable and possibly would diminish their reactions. Or maybe I had the haunting suspicion that if I went back over it, I might stumble on something, unseen at the time, that would answer the questions.

But I believed I knew the story as it happened. Even the night I called Ron, to tell him I had decided to write about the Saints' club, even when he paused and said, 'Then we'd better talk,' even then I thought I knew the whole story of this improbable club.

So he came to my apartment and we started to talk, to remember, to laugh, to argue the differences in our memories of single incidents. But suddenly, abruptly, he stood up and walked the length of my living room. 'If it weren't for you,' he said, 'I'd be in Kingston Penitentiary right now. I got something to tell you and I want you to remember that while I'm telling you.'

It was the tone of his voice. Absurdly I thought of the department-store executive, the day I asked him to give Paul a job, '. . . and some day, when he's a contributing member of society . . . we'll cry . . . because I was responsible for it.' I wasn't responsible for this tall, straight, 'contributing member of society.' I had done nothing but participate in a friendship which had been the most rewarding and dependable of my life. But there was something in the tone of his voice.

'If you're going to tell the story of the Saints,' he said, 'you have to know the whole truth. It makes a different story. And it's part of the reason why I'm here in this apartment, instead of behind bars.' He went back to the chair, to sit down and face me, deliberately, ruefully, seriously. 'You never did guess, did you,' he said, his voice full of the indulgent, affectionate exasperation it held in the old days when he would beg me not to be stupid. 'You never did guess,' he repeated.

Chapter Thirty

A cool wind slithered across the balcony, but it was warm in the apartment. The cry of a siren sounded in the distance, screeching across the sad music of a folk ballad from somewhere in the building. Lisa, my Yorkshire terrier, was curled asleep at my side. And Ron, my old friend, sat where he had sat innumerable times over the years. Everything was familiar, except the tone of his voice.

'The Saints' club was organized originally as a front, a cover,' he said flatly. His gaze turned inward, a man peering back to another time, another incarnation of himself. 'We were a bunch of working thieves. We set out deliberately to use you.'

There was absolute stillness. 'A front,' I repeated, as if I were considering a suggestion for the ending to a story. 'A bit melodramatic, but it's an interesting twist.'

'Listen to me,' he demanded, leaning forward. 'A bunch of us had been together a long time. Sometimes somebody would get caught,' his eyes glinted with irony, 'like your friend, David. But we were doing okay. Then you came along.' He spread his hands, hands a magistrate had once termed lethal weapons. 'It was the chance of a lifetime. Experienced guys, working under the cover of a club organized to fight delinquency.'

'A front?' I repeated again, disbelief crashing into the intensity, the undeniable honesty of his expression. And memory punched up images, my first Saints' meeting, the watchful teenagers, the flamboyance, the cynicism, the hostility, the laughter. And my own reaction: 'if they had decided to shift into a new life, I had news for them. They were trailing remnants of the old one.'

'All of you?' My voice skidded up. I could hear my voice, but all emotion had gone into hiding. 'You mean all of you . . .'

'No,' he put out a hand, halting the flight, while my mind leaped back and forth, 'no, not all. It seemed better when we were organizing it to have some guys who were for real.'

'For real?' I was trying to connect the pieces, to make sense out of this ludicrous revelation.

'Listen to me,' he said sternly. 'Don't get excited. Don't get mad. Just listen to me. I said it seemed better when we were organizing it to have some guys who were for real, I mean guys who didn't know the true purpose of the club – that it was to be a cover. Some guys were just drifting,' a half smile flickered, 'not . . .'

'Working thieves,' I supplied helpfully, as if it were all quite sensible and understandable.

'That's right. They were invited to join the Saints' club. And sure, they thought it was going to try to keep guys out of trouble. They weren't exactly crusaders,' – the smile widened – 'but they kinda liked the idea of being together in a club.'

David's voice, the day in my office: 'We'll be together . . .'

'I know,' I interrupted again and sarcasm crept into my tone. 'David explained the club's philosophy when he was persuading me to join you. It would keep the guys off the street, give them some place to go, something to do, a chance to be together.'

Ron ignored the sarcasm. 'That's what brought some of them in,' he said seriously. 'And there were even a few,' he sounded a little surprised, 'who really liked the idea of fighting delinquency, I mean helping guys keep out of trouble. They came in too.'

The 'genuine core,' I thought, and the 'unconverted.' Laughter prodded. Laughter at myself. I had figured it out. 'There would be the sincere ones and the ones open to persuasion.' Sound analysis. But I'd put the wrong ones in the classifications. I'd had it upside down.

'And Father Orr?' I was snatching at the questions as they hopped in my mind. 'You chose him deliberately?'

'The church,' Ron said cryptically.

The probation officer's voice whispered in memory: 'I wonder why they'd choose a church as headquarters? A father-figure . . . or?'

'Respectability,' I said aloud, my voice shrinking back to a dazed whisper.

'Sure.'

'Beginning with David.' I pounced on the name as if it were a clue.

'That's what I've been trying to tell you,' Ron said patiently. 'Your offer to help him. Then the magazine article.' Laughter glimmered in his eyes again. 'Like it said, you were your burglar's best friend.'

'David,' I repeated. And I was back at the beginning in my bathroom, the limp boy at the Don Jail, the governor's ridicule, the offer of friendship and my scrutiny of his letter, trying to find traces of cunning because I questioned his swift acceptance of that friendship when 'you can't get through to him.'

'That's why he was made president," I said.

209

'To bring you in, of course,' Ron confirmed. 'It was a beautiful set-up,' he said with a dreamy, self-mocking nostalgia, 'You got to admit it was a beautiful set-up.'

'Did it ever occur to anybody what you might have done to Father Orr?' I asked slowly.

Ron shook his head vigorously. 'We had a rule. You and Father Orr weren't to be made fools of. No, wait,' as I started to speak, 'remember the club was supposed to be fighting delinquency, but you knew all the members weren't converted. That was the whole point, to convince guys that they –'

'Didn't have to lead a life of crime,' I chanted. David.

'Sure. So if somebody – I mean in our own group – got caught, you couldn't be blamed. Don't you see?' He paused. 'And remember how you seemed to us,' he said gently.

My comment to Paul's informer. 'You know where to find the easiest mark in town.' But also, I thought, symbols of a society to be outwitted.

'You were gullible,' Ron said, as if he were reading my thoughts, 'but you and Father Orr were both on the level.'

'Beginning with David,' I said, and his thin ghost glided into the room, to smile engagingly, to tilt his head inquiringly, to say, 'I'll do or say anything you want,' and 'After all, I owe you a lot' when he made that offer of – manic laughter swelled again – of that hot lingerie. David had recognized the possibilities in the first meeting at the Don? When I visited him at Guelph? When he read the magazine article? The night of our first dinner, during his 'confession'? Mentally I denied it. He might have sensed a potential, but it would take another kind of mind, a shrewder, better mind, to turn that potential into a workable reality.

Ron was quiet. He was waiting for the real question. The important question. He had said, 'If it weren't for you I'd be in Kingston Penitentiary right now. I want you to remember that when I tell you the truth.' And he had said 'we' and 'us.'

I met the steady look. 'And who was the brain, the organizer, the head of this little crime ring?' I asked carefully. He smiled. Faintly. Silently. 'You,' I said. 'Of course. All the time it was you.' Memory dipped and swung back. My instinctive recognition of him from the beginning as the real leader. That indefinable, undeniable sense that there was something I didn't understand. 'All the time it was you,' I said wonderingly.

210

'There was a bunch of us,' he said. 'The idea kinda grew.'

I didn't have to ask the details. I could see them, huddling together in their spiritual home, the restaurant, listening to David's account of me, reading the magazine article, young eyes brightening or widening, someone – Ron? – shouting, 'Hey! I got a great idea!' This would be the real kick, the true thrill, the impossible dream made possible.

'And appointing yourself my bodyguard?' Slowly now. 'That was part of the plot?'

The probation officer's voice again: '. . . a message, lay off, fellas, or meet me in the alley.'

'No,' he said simply.

'Why?'

His shoulders, powerful still, lifted slightly and dropped. 'I don't know. You seemed to need protection.'

'But all the time it was a front? All the time, all those months, all – '

'No,' Ron said emphatically, impatiently. 'That's what makes the story different. That's why I wanted you to know. I said it was organized originally as a front. Originally.' He met my look with candid, steady eyes. 'That didn't last long.'

I couldn't absorb it all. 'What do you mean that's what makes the story different?'

'Look.' He leaned forward again, exasperated by my bewilderment. 'It's one thing to have been part of a club that was organized by a bunch of reformed bandits trying to fight delinquency,' he said slowly. 'So in that story you and Father Orr and the' – he grinned – 'the reformed bandits had certain experiences. Okay, that was your story. Right?'

'I guess so.'

'But it's another thing to have been part of a club, organized by bandits who weren't reformed at all, who were using you deliberately, when you didn't know it and,' he spread his hands eloquently, 'to have some of those bandits reform. In spite of their other intention. Understand?'

The light was beginning to break. 'But when did this beautiful set-up, this front idea, begin to fall apart?'

'Not long after you joined us,' he said quietly.

'Why?' I demanded again and this time the question lost personal significance. Now it was bunting into something else.

He stood up, to walk to the windows and look out over the city. 'I don't honestly know,' he said. 'It just did. A lot of things happened.

I don't mean,' he swung to face me, 'that we were all suddenly converted. In our own group, I mean. Some guys got kinda interested.' He laughed. 'You and Father Orr were kinda highpowered in a lot of ways. Other guys went on stealing, independently.' A frown gathered, as if he were trying to remember how it had been. 'Some just left the club.' He stopped, helpless among the recollections.

'And you?' I asked.

'You,' he said, as if the single word held the full answer.

'I don't understand.'

'I don't either,' he looked rueful, even embarrassed. 'I was a very experienced young hood. I started in young. Remember those tapings for the CBC show and your interview sessions? Remember you were surprised when I said kids began to steal, for real, at five or six. You shouldn't have been surprised,' his voice chided, 'not when you knew there were two brothers to teach the ropes. Not when you knew about that. I had a good education. I was a very experienced young hood.' He paused again. 'Beginning at age five.'

The experienced young hood, with whom I had made no covenant, to whom I had made no vow of unconditional help. The experienced young hood, who had worn no label for me – not even that of the reformed bandit. I thought of the day in court, the day of our crisis, when, searingly, the unknown dimension had been revealed and my response had been only the storming, raging determination that this life would not be wasted.

'But what made the difference?' I insisted. And to know, to isolate the reason, the factor, that made a difference within this one human being was abruptly urgently important. In that instant it was no longer probing a revelation. It was to stand on the brink of discovery, to solve a tragic riddle, to burrow into the heart of the disease of crime and to find the cure hidden, but present, in that heart.

It had begun to rain, a soft hissing rain, blowing inward across the balcony onto the apartment windows. Light shivered on the droplets of water. I thought of Bill, the question that day, 'what would cure you?' and his sighing, defeated, 'damned if I know.' Bill, the most incorrigible man in Canada. And that other day, after the trial: 'This is the first time this family ever got a break. You'll never have to worry about us again.' A promise made. A promise never broken.

'I don't know,' Ron said from the window. He turned to face me again. 'Remember the time you told the cop to tell me to go to hell?

212

When he gave me the message – and he wanted you to mean it – I said "she might say that, but she'd never let me go." I knew. You see? I knew.'

'That summer . . .' I was still among the memories. 'That awful summer.' When the gifts of experience deserted the experienced young hood. Because of a secret wish to be caught?

'I thought I was headed for Kingston,' he said and shuddered.

'It would have destroyed you.'

'It might have turned me into one of the great bandits of our age.' He smiled. 'You may have ruined one of the great criminal careers of our time.' He went to the chair, to sit down and lean back, to look up, sorting his own memories.

Father Orr's voice now, the day of the rumble threat. 'Some day he may want you to know all there is to know. How you receive it may make a big difference. Especially to him.'

'But I knew,' Ron said. 'I don't know how I knew, or why it made a difference. But I'm here, in this apartment, instead of in Kingston Penitentiary. I have kids, a business, a good life. And I owe all of it to you.'

I tried to remember Robert Frost's poem, in which he talks about all of us making ourselves 'a place apart' behind light words, but waiting, with agitated hearts until someone really finds us out. Frost was referring symbolically to the old game of hide-and-seek, but it applied to all of us who know uncertainty and fear and that special lonely need, to all of us who wait, in agitated aloneness, until someone really finds us out.

'It doesn't work that way,' I said from the welter of thoughts. 'You don't owe any of it to me. Nobody can give you anything you're not willing or able to use.'

'But you were always there when I needed you,' he said.

'And you've always been there when I needed you,' I replied, and memories tumbled again, especially of a time, long after the Saints' club had folded, when my life shuttled into a darkness, filled with emotional turmoil. I had given Ron none of the details. I didn't need to – 'the wounded sense things.' But he knew I had entered a troubled time, and he knew what trouble can mean, even to the practicalities of life. One afternoon he came to the apartment on the pretext of needing help on a contract. Instead he pulled an envelope from his pocket and tossed it on the coffee table. 'That's from a couple of us,' he said. 'The money isn't a loan and it isn't as much as we'd like it to be. It's just to help maybe a little.' And he had added, 'after all, you were always there when we needed you. Only you were there faster.'

213

'It works both ways,' I said now and he smiled.

A thousand questions begged to be answered. Was Aaron part of the original plot? No. Bruce? A silent, eloquent look. My shy, half-embarrassed question: 'David. Did he laugh much about me. It must have seemed very funny to him.' The direct answer. 'He laughed once. Just once. He never laughed again.' And 'Did he tell you he intended to kill me that first night?' A startled 'No!' and a shrug, 'probably that wasn't true.' David. 'Do you think if I'd been smarter, I could have helped him?' Another direct answer. 'I doubt it. He needs a lot of . . . you know, trained help.' And 'Were there many who went on stealing, despite the breakdown of the organized front?' Another shrug; 'We didn't keep score. But,' a smile passed over his face, a ripple of delighted satisfaction, 'I gotta tell you this. Remember the day the CBC taped the show? Remember how the cops from Number Six all crowded around, as fascinated as we were by the cameras, kinda forgetting their duties? Remember some Saints were missing?' Appalled laughter. 'You mean?' And laughter from Ron. 'Sure, they were just doing their thing. It was too good a chance to miss.' And the memory of my own petty, sour satisfaction at defeating Detective x.

'About the disintegration of the club?'

'Some guys got bored, I guess. Happens all the time in clubs.'

I thought of the resignation, 'I do hereby rezin . . . becuz the Young Men's Saints' Club has not cept up to its name.' And disenchantment after the trial of a vice-president? Followed by the betrayal of a president and again a vice-president?

'The Inspector,' I said suddenly. The good Inspector, justified in his suspicions. Ron's buoyant laugh filled the room. 'But if we'd taken his assessment, tried to follow his lead . . . what would have happened?'

'Easy.' The 'lethal weapons' spread apart. 'I'd be in Kingston right now. So would a lot of other guys.'

'Some are anyway,' I reminded him.

'Sure. Not many, but sure some are. What do you expect, a full-scale miracle? Remember Millbrook?'

The Colonel's voice: 'We'll break this man's spirit.'

'Remember Bill?' Ron said softly.

Remember Bill. Remember all of them. How lovely and sad and joyful and tragic were the memories, fading and vivid, overshadowing all Ron had said, spreading longing and silliness, laughter and, yes, satisfaction. I felt suddenly lonesome for those days, even as this revelation changed the story, shattered some memories and threw a new

214

shining light on others. And abruptly they were there, the ghosts of the young men who had made the headlines, crowding into the apartment, to smile and giggle, or stare solemnly at me. Tim, at university now; Aaron, busy with his worrying responsibilities of a family; Bruce, in a new life with the old one a bad dream; Ernie and Mary, with three children; Peter, the musician, somewhere in the States; Tony, still bouncing, still hunting excitement; the sad ones – David. I looked at Ron.

'Why did you never tell me before?' I asked.

'You never asked,' he grinned.

'I didn't ask now.'

'But you're writing about it now. Some Saints will read it. Can't have you looking an idiot.' The familiar code-grin. 'And you might have come up with some damn-fool theories about guys like us . . . I mean, with that other story. Anyway, I thought you should know.' He leaned forward. 'I've been thinking,' he said, 'there are a hell of a lot of kids who need help. The whole new crop . . .'

'The next generation,' I said and sighed.

'There have been some reforms,' he conceded, 'a few halfway houses, legislation, stuff like that, but all that's for after the trouble has started.'

'And more people are beginning to understand,' I interrupted.

'Most people still don't give a damn,' he said flatly, 'and you know it. They're too indignant about the young punks, or too selfish – ' he halted. 'Isn't that funny,' he said, 'that's what I said made kids steal, when you were interviewing us, but I guess it works both ways. People are too damned selfish.'

Or too indifferent, too apathetic, too full of irrational prejudices and fears that can't be legislated out of people, too bound by faith in the ultimate rightness of our system, I thought, remembering the Markham detective's call and the night of my own gloomy sadness. The civil-rights battle raged on. But it still ignored what could be one of the most vital set of victims.

'Anyway,' Ron said, excitement building, 'I've been thinking. Maybe we could start another club for the younger kids. They do start in young. Go right where the action is. After all,' he added, 'we know where it's at, because we've been there. Both of us.' He stopped at my sigh.

'Oh sure,' he said, 'I know you got to get this book done, first.'

'No, I was thinking,' I said, and the old frustration welled up. 'You're right, it's a different story with at least one happy ending, but no answers to the questions of "why" or "how" or. . .'

'Does it matter? Does it really matter how or why it happened? Didn't you say once that motives and methods aren't really what count? Didn't you say all that's really important are the consequences?' He laughed, the old, indulgent, affectionate laugh. 'Like I've been telling you for years – don't be stupid.'